1st Edition 2019
Copyright ©2019 by Björn Bundschuh
www.thebundschuhs.de

Author & Publisher: Björn Bundschuh, Am Stadtgraben 6, 64823 Groß-Umstadt, Germany
Illustrations and Pictures: Björn Bundschuh
Cover design: Björn Bundschuh
Translation: Björn Bundschuh

All rights reserved. No part of this publication may be reproduced, distributed, or transmitted in any form or by any means, including photocopying, recording, or other electronic or mechanical methods, without the prior written permission of the publisher, except in the case of brief quotations embodied in critical reviews and certain other noncommercial uses permitted by copyright law.

Although the author and publisher have made every effort to ensure that the information in this book was correct at press time, the author and publisher do not assume and hereby disclaim any liability to any party for any loss, damage, or disruption caused by errors or omissions, whether such errors or omissions result from negligence, accident, or any other cause.

The author acknowledges and wishes the audience to acknowledge also that trademark signs and such similar marks are not in any way promoted and endorsed by such holders of trademarks and such similar marks. Where a mark is protected by statute and or under the law of passing off, it is to be acknowledged that the authors use of these marks amount only to fair use and does not seek to gain an unfair advantage from there use or seek to harm or damage the reputation of such protected marks. The publication and use of these trademarks are not authorized, associated with, or sponsored by the trademark owners. It therefore should be borne in the mind of the audience that there is no association between the author and the owners of these protected signs.

LEGO, LEGO-Minifigures, MINDSTORMS and LEGO-Bricks are trademarks of the LEGO-Group
Rubix Cube is a trademark of Rubik's Brand Ltd.

This book contains references and links to other Third-Party products and services. Some of these references have been included for the convenience of the readers and to make the book more complete. They should not be construed as endorsements from, or of any of these Third Parties or their products or services. These links and references may contain products and opinions expressed by their respective owners. The author does not assume liability or responsibility for any Third-Party material or opinions.

Content

Preface 4
How to use this book 5
Program creation 6
    Creative Canvas 6
    Programming for Experts 7
    Define sub-routines as programming blocks 7
Ball-Booster – The marble run 8
    Build 8
    Code 42
    Play 43
Bob-It-Booster – The Party-Game 45
    Build 45
    Code 48
    Play 50
Weight-Booster – The Balance 53
    Build 53
    Code 61
    Play 62
Boost Writer – Write, Draw and Copy Bug 64
    Build 64
    Code 78
    Play 81
Egg-Booster – Multi-colored chicken eggs 85
    Build 85
    Code 102
    Play 107
Cube Booster – The cube-solver 110
    Build 110
    Code 122
    Play 126
Controlling the Move-Hub by PC and Python 131
Acknowledgements 131
About the author 131

Preface

LEGO-Boost was the first set of the Powered-Up technology platform. So far, the set and the new platform are not recognized as a serious extension of the existing motors or Mindstorms set, yet. The Boost-Set will gain more importance by the expansion of the Powered-Up technology into other sets. This book wants to show that you can achieve highly sophisticated results with the simple Boost-Set alone. Although the set is missing a wider variety of Lego-Technic elements and the Boost-App is designed for small kids, the possibilities shown in this book are quite amazing.

Additional program versions, videos and part lists are available on the web resources of the author:
        thebundschuhs.de/boost
        rebrickable.com/users/bundy/mocs

How to use this book

The book is based on model descriptions for the Boost-Set. Each model description is segmented into the three sections "Build", "Code" and "Play".

Build

The easiest way to work with the models is to follow the step by step building instructions and create the illustrated programs within the Boost-App. There is already a lot to be learned about the operation of the model from its design.

Code

Each program is illustrated in detail. The program sequences and sub-routines can easily be created in the Boost-App. The general operation of the model and its basic start-up procedure is explained.

Play

This section describes some specialties of the programming blocks in use. Please be aware that programming blocks explained in one model are not described again in any of the following models. Therefore, it is recommended to build the models one after the other. The complexity of programming increases towards the end of the book.

The following table gives an overview over the content and functions used in the models:

Model	Build	Code	Color-sensor	Motion-sensor	Rotation-sensors	Motors	Local variables	Global variables	Parameter values
Ball-Booster	complex	easy	✓			✓			
Bob-It-Booster	easy	medium	✓	✓	✓		✓		
Weight-Booster	easy	medium		✓	✓	✓	✓		
Boost-Writer	medium	complex	✓		✓	✓	✓	✓	
Egg-Booster	medium	complex			✓	✓	✓	✓	
Cube-Booster	medium	complex	✓		✓	✓	✓	✓	✓

Program creation

Creative Canvas

To create your own program code, you must move to the creative canvas. To do so, just follow these simple steps:

1. Open the window shutter on the ride hand side

2. Tap the window

3. Click on the large plus symbol (+) in the upper left corner to open a new program. The name and icon of the new program are automatically assigned and can be changed in a later stage.

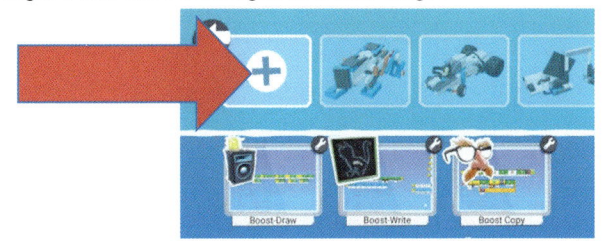

Programming for Experts

1. To enable the use of all expert functions the program must be set to expert level (Level 3). To switch to level 3, you click the tool symbol of the program icon.
2. Click the stacked Lego-plates on the right-hand side of the program icon.
3. Choose the three stacked Lego plates to enable level 3

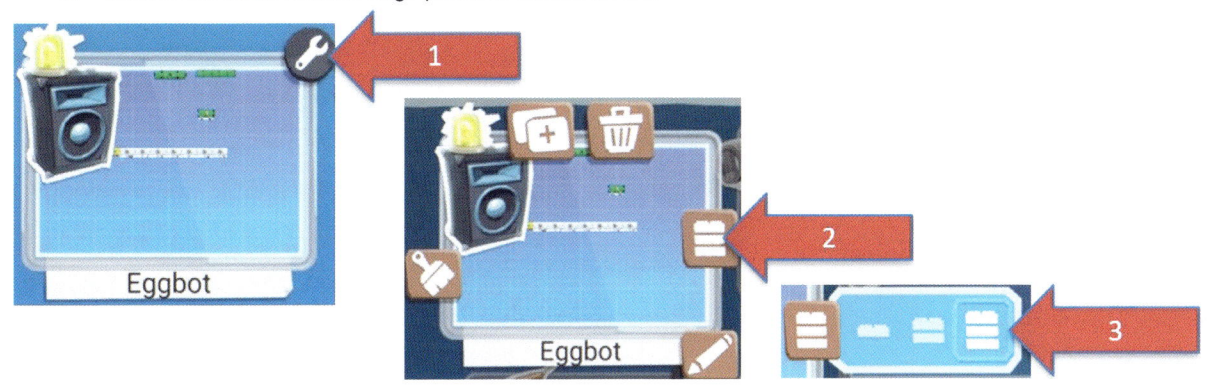

Define sub-routines as programming blocks

To create sub-routines as programming blocks you can perform the following steps.

1. Within a program click the grey block library in the lower part of the screen.

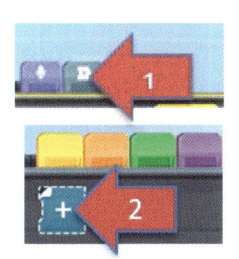

2. Click on the „+". A new programming block will be created.

3. Click into the dark blue window above the new programming block.

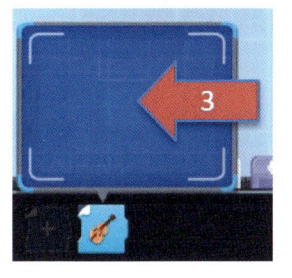

4. You can change the icon from within the new programming block. To do so, click the icon in the upper left of the screen.

5. While selecting an icon, it is recommended to choose the same icons as used in this book. This simplifies the understanding and debugging of the code. Confirm your selection by clicking the green check mark.

6. Code within the subroutine is created the same way as in the main program. Click on the red arrow in the upper left corner to exit the subroutine and save all changes. Attention: When exiting an empty subroutine, the subroutine will be deleted.

Ball-Booster

Ball-Booster – The marble run

The programming of the marble run is quite simple. However, with its voluminous structure it is the most laborious model in this book. Building requires a good skill level. All needed bricks are included in the original Boost set. You only have to add a suitable marble. Ideally, a Lego-soccer ball or Lego-basketball is used. Alternatively, you can use any kind of ball (e.g. glass marble) with a diameter of approximately 14mm.

Build

Although the building instructions only use the bricks of the original Boost-Set, the marble run can easily be extended on both sides by using bricks from your own Lego-collection.

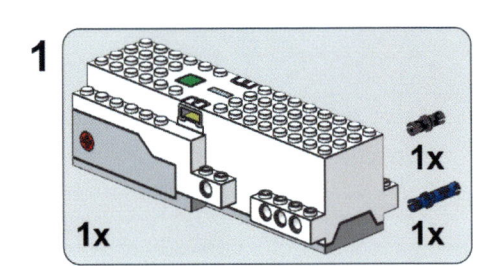

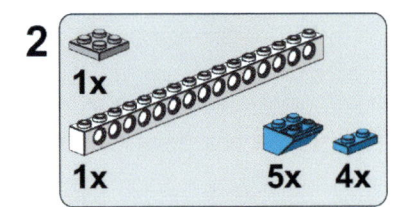

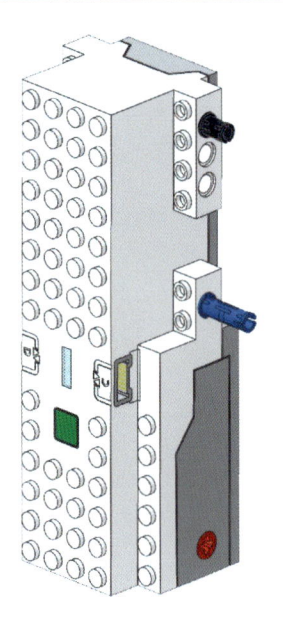

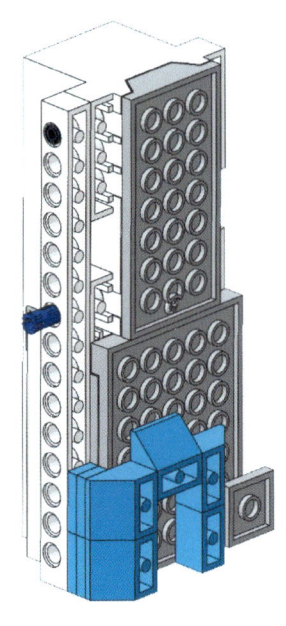

Ball-Booster

BUILD

1 1x 1x

2 1x 1x

3 1x   2x

3

4

1 1x 1x 1x 1x   5 4

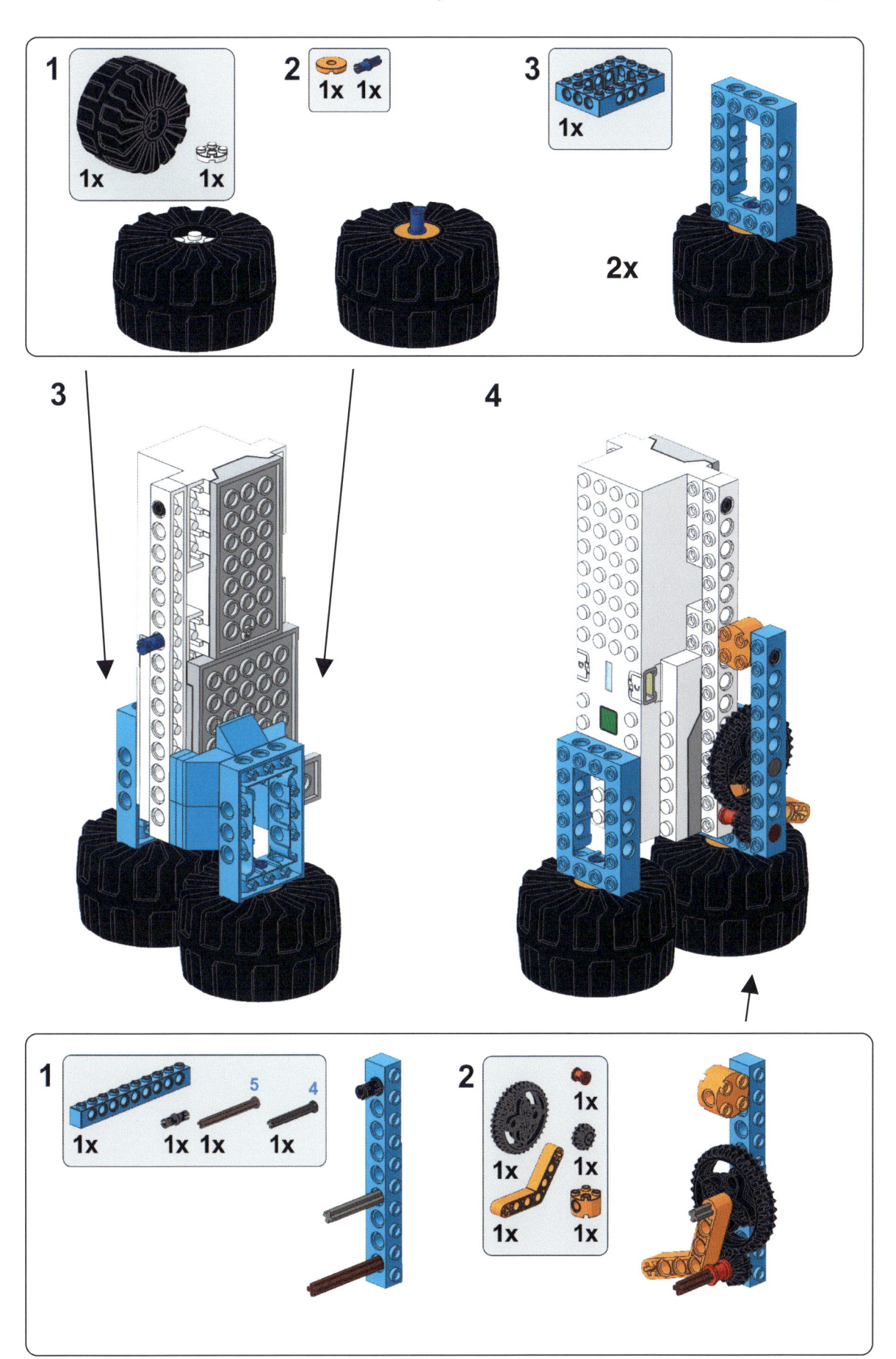

2 1x 1x 1x 1x

Ball-Booster

5 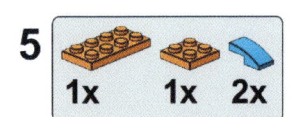 1x 1x 2x

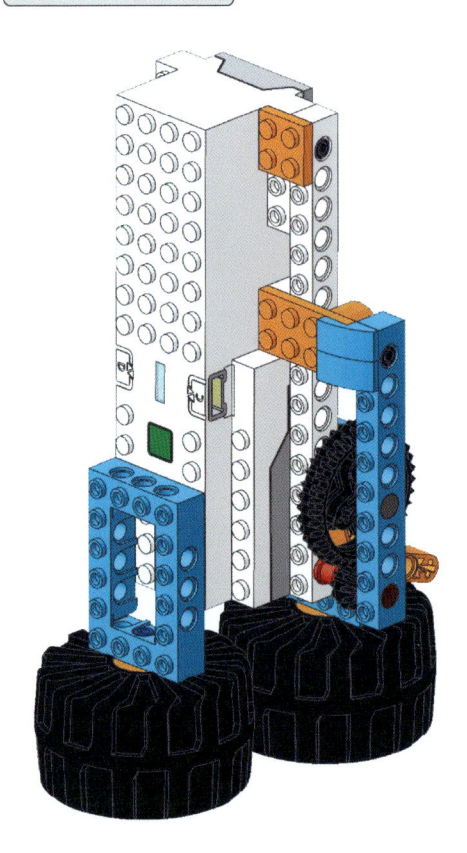

6  1x 1x 3x 1x

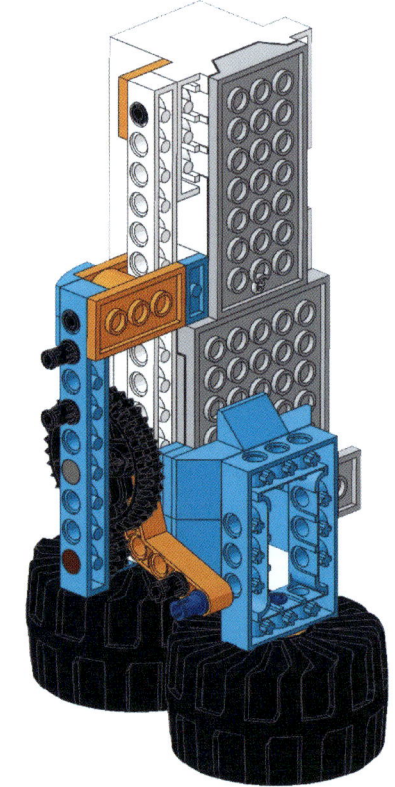

Ball-Booster

BUILD

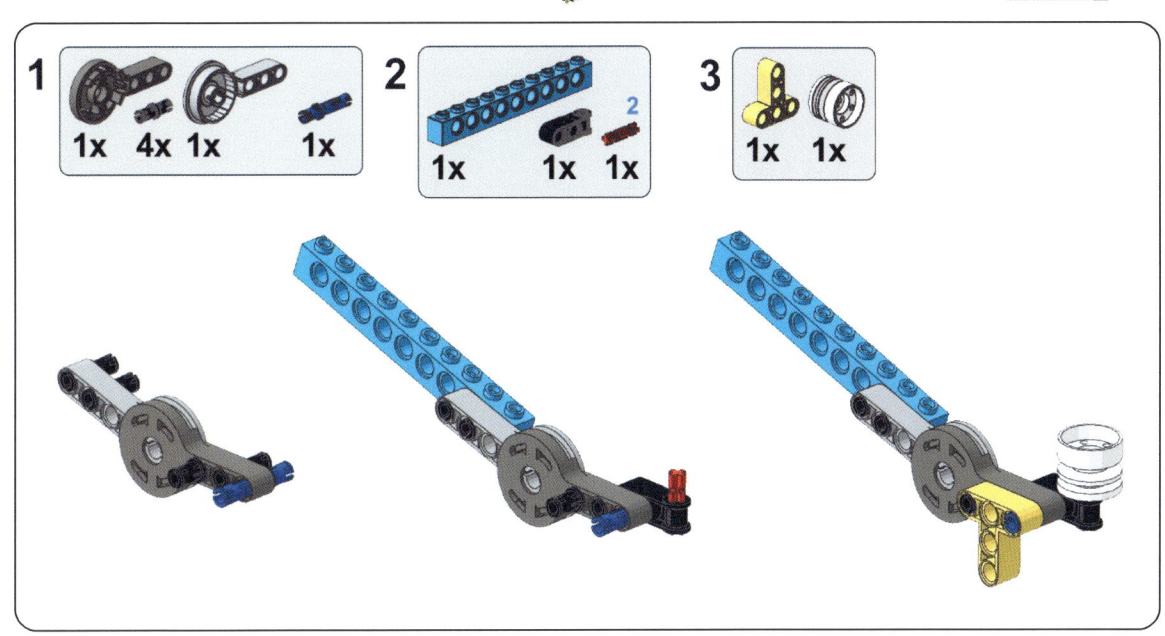

1 1x 4x 1x 1x

2 1x 1x 1x

3 1x 1x

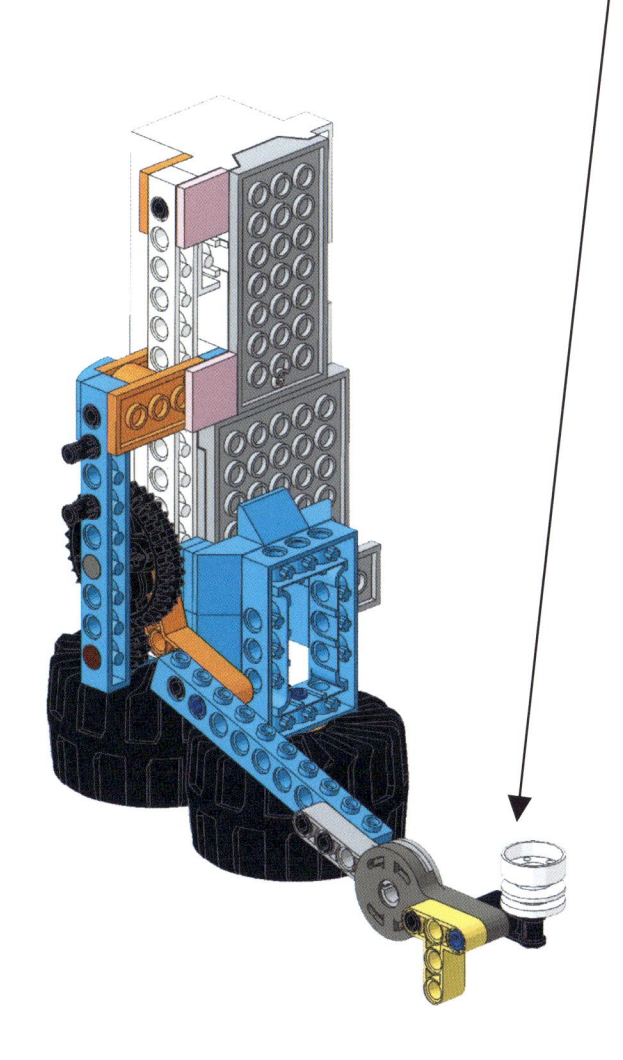

7 2x

Ball-Booster

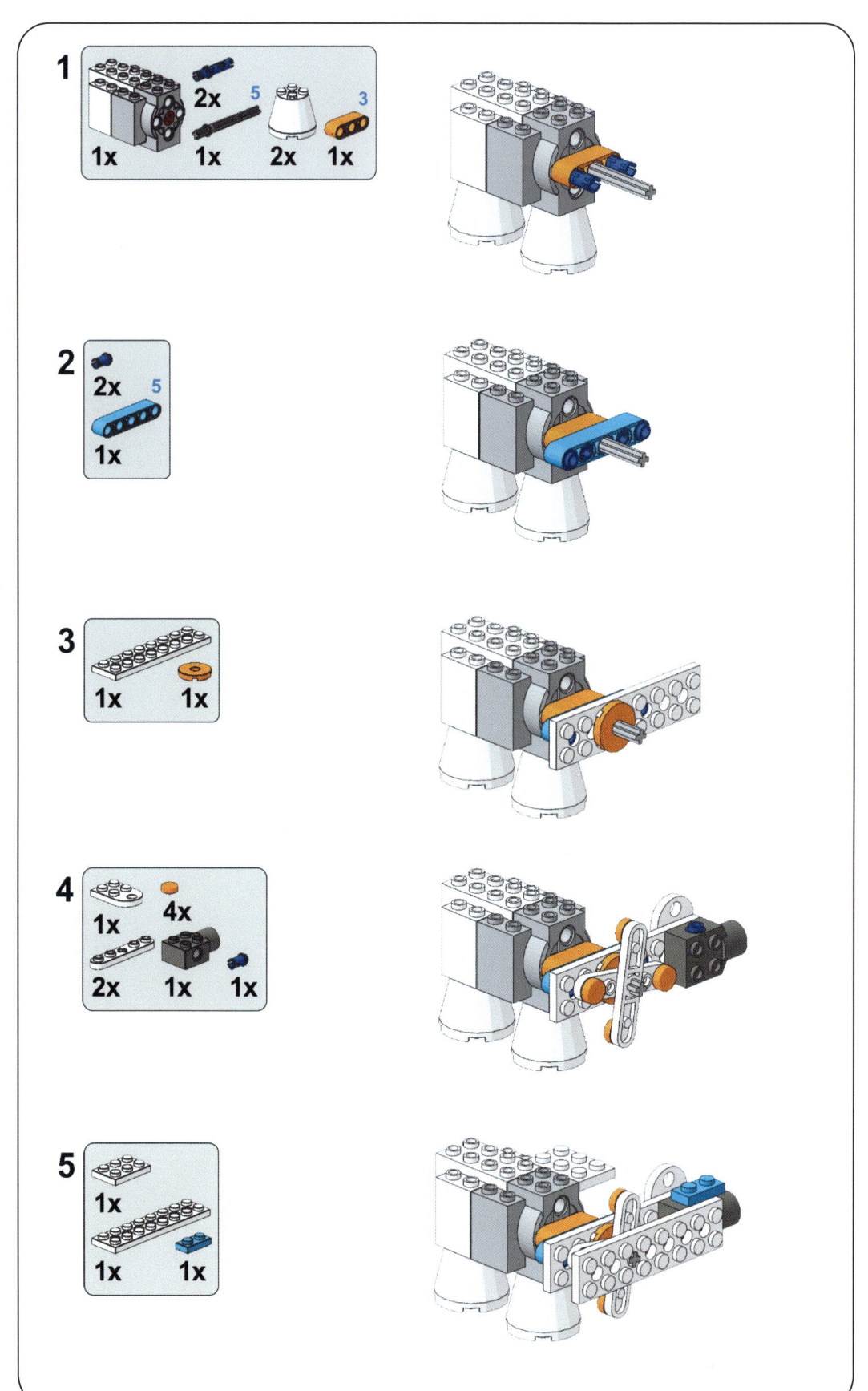

Ball-Booster

BUILD

6 1x 2x 2x 1x 1x

7 1x 1x 1x 1x 1x

8 2x 1x 1x

9 1x 2x 1x 1x 2x 1x

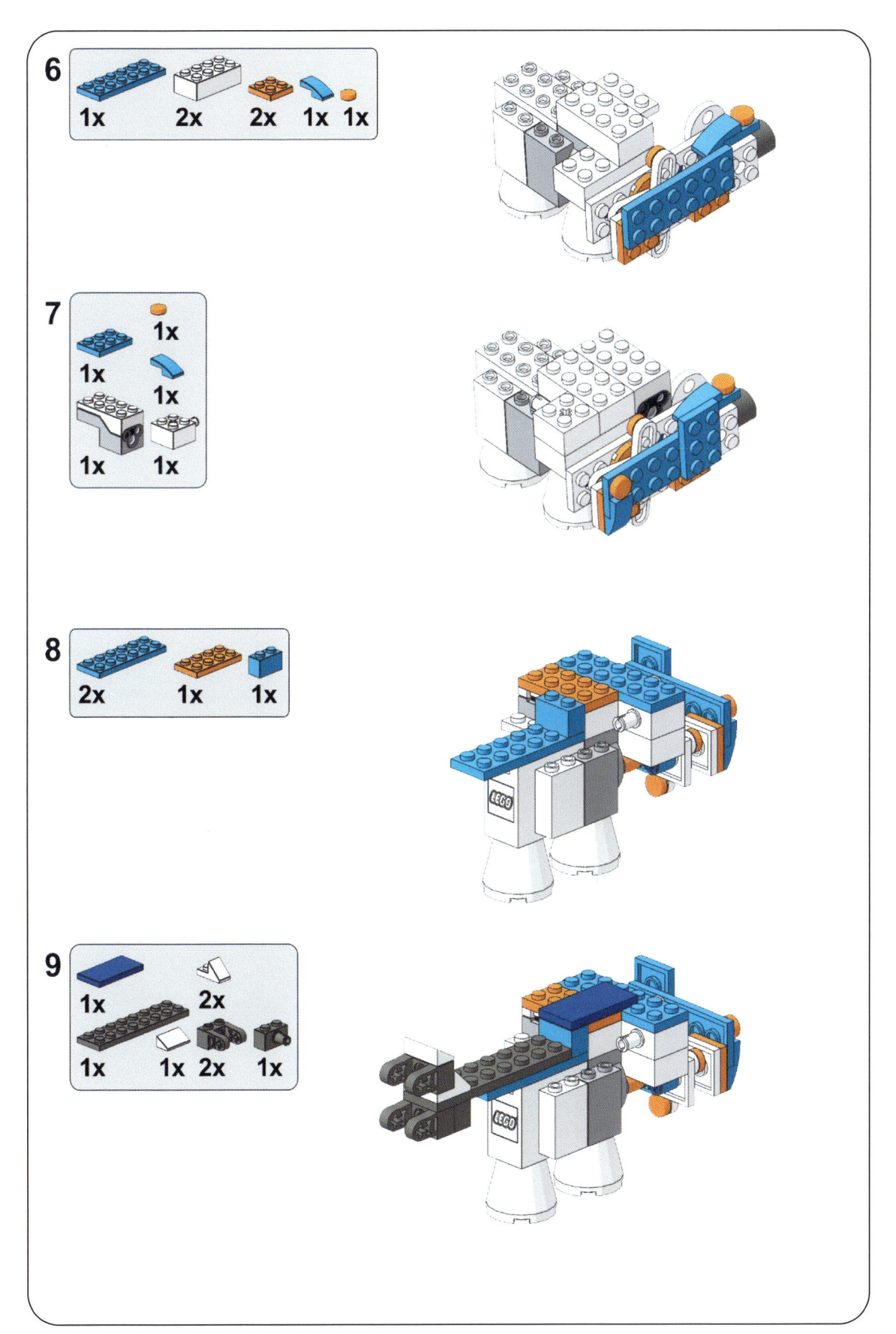

13

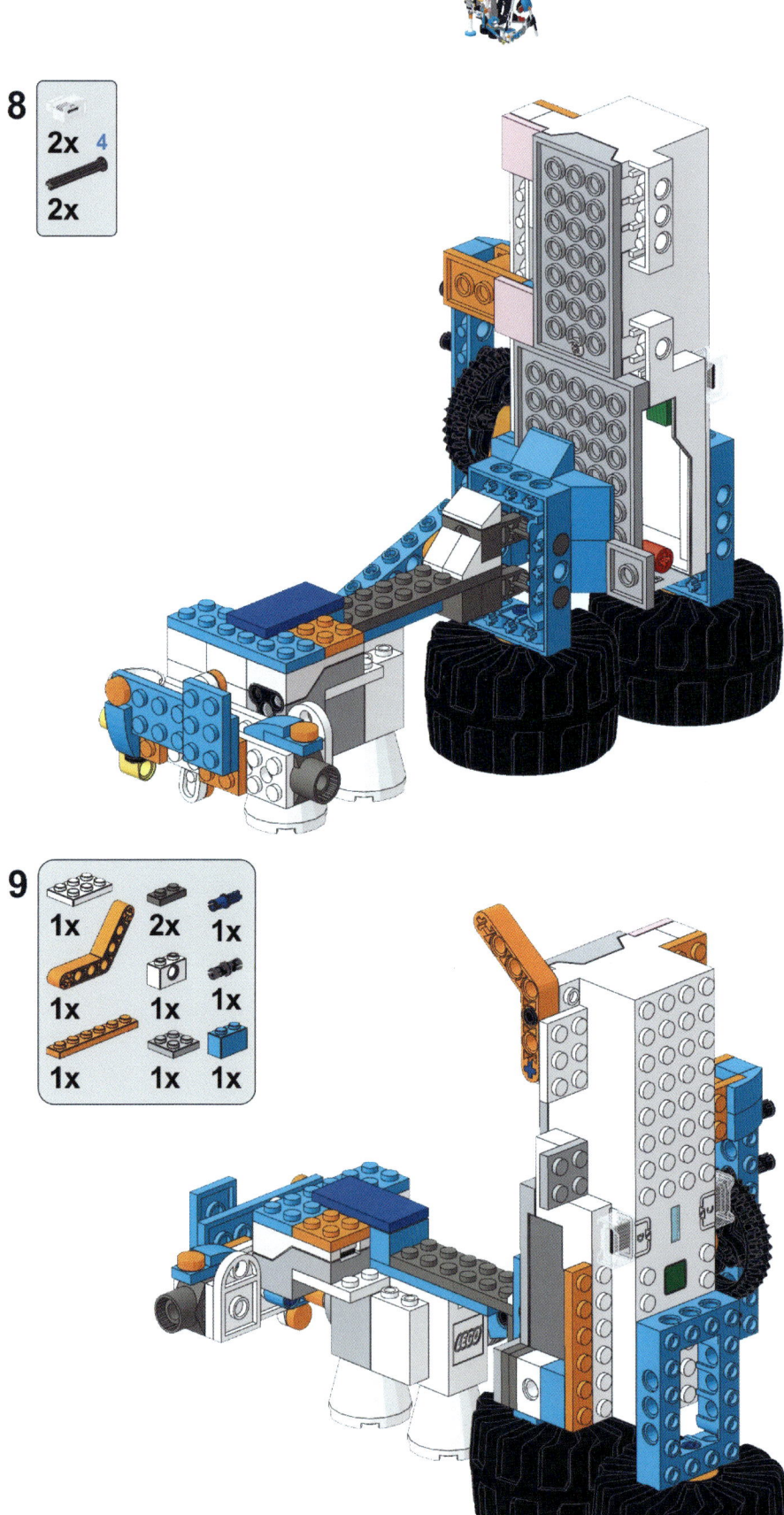

Ball-Booster

8
2x 4
2x

9
1x 2x 1x
1x 1x 1x
1x 1x 1x

14

Ball-Booster

BUILD

10
1x 1x 1x 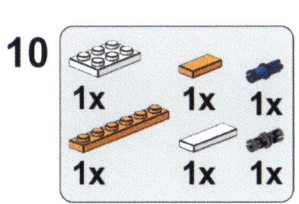
1x 1x 1x

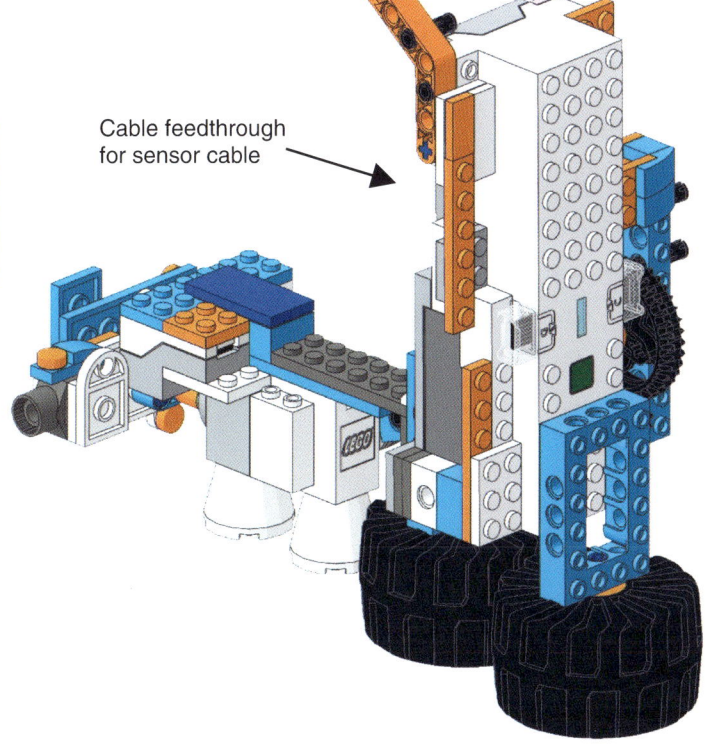

Cable feedthrough for sensor cable

11
1x 1x
9
1x 2x 1x 1x 1x

15

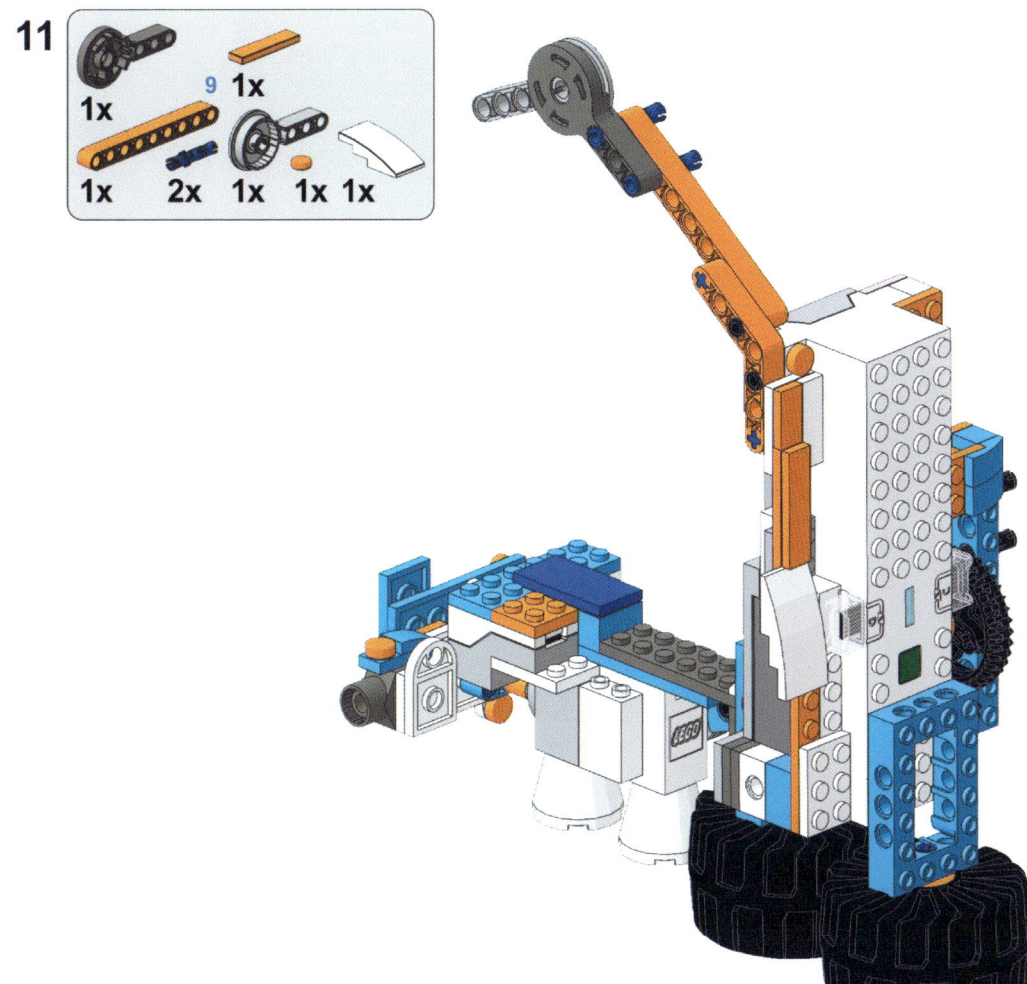

Ball-Booster

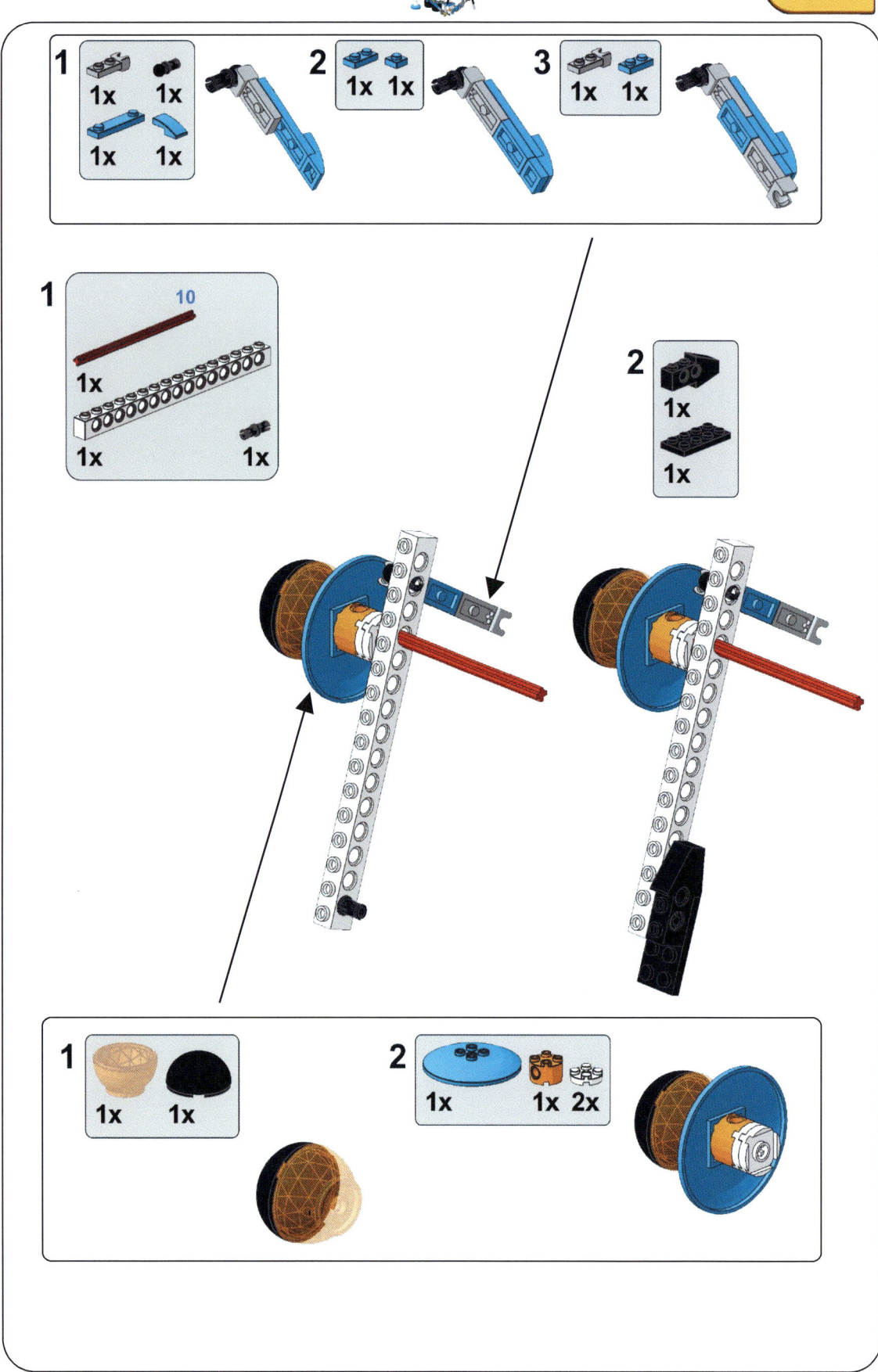

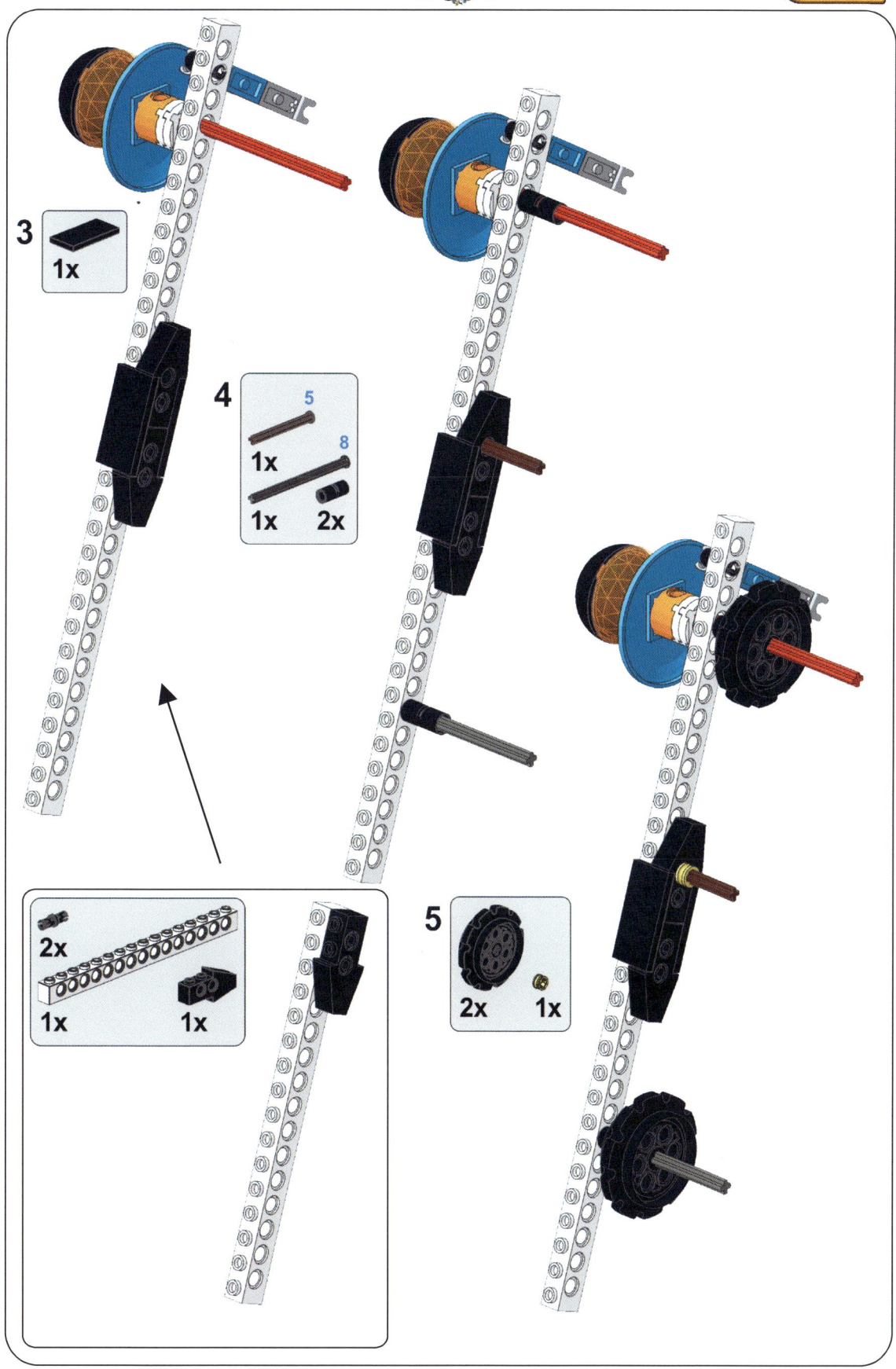

Ball-Booster

3 1x

4 5 1x / 8 1x 2x

5 2x 1x

2x / 1x / 1x

17

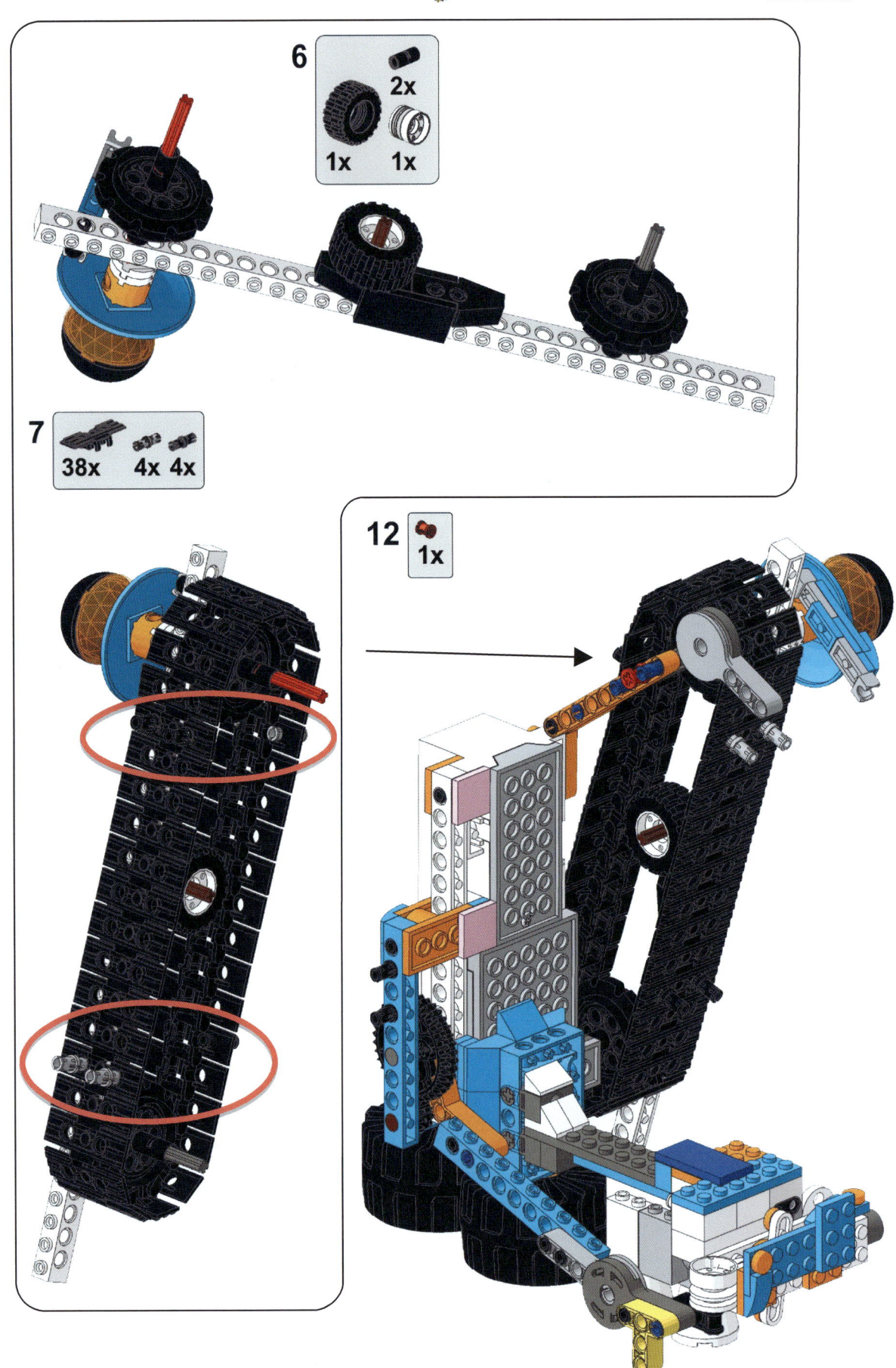

Ball-Booster

6
1x 2x
1x 1x

7
38x 4x 4x

12
1x

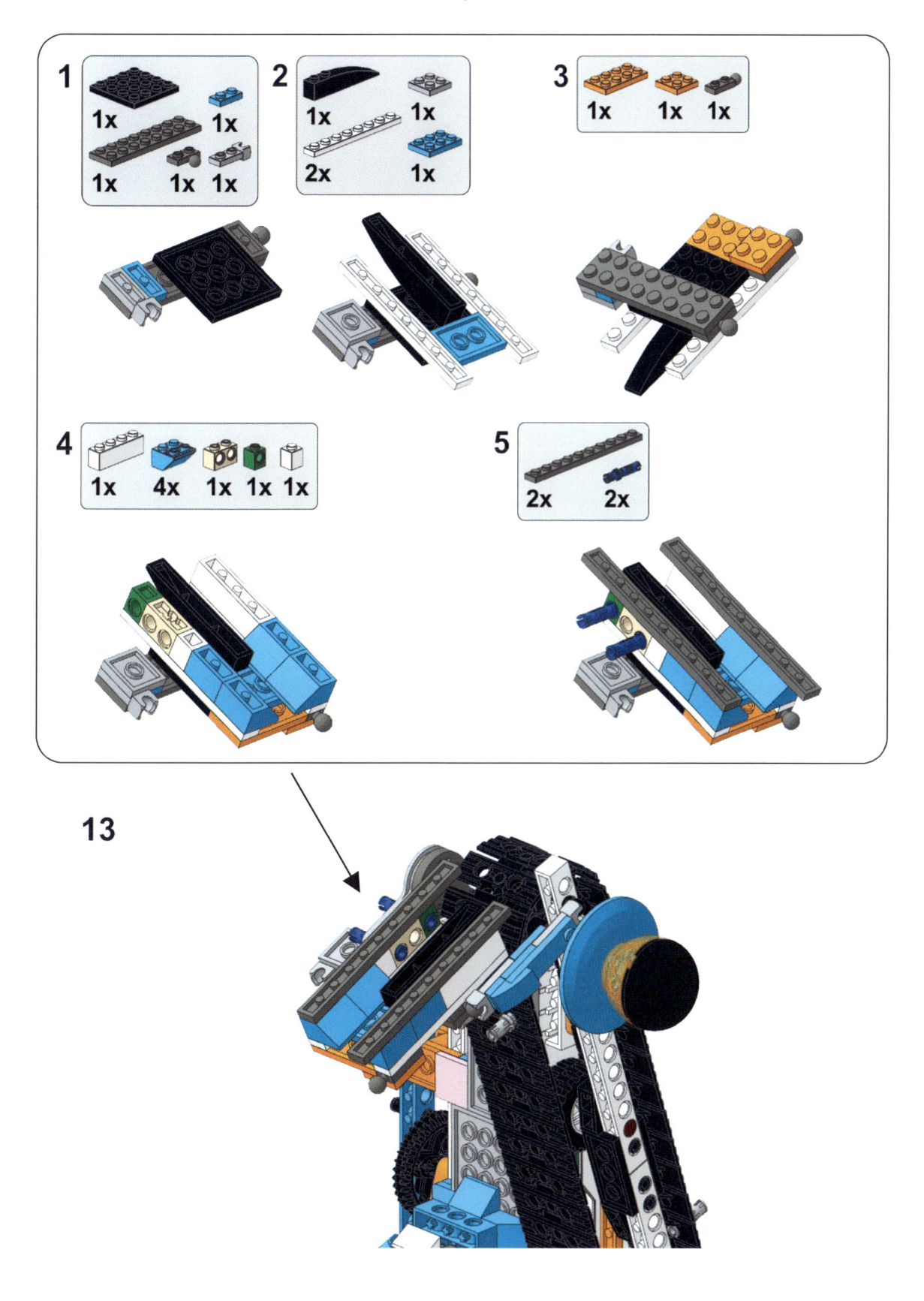

Ball-Booster

1 1x 1x 1x 1x 1x

2 1x 1x 2x 1x

3 1x 1x 1x

4 1x 4x 1x 1x 1x

5 2x 2x

13

Ball-Booster

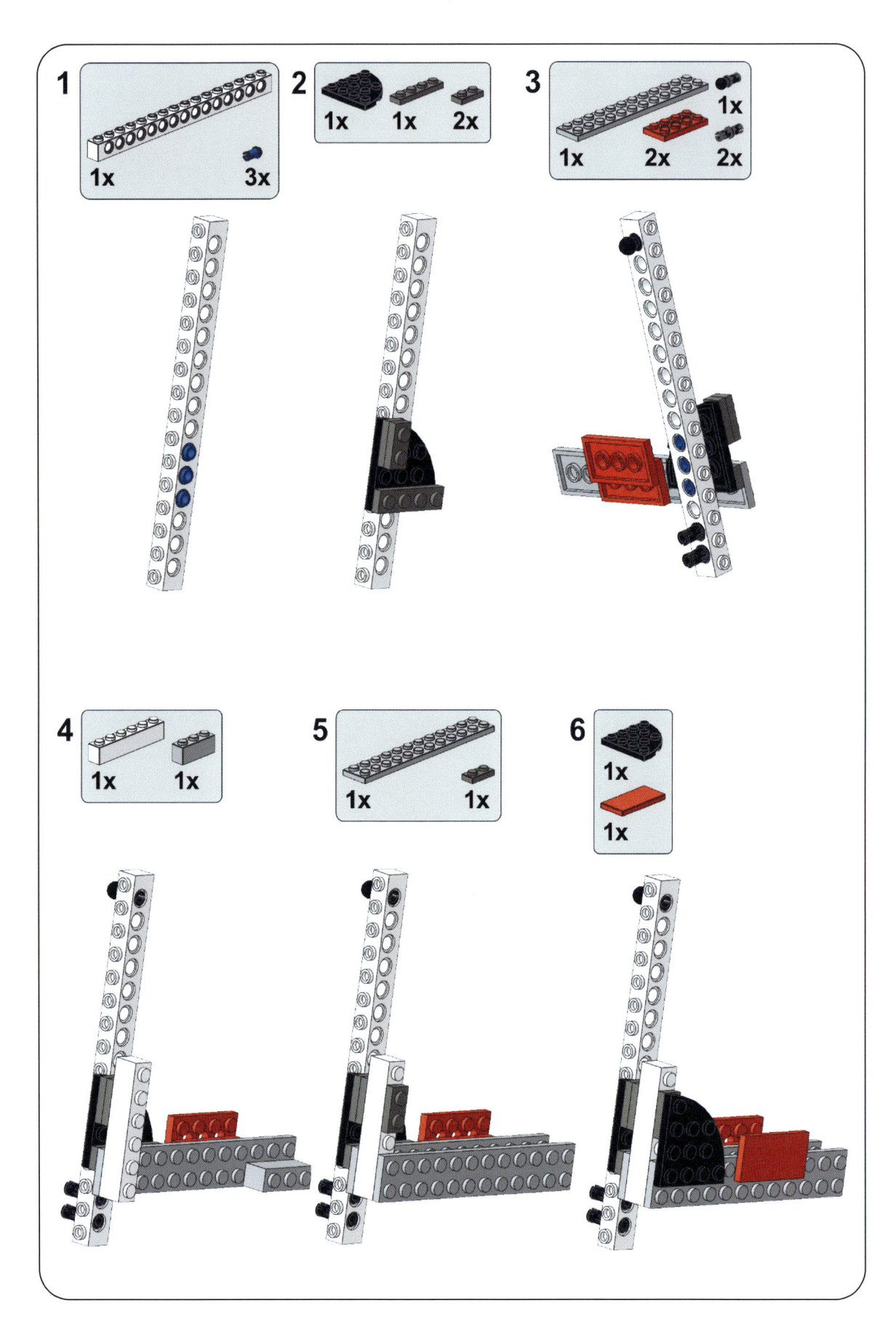

20

Ball-Booster

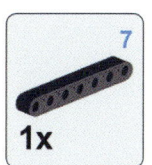

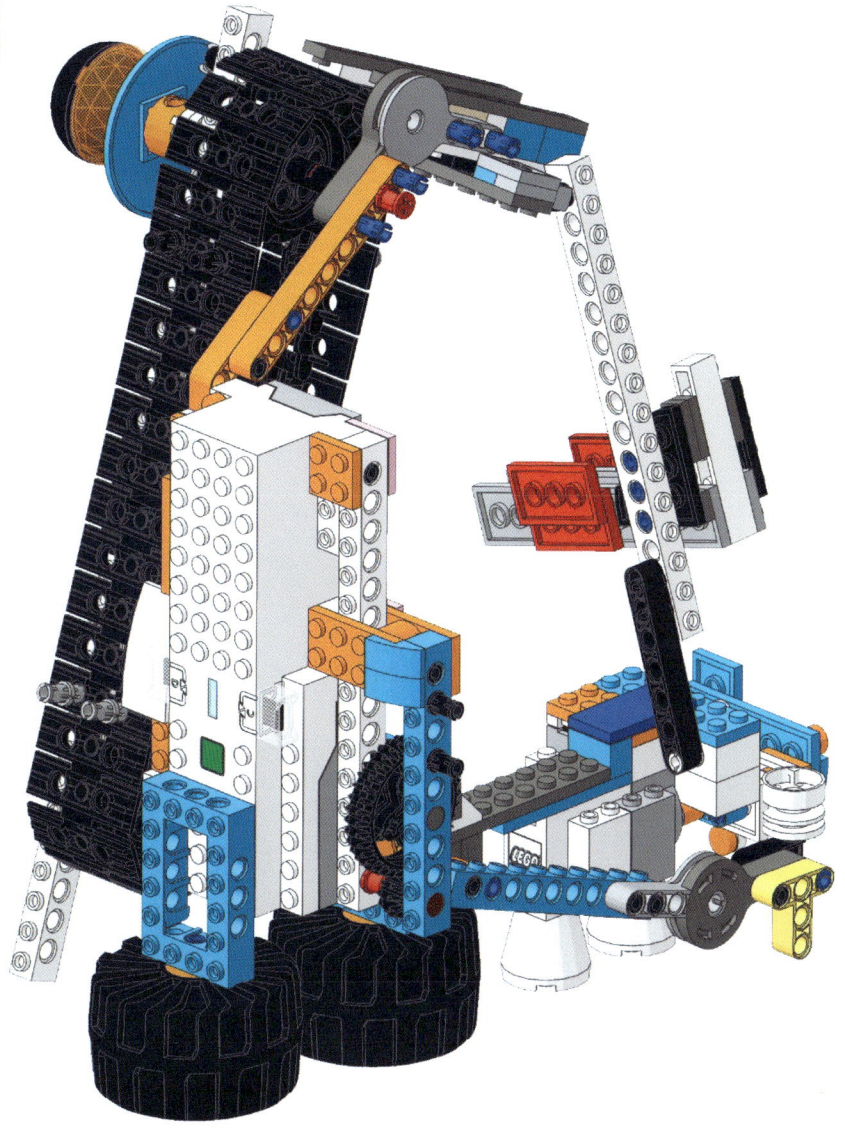

14 1x 7

Ball-Booster

BUILD

1 1x 1x 1x 1x 1x
2 1x 2x
3 1x 3x
4 3x 1x 1x 1x
5 1x 1x 1x
6 1x 1x

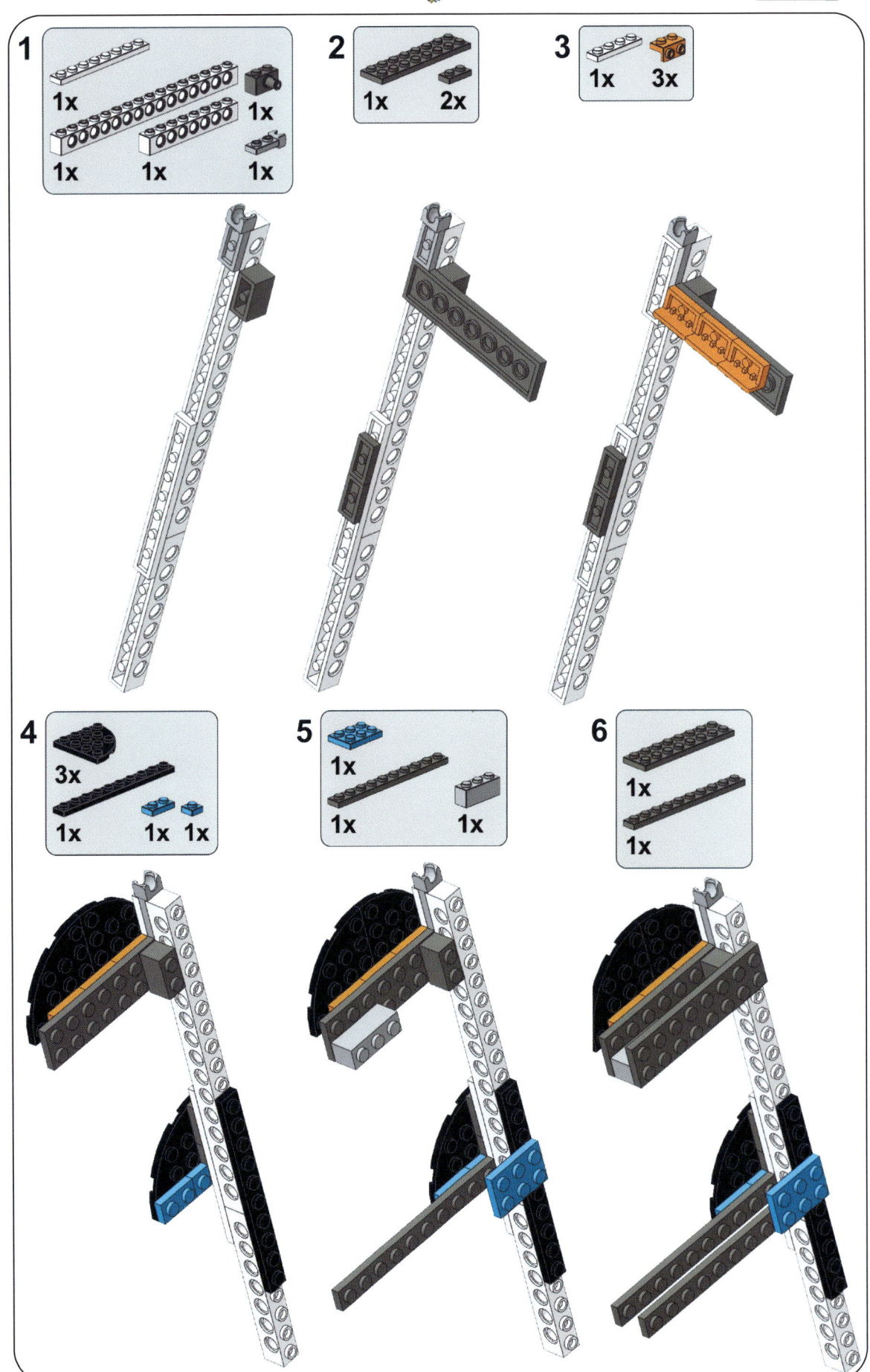

22

Ball-Booster

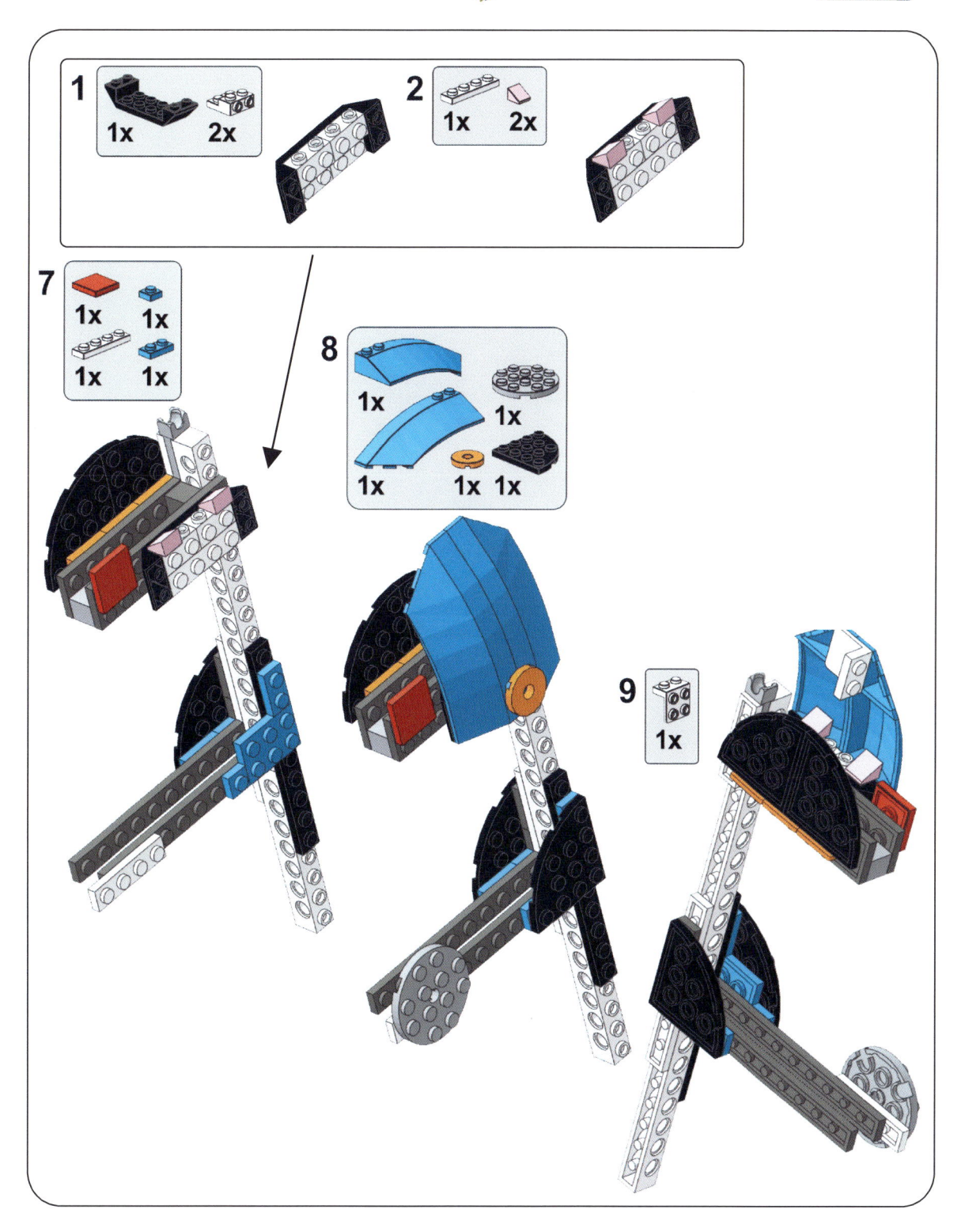

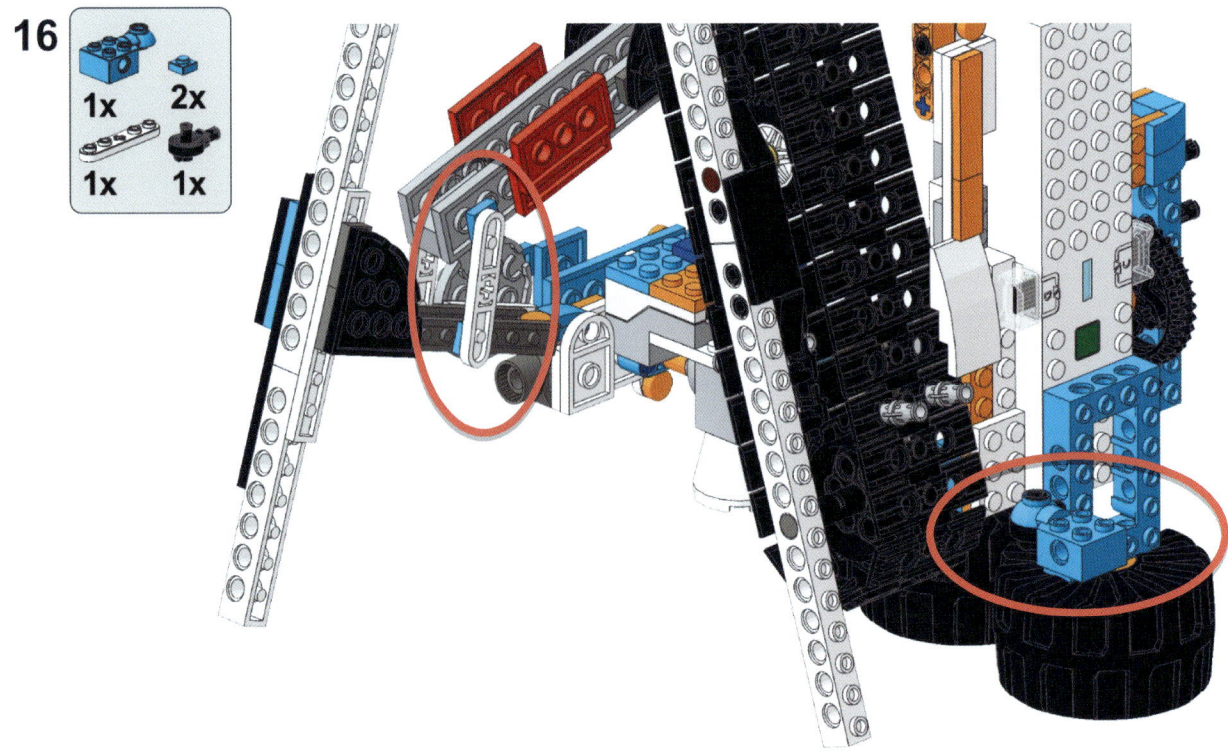

Ball-Booster

15 1x 1x

16 1x 2x 1x 1x

Ball-Booster

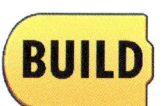

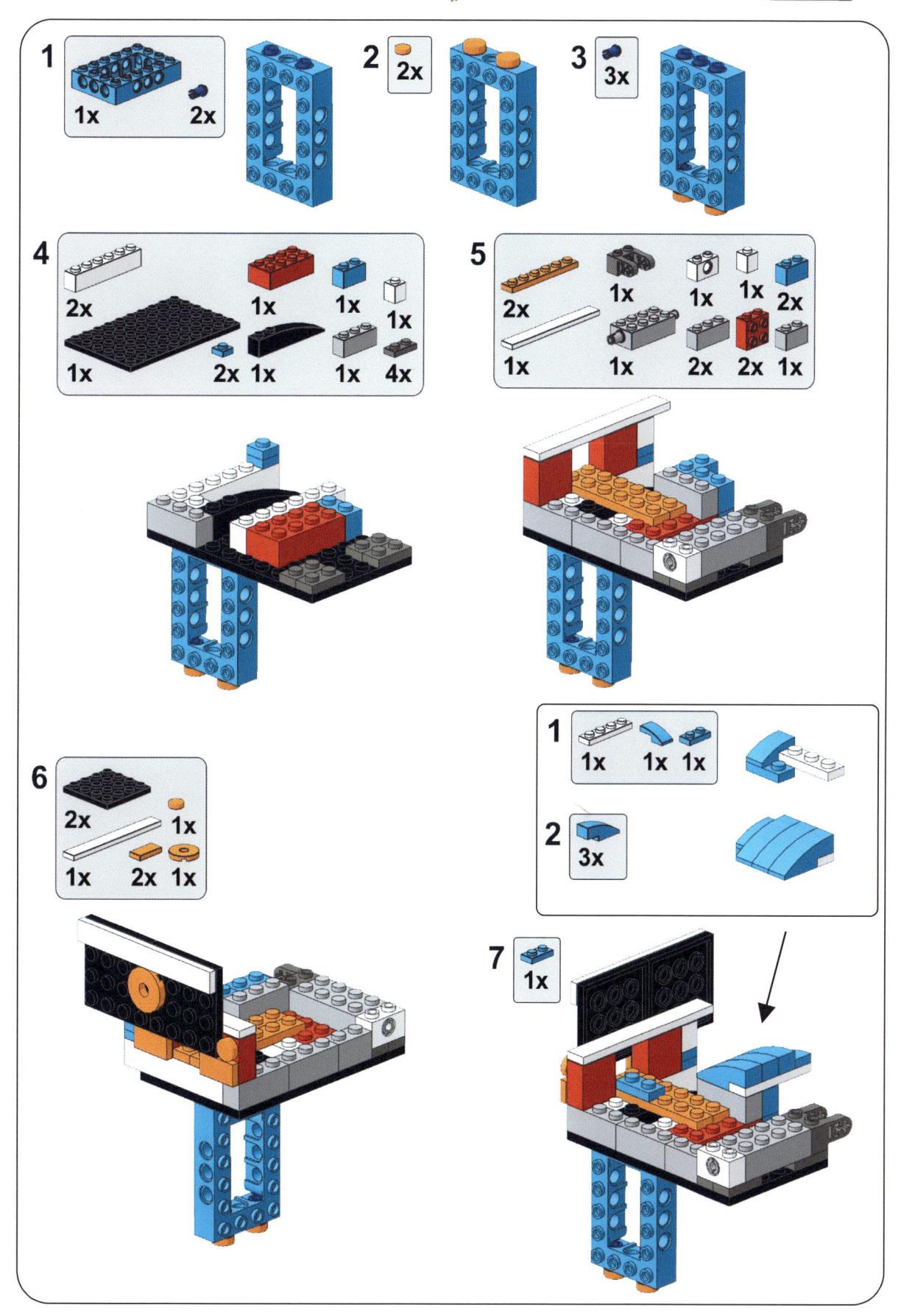

25

Ball-Booster

BUILD

8

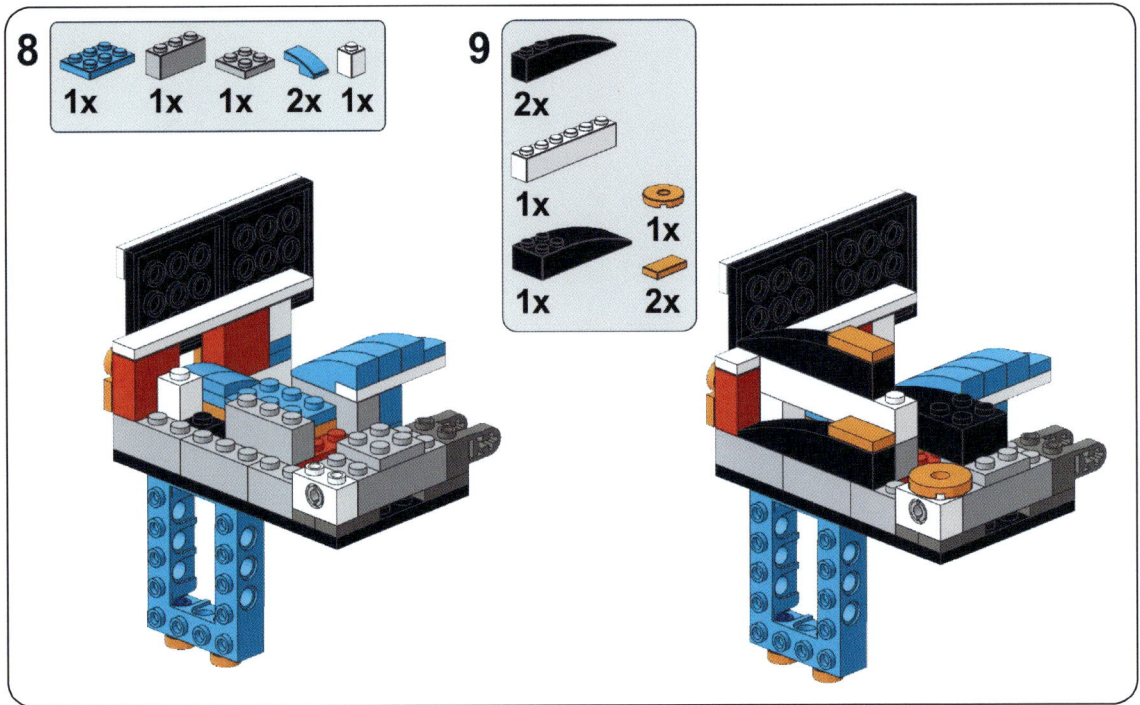

9

17

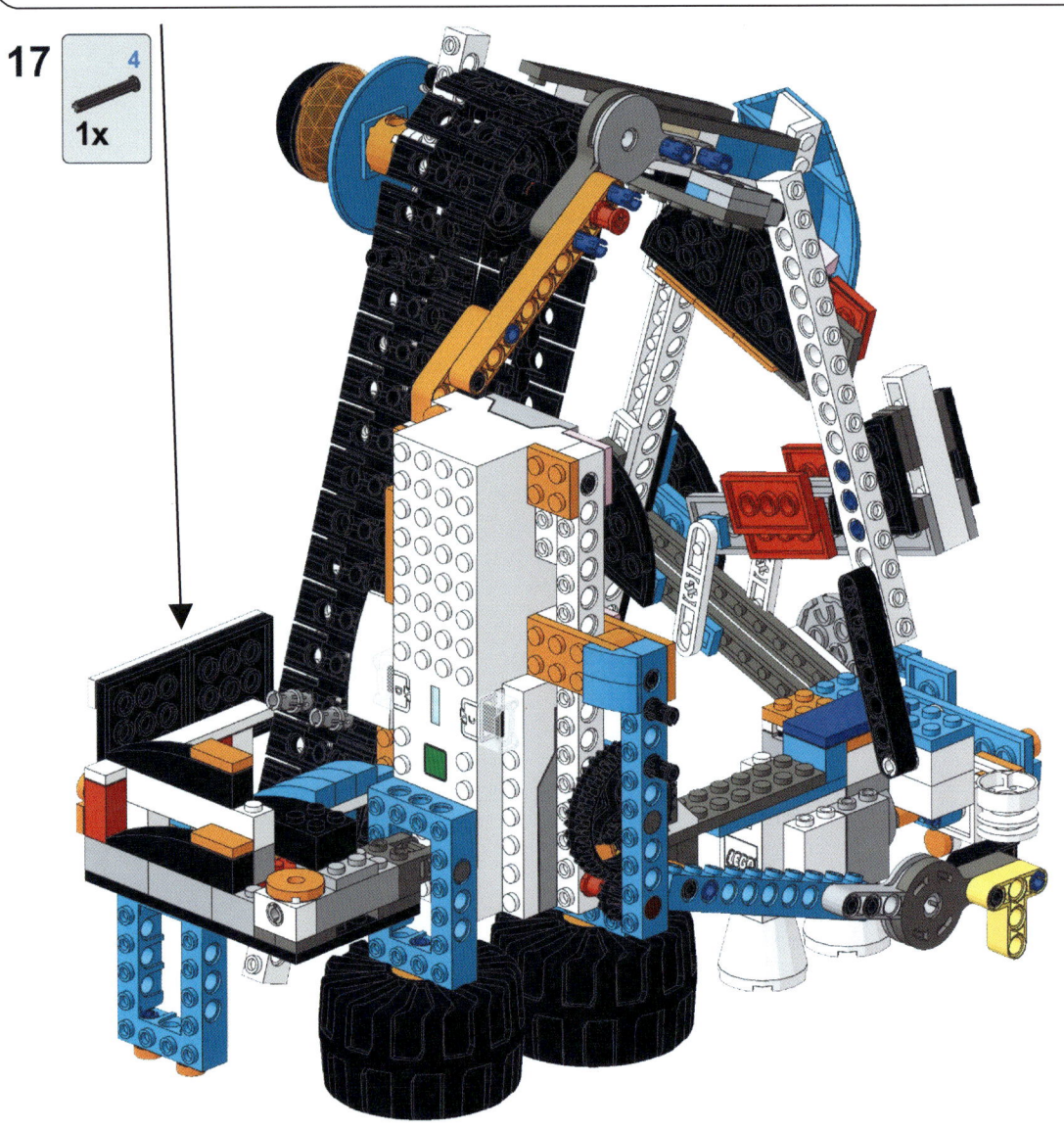

Ball-Booster

BUILD

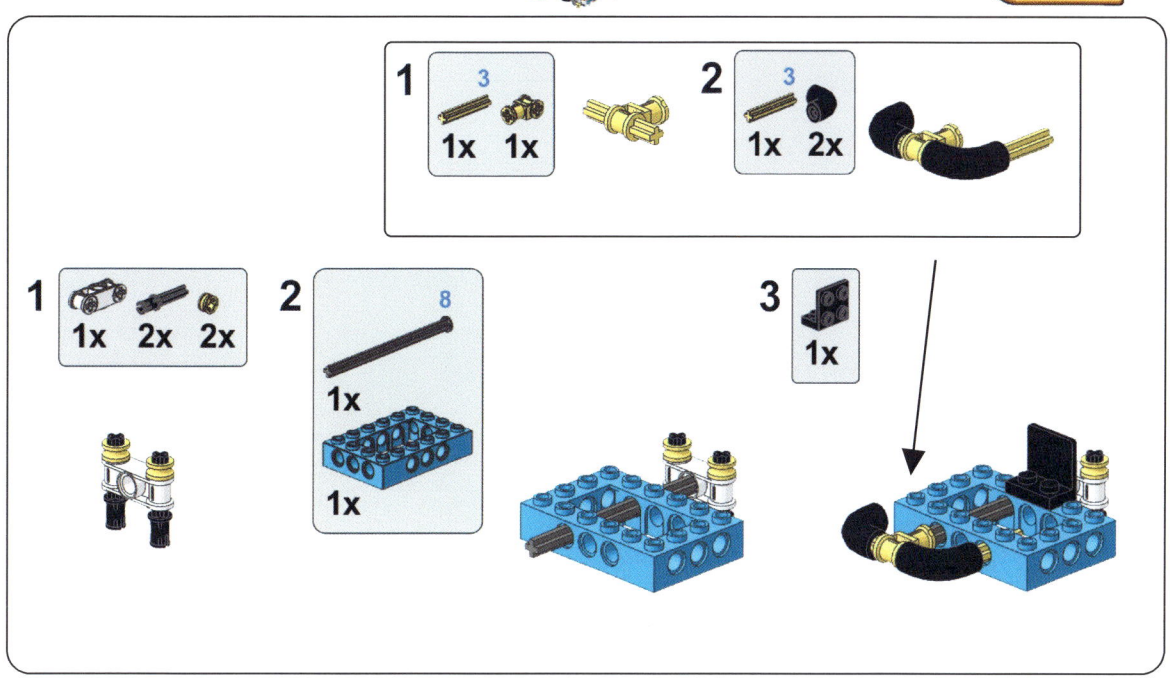

18

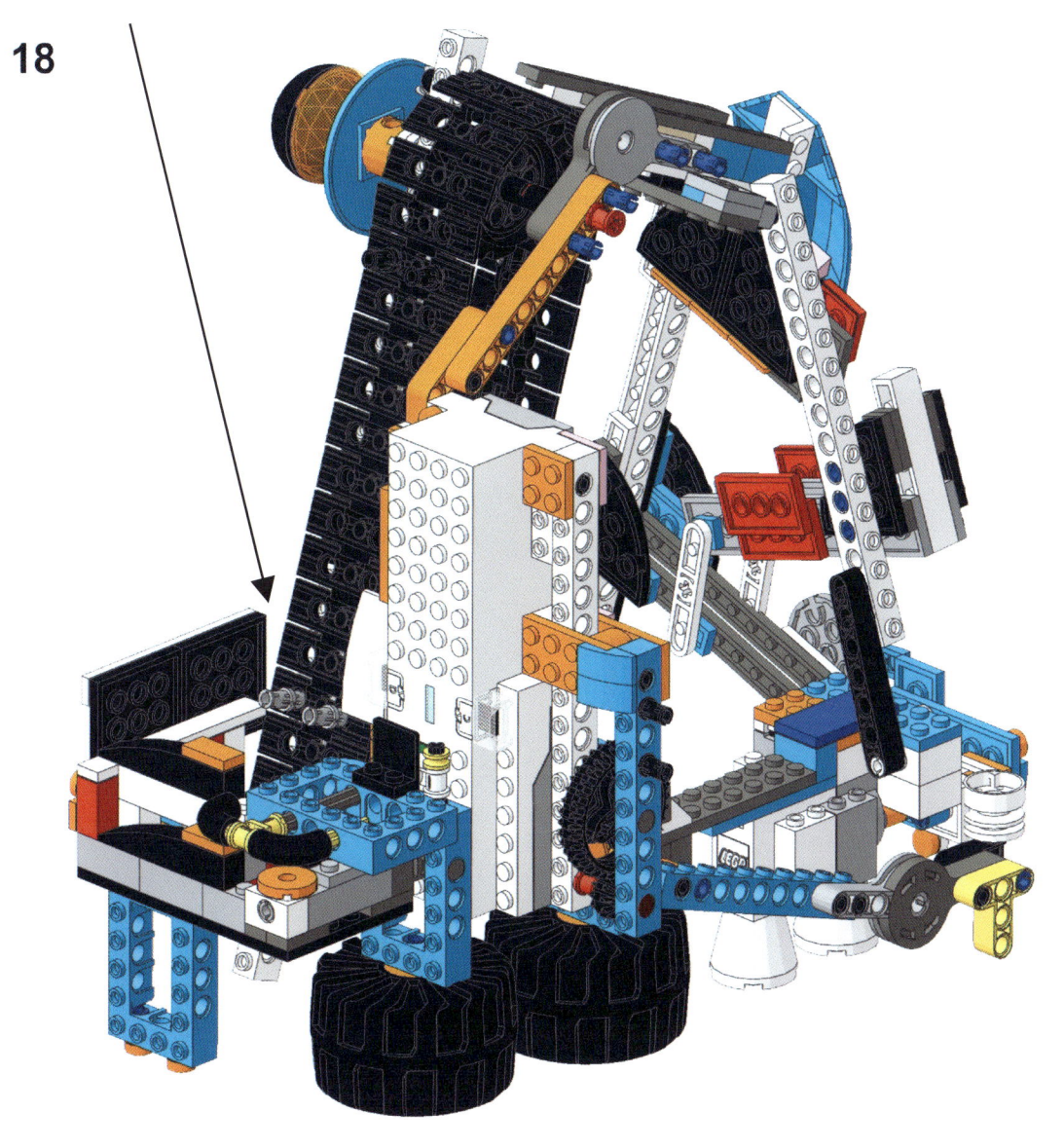

Ball-Booster

19
1x 1x 2x 2x

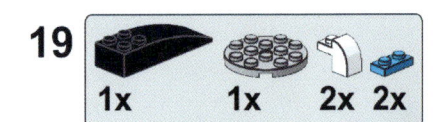

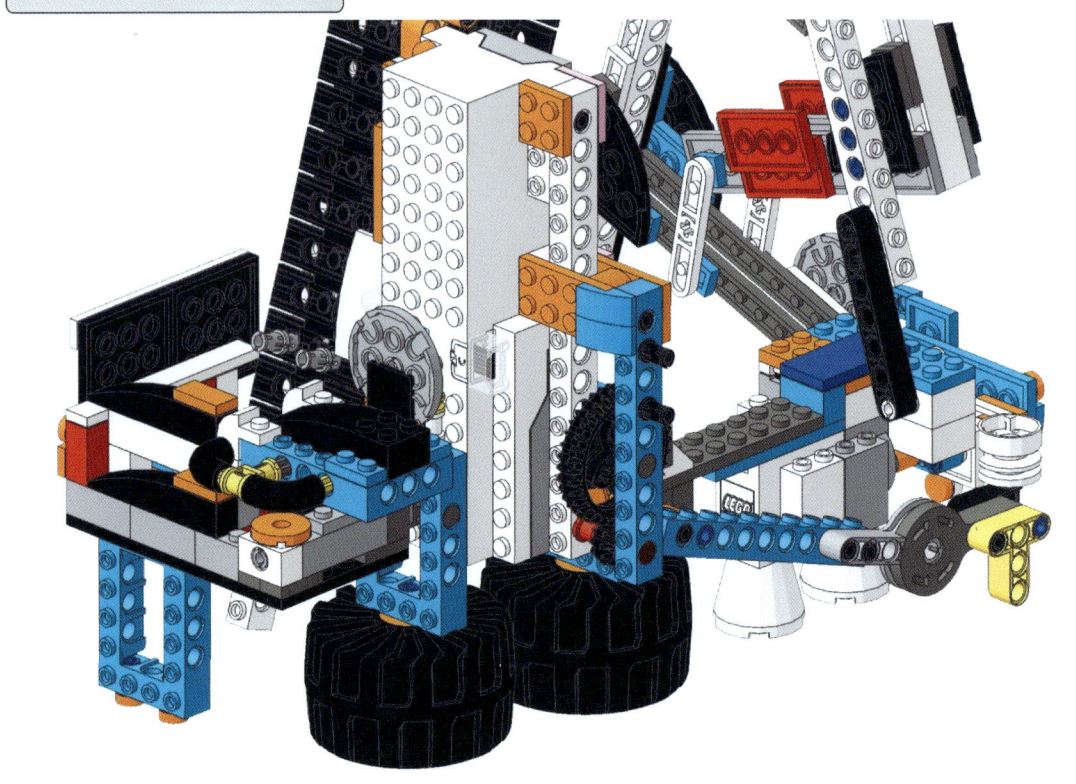

20
1x 2x 2x
1x 2x 1x 1x

28

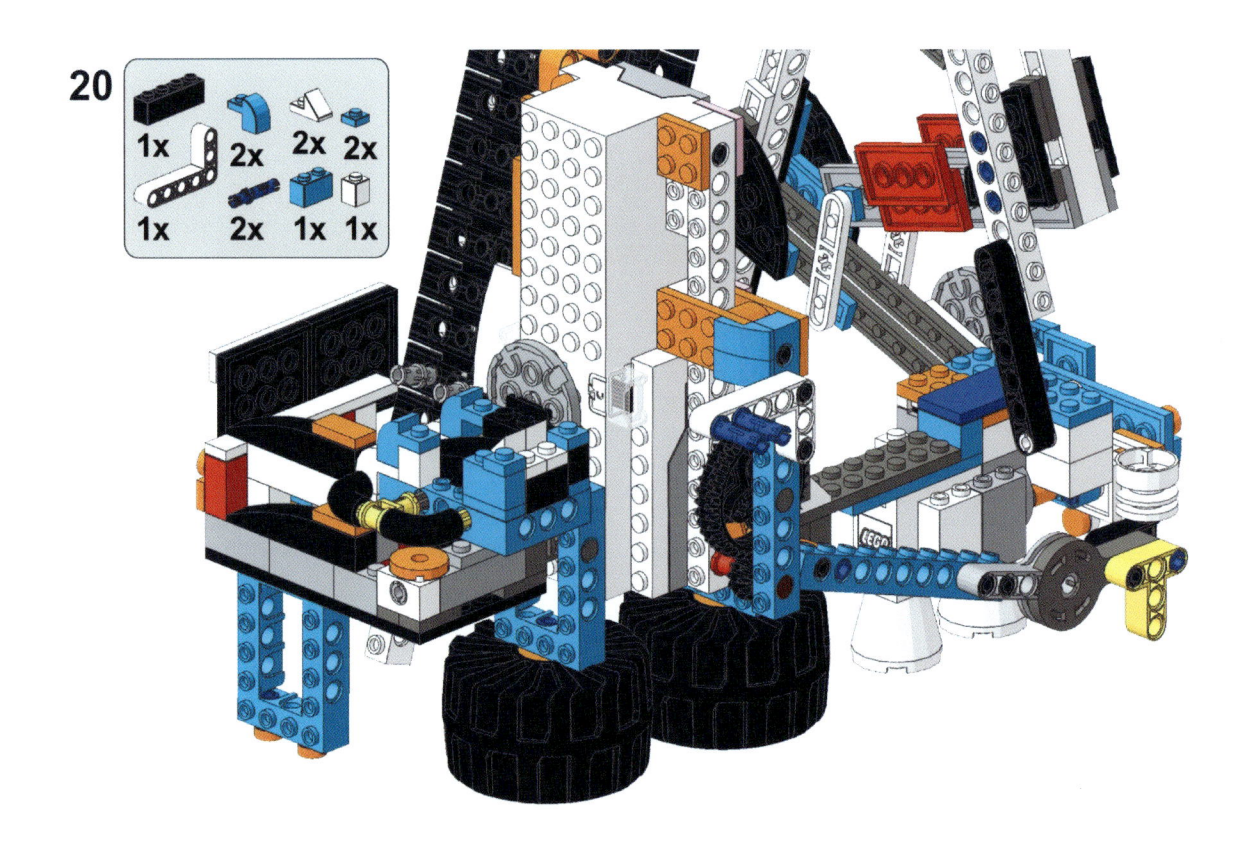

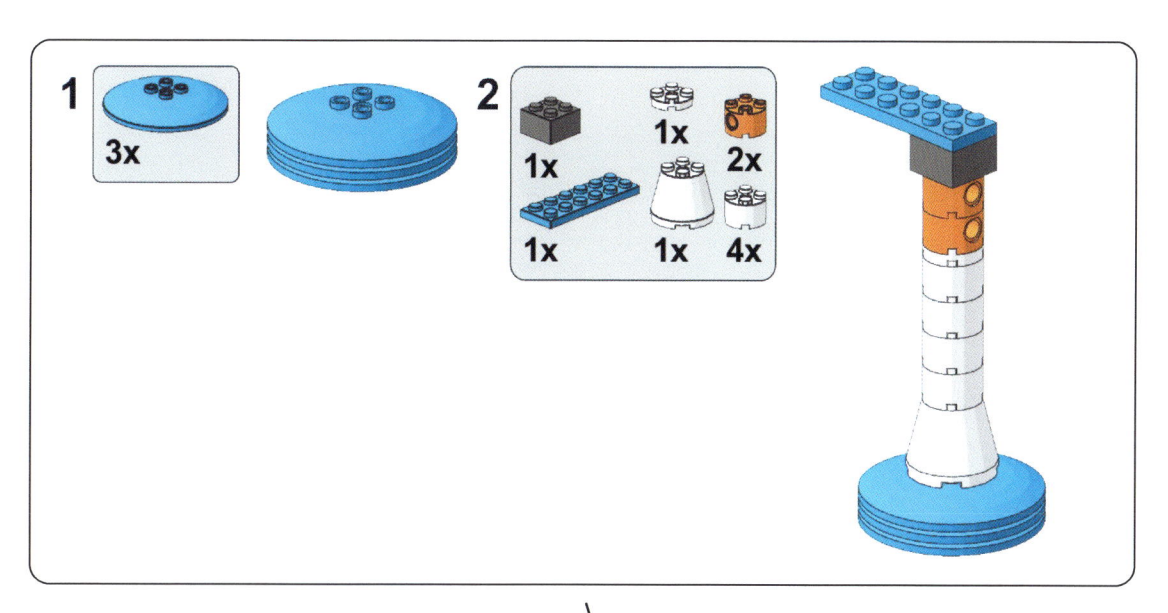

Ball-Booster

BUILD

1 3x

2 1x, 1x, 1x, 2x, 1x, 4x

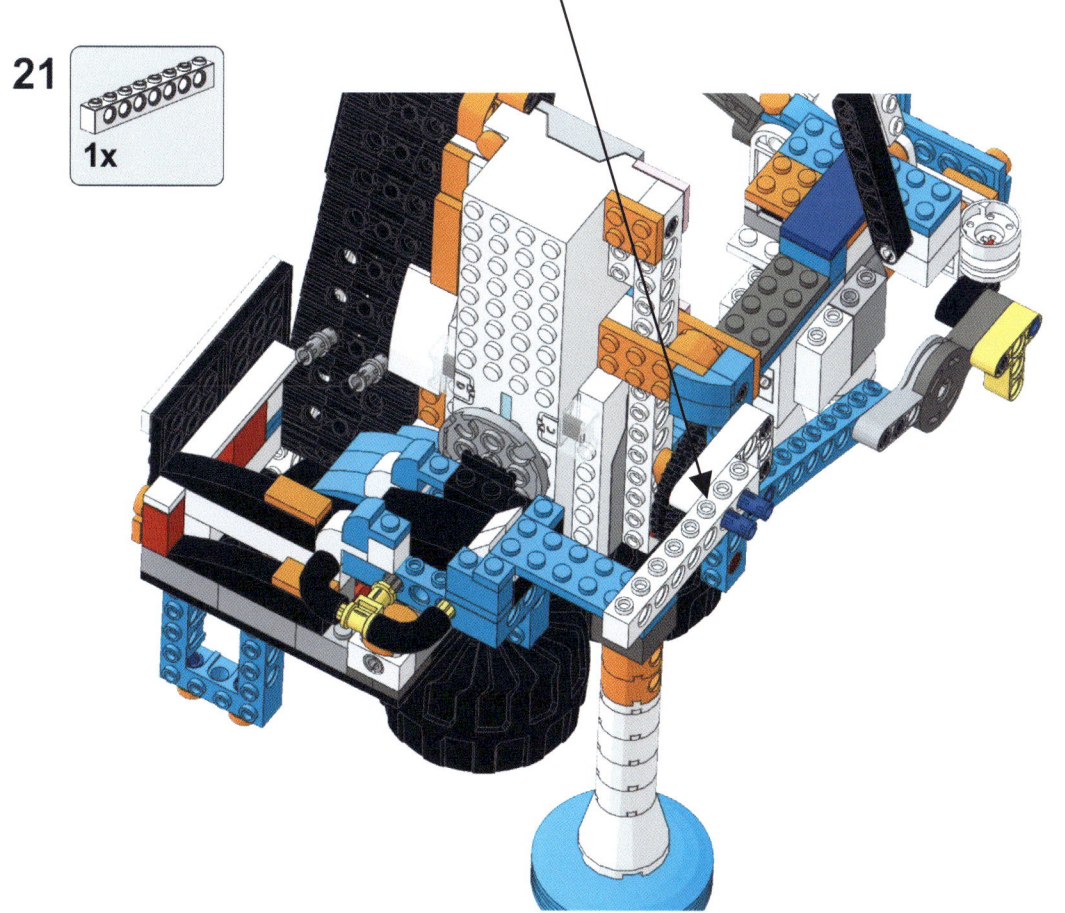

21 1x

Ball-Booster

22 2x 1x 1x

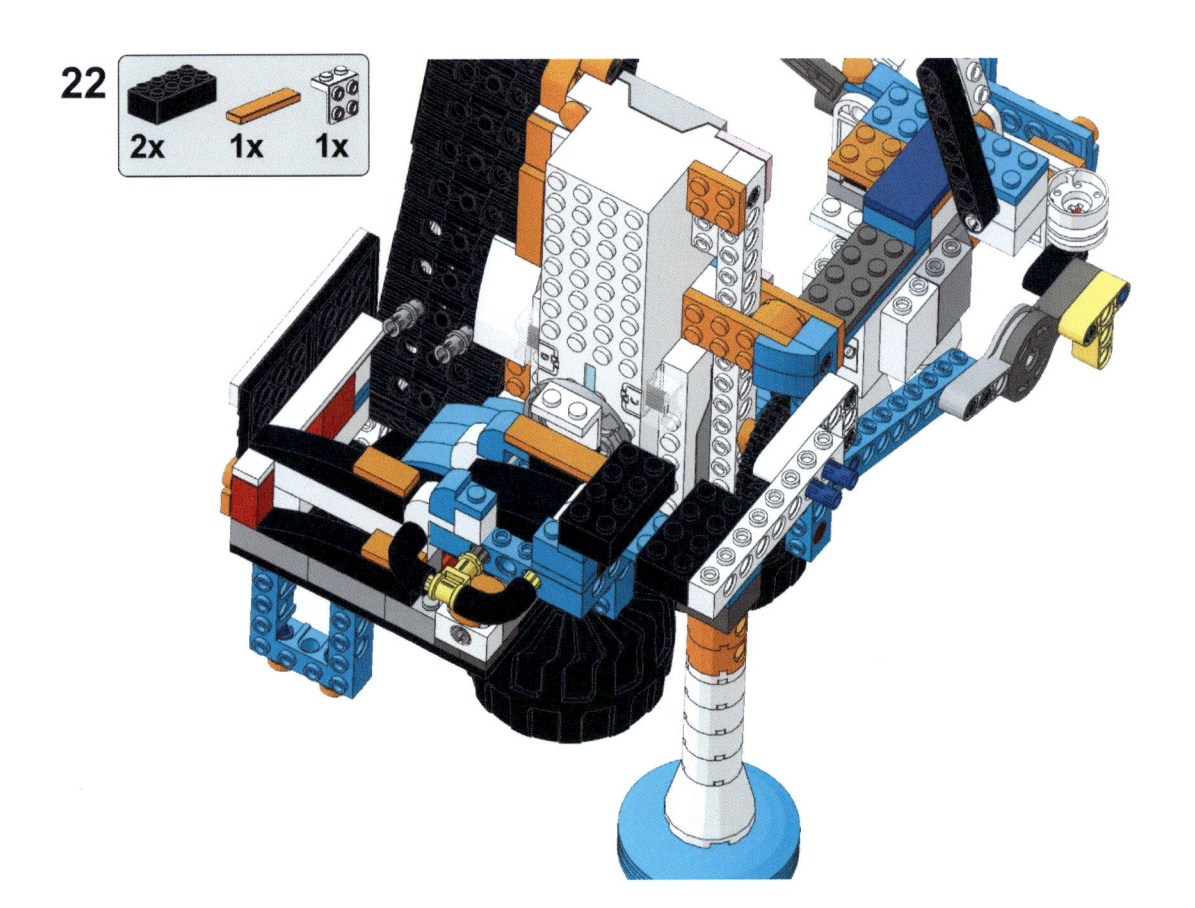

23 2x 1x

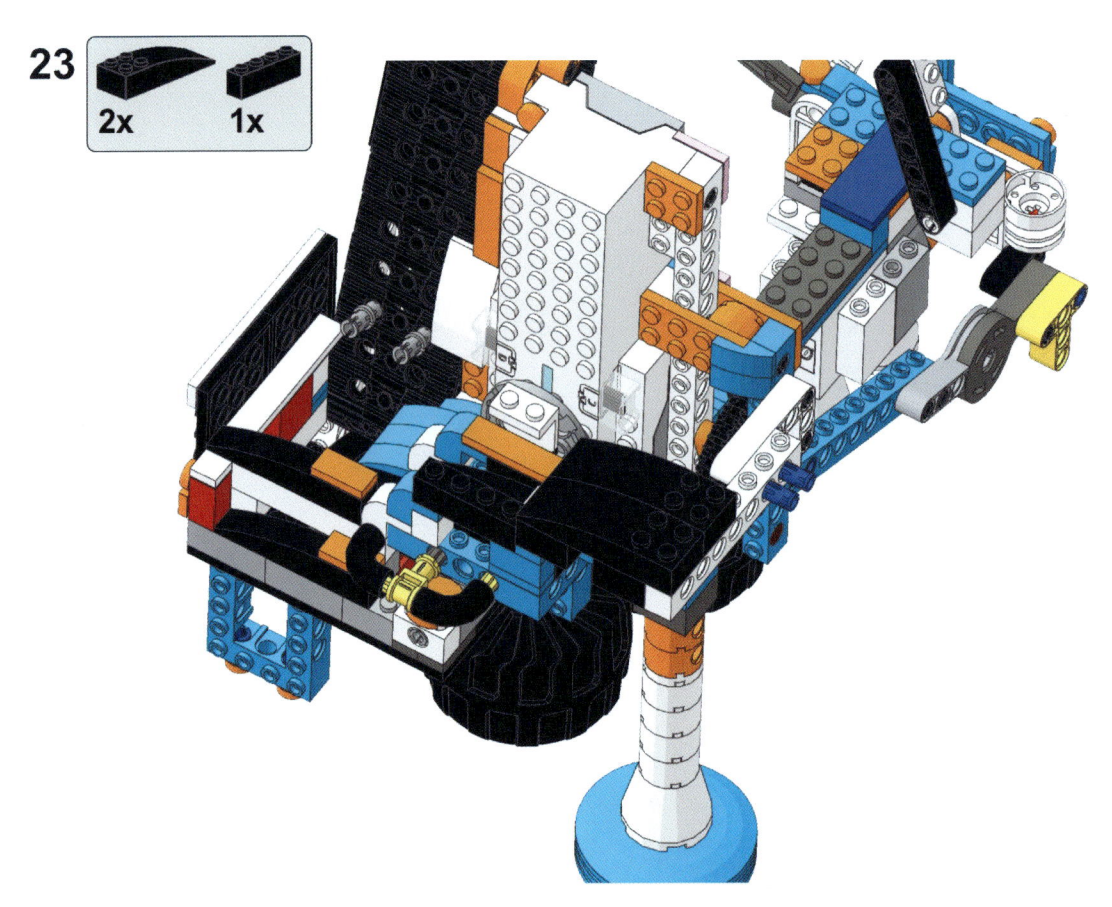

Ball-Booster

24 1x 1x 1x

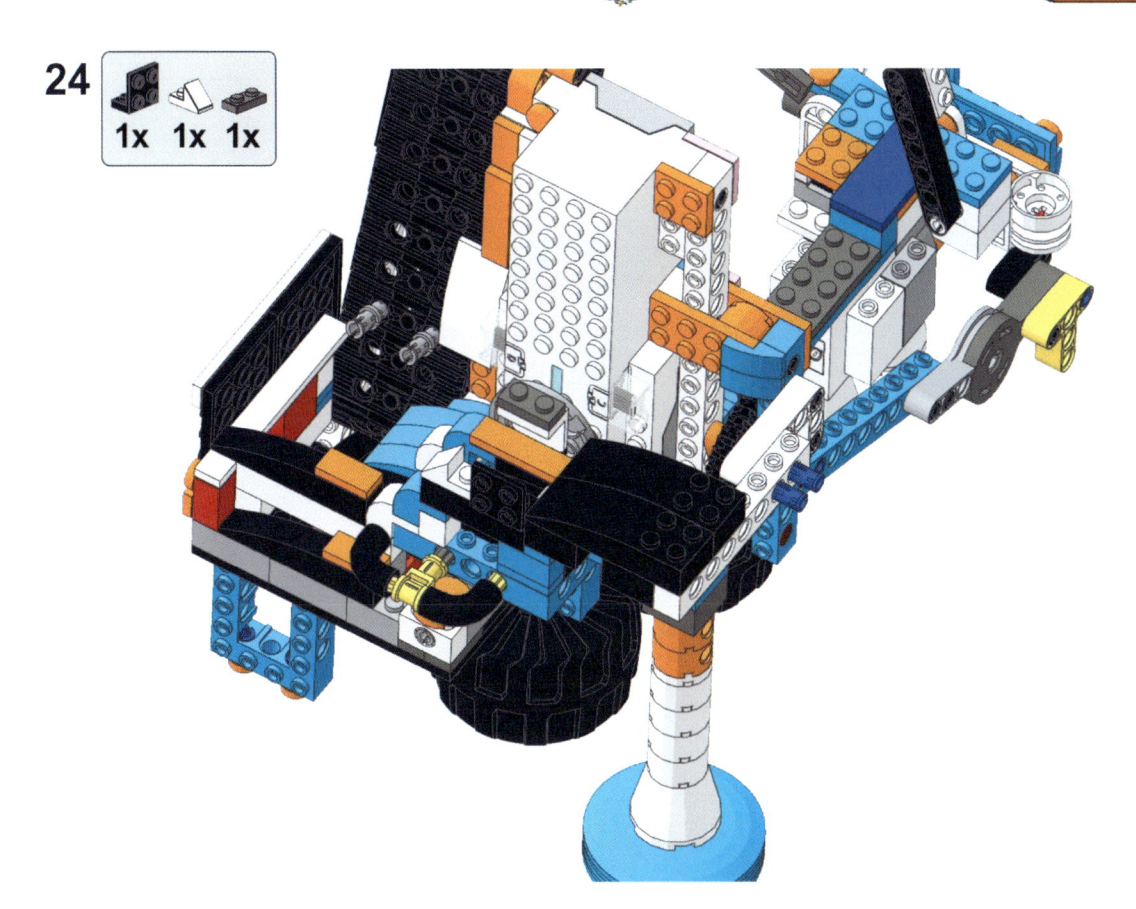

25 1x 1x

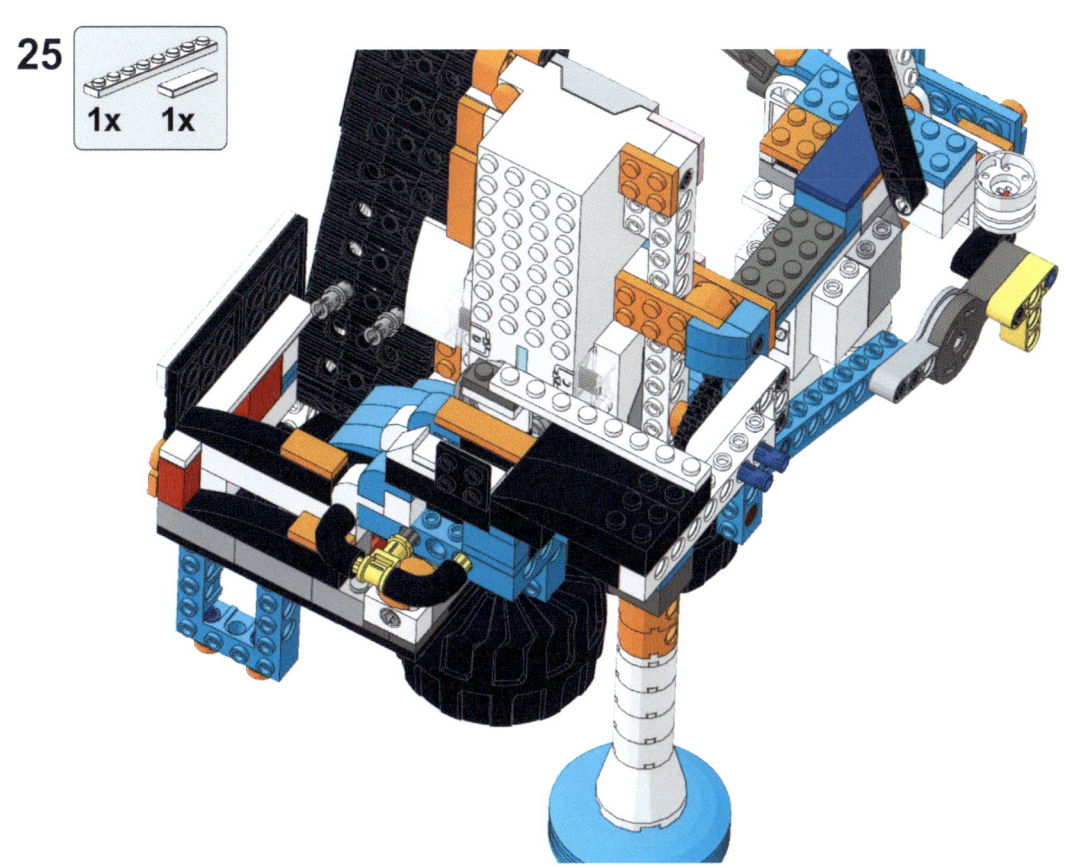

Ball-Booster

26 1x 3x

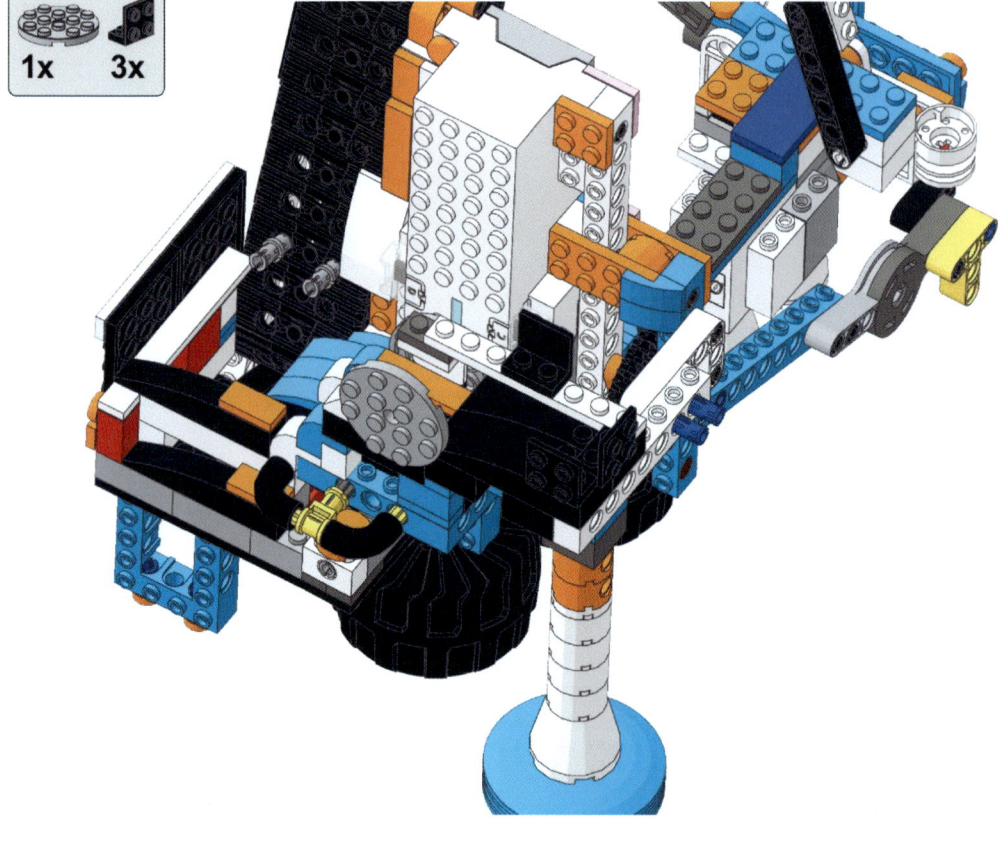

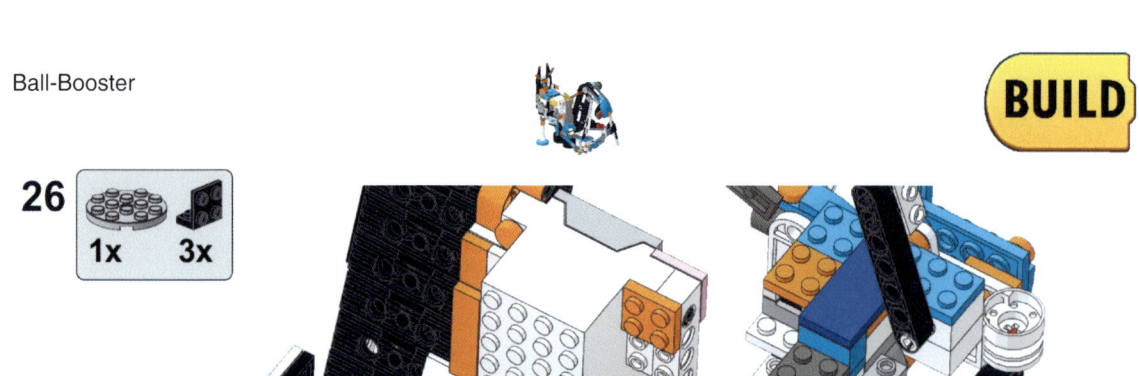

27 2x 1x 1x
    1x 1x 3x 2x

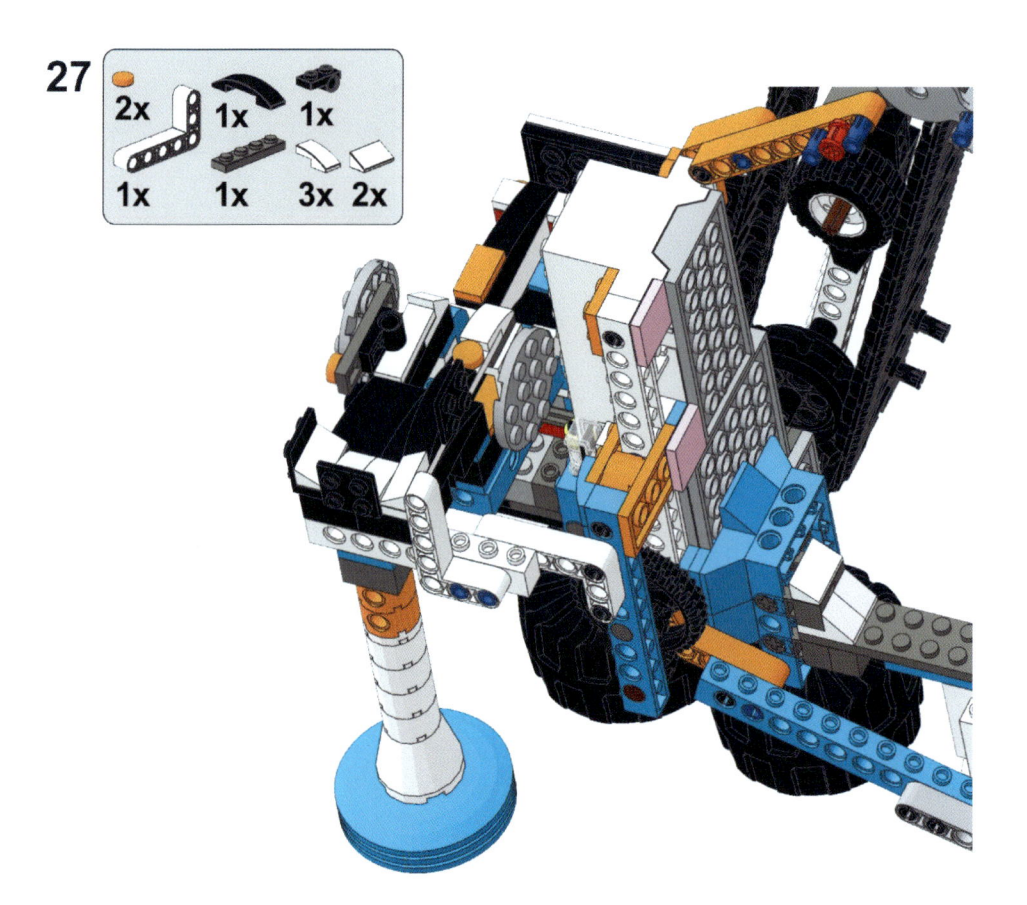

32

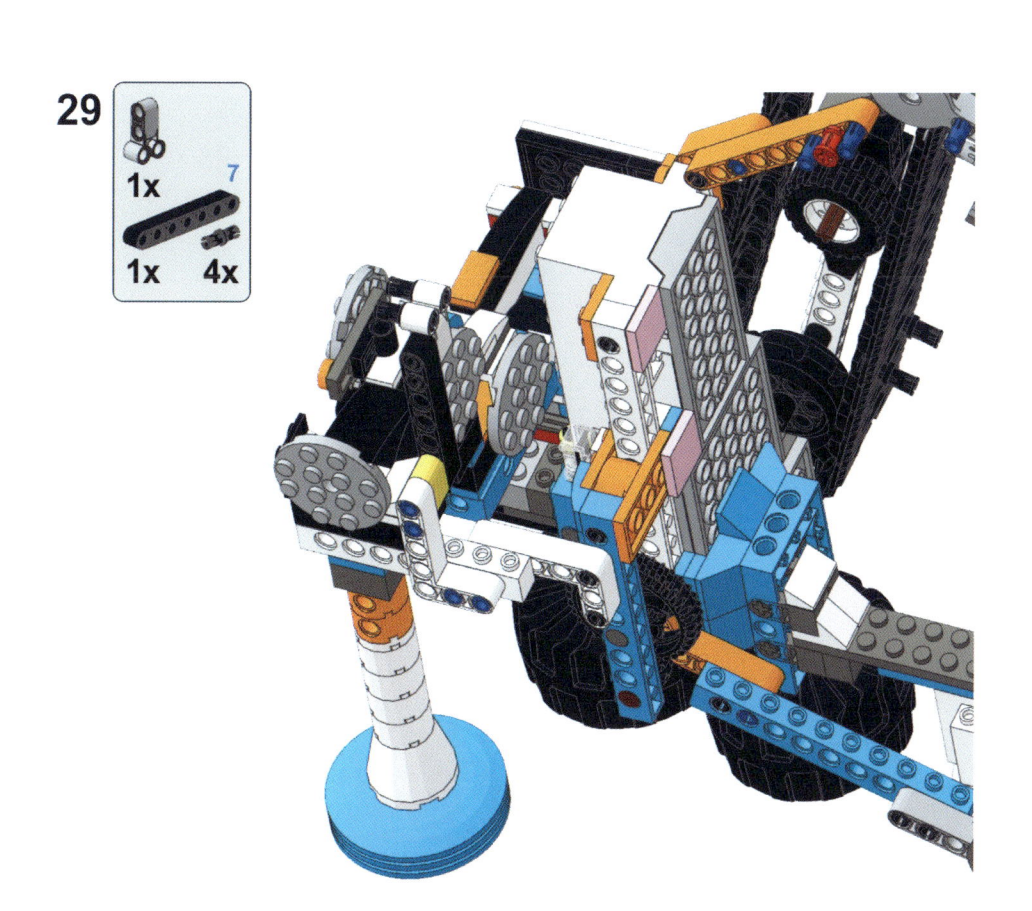

Ball-Booster

28 2x 2x 1x (2)

29 1x 1x 4x (7)

33

Ball-Booster

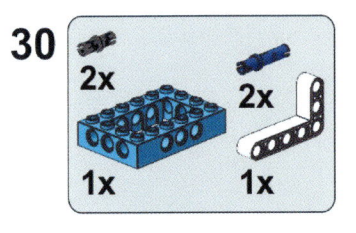

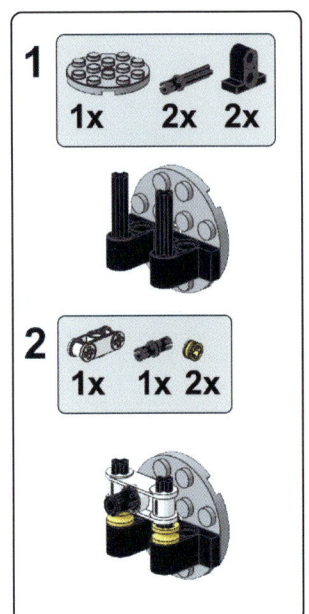

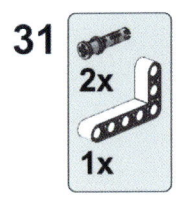

30

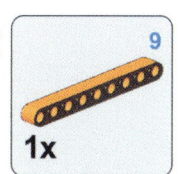

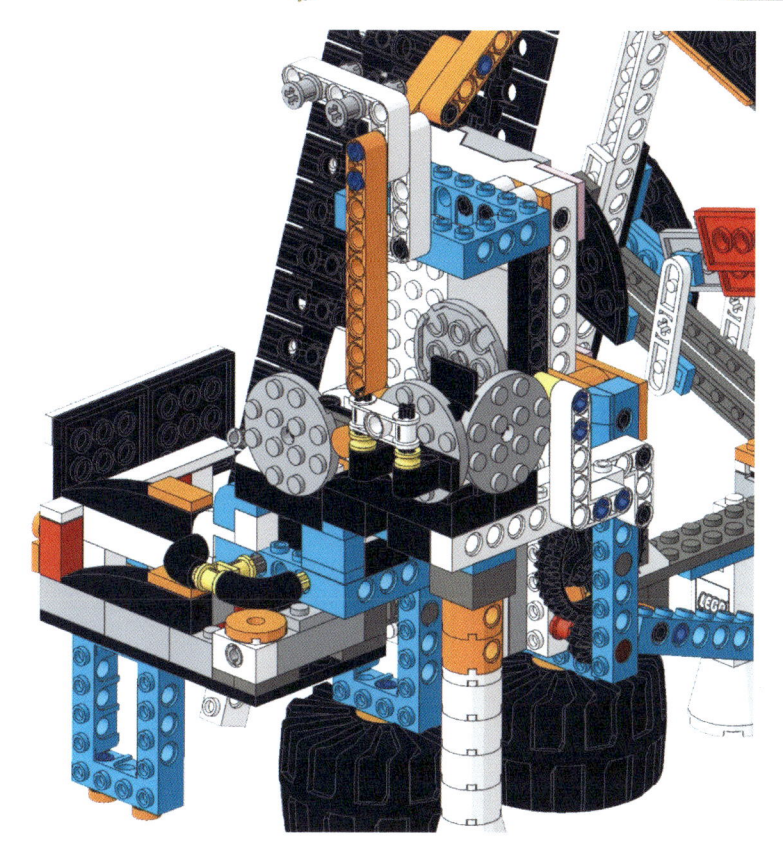

Ball-Booster

32 1x (9)

33 3x, 1x (5)

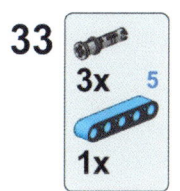

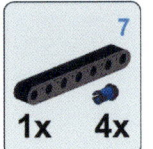

Ball-Booster

34 1x 4x

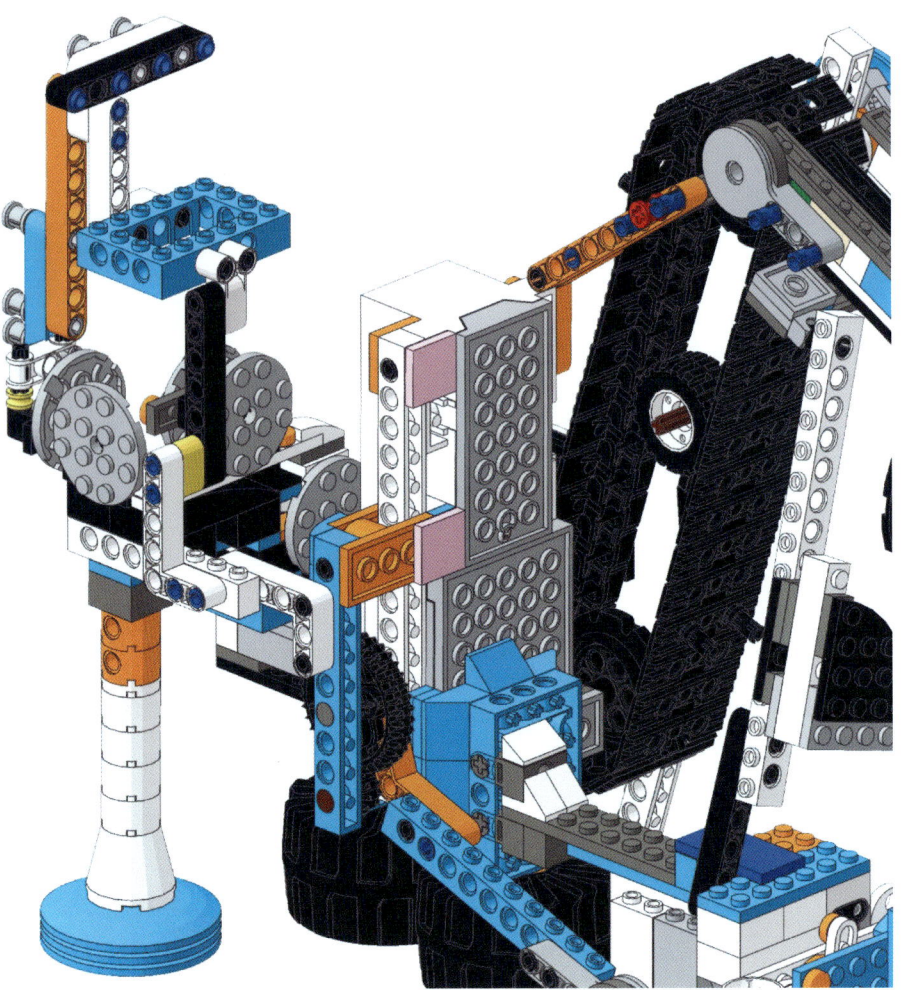

35 1x

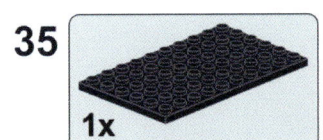

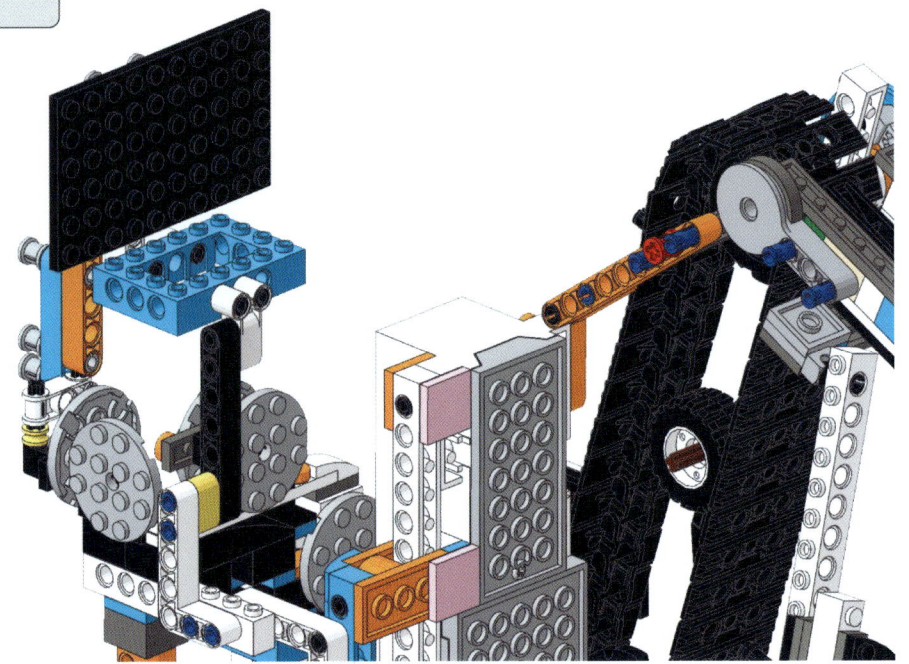

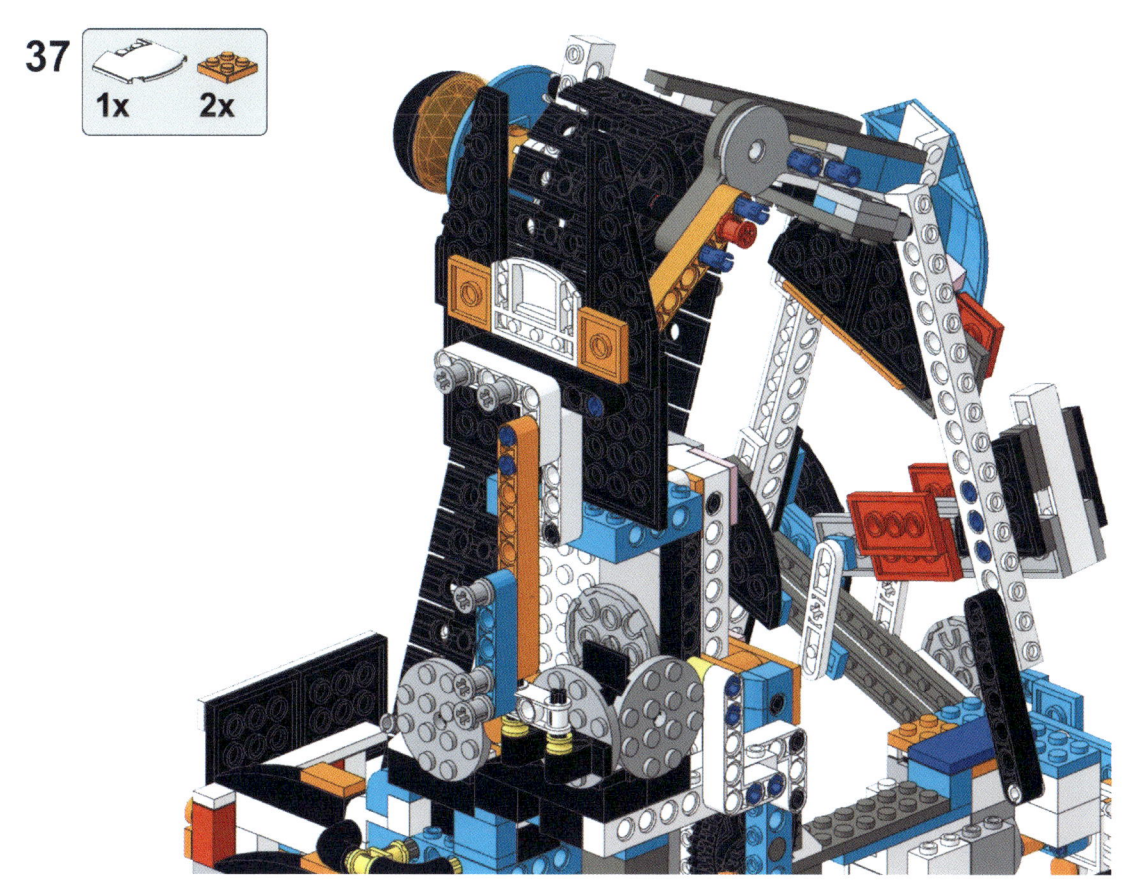

Ball-Booster

36 1x 1x 1x

37 1x 2x

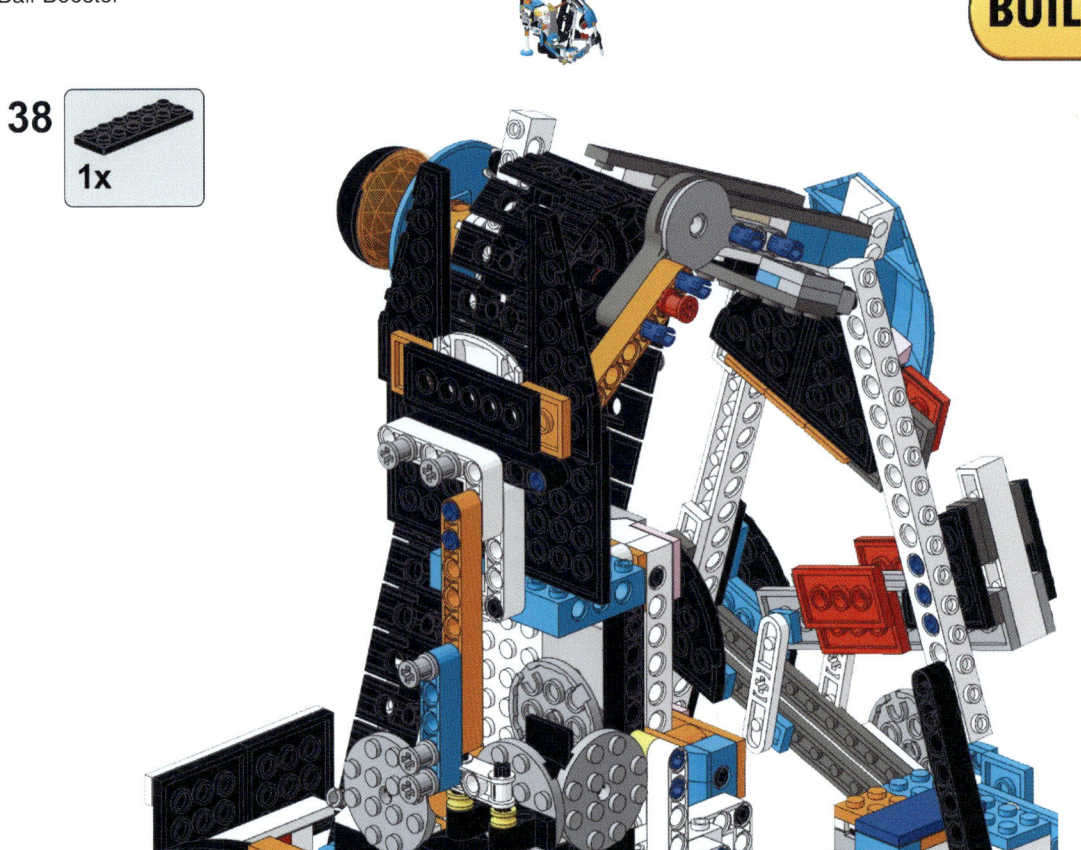

Ball-Booster

38 1x

39 2x 2x

Ball-Booster

BUILD

40

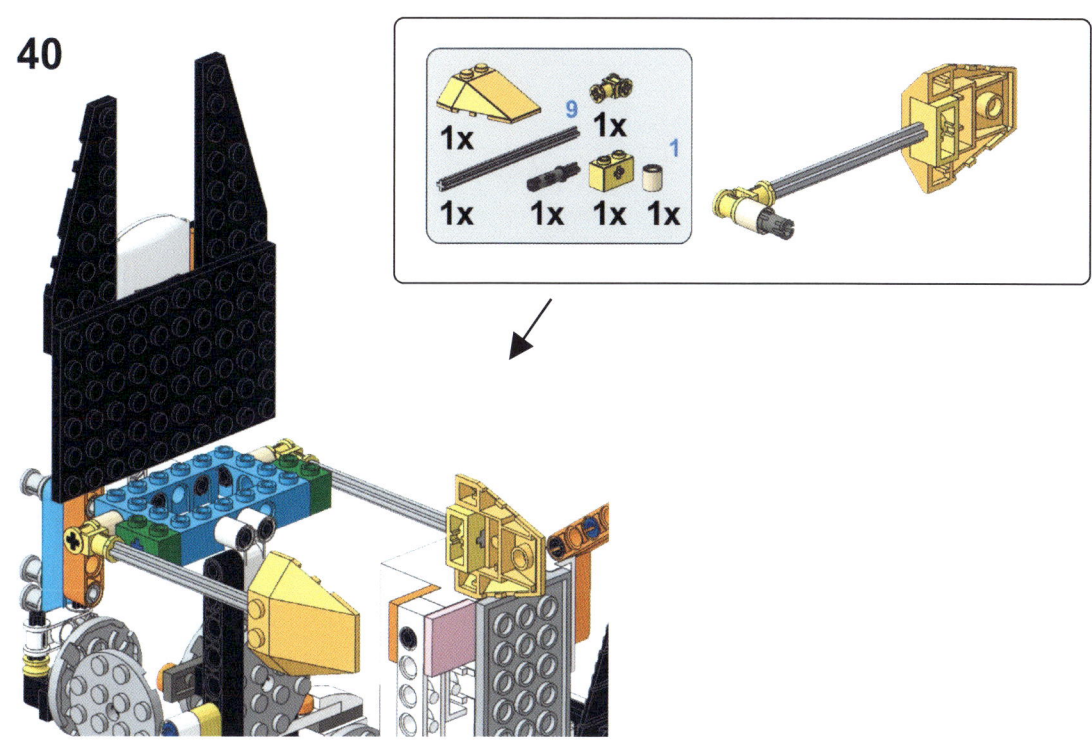

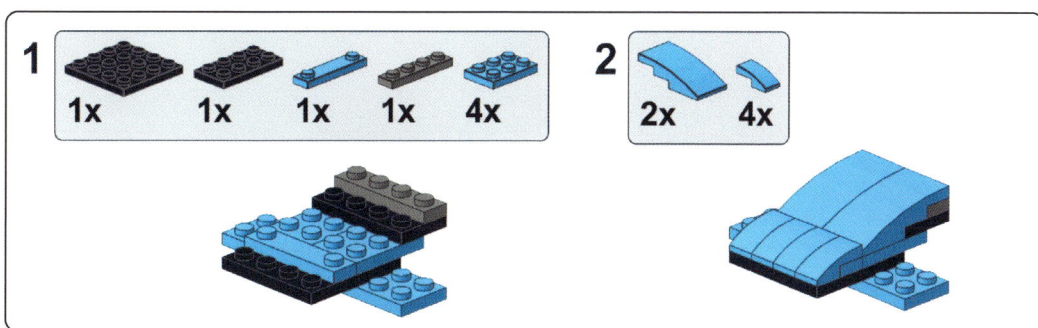

1
1x 1x 1x 1x 4x

2
2x 4x

41
3x 1x
1x 2x 2x 2x

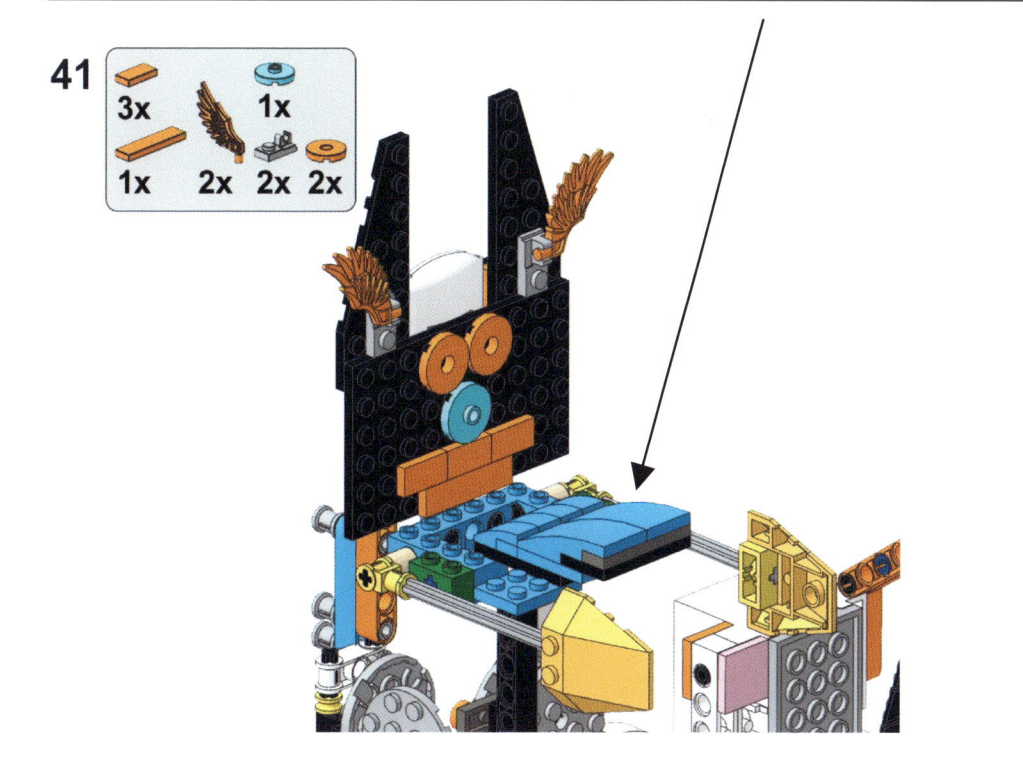

Ball-Booster

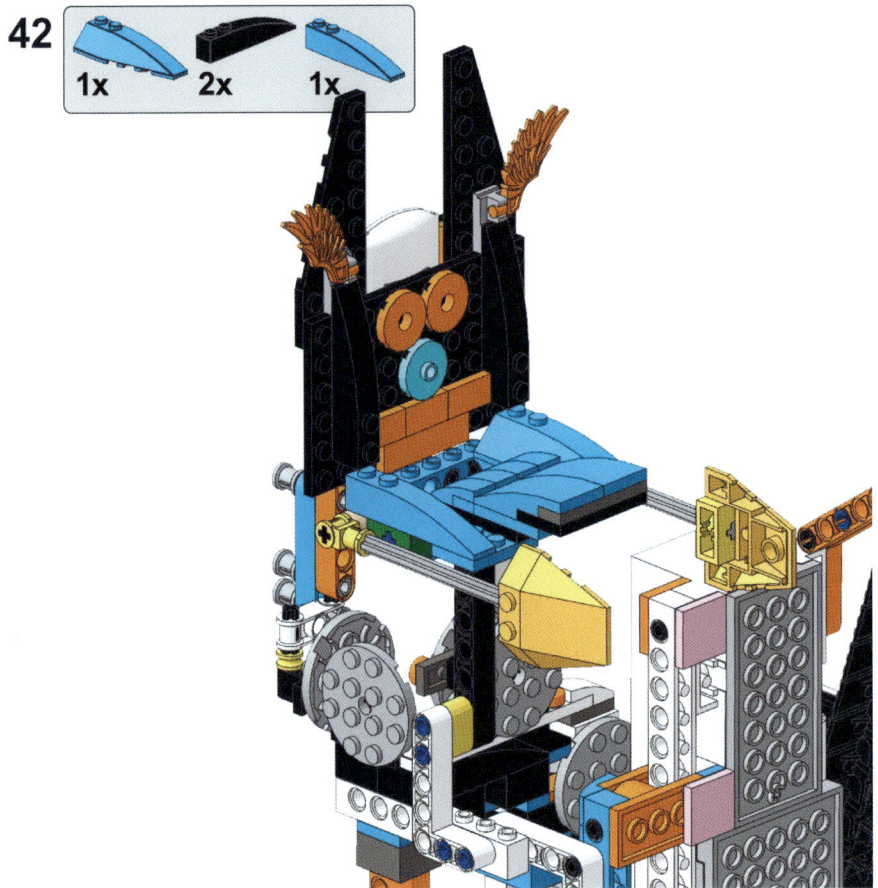

42 1x 2x 1x

43 2x

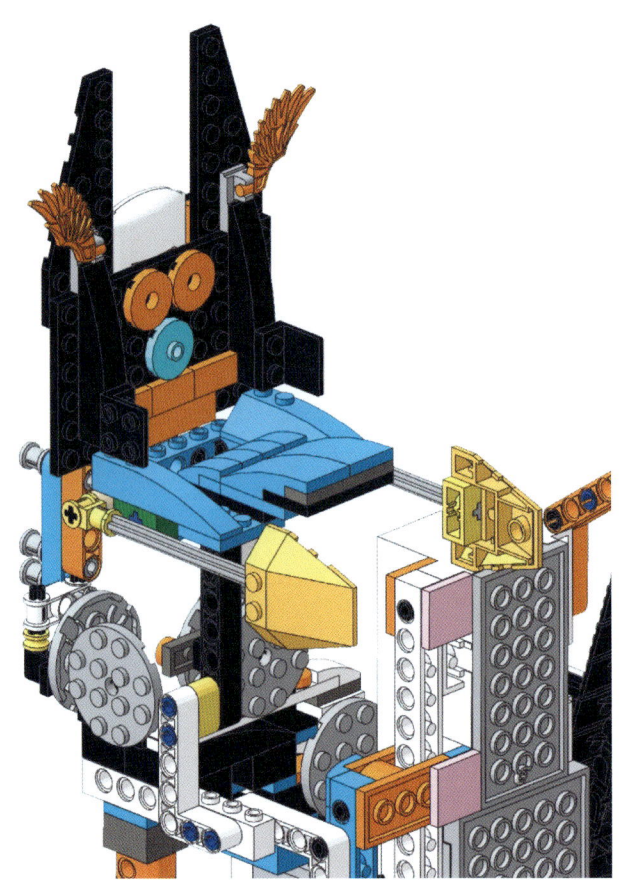

Ball-Booster

44  2x 3x

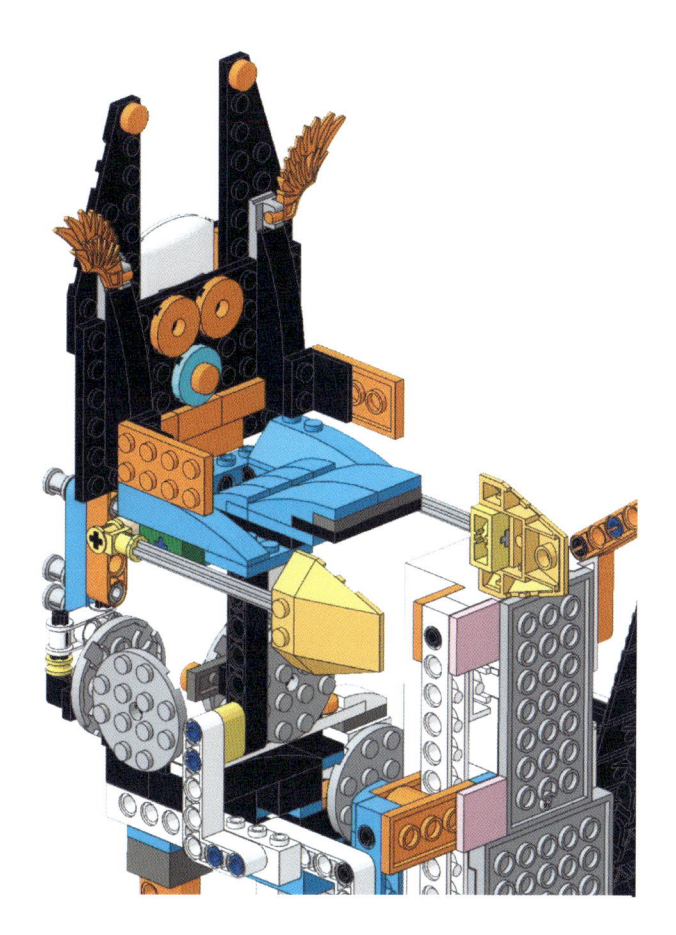

45 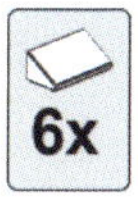 6x

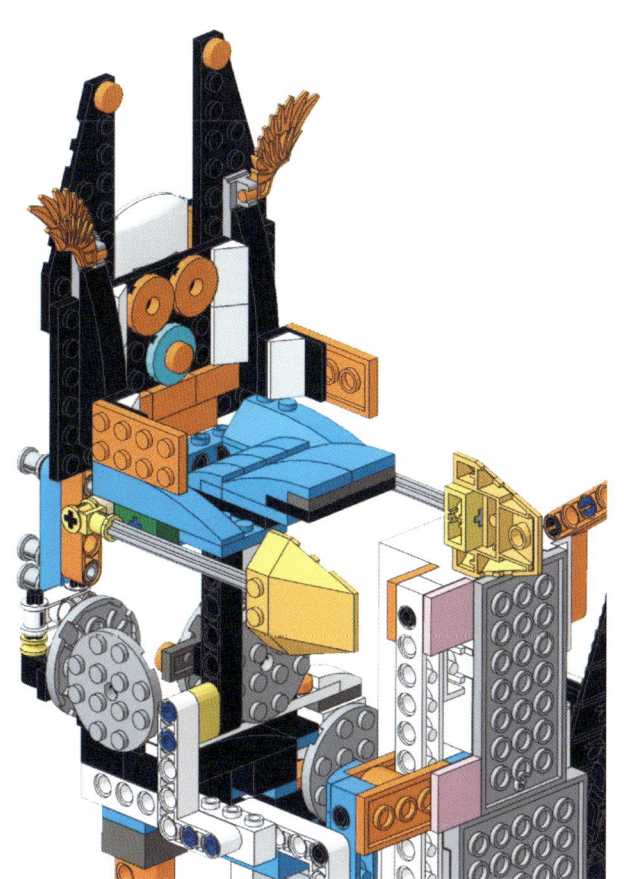

41

Ball-Booster

Code
The program must be entered in a new and empty program window. To create the program, you must drag each symbol from the color-coded menus at the bottom of the screen.

Before starting, you put one or several marbles into the hopper at the lower end of the conveyor belt (1). To activate the Move-Hub you push the mechanical „remote" for the green button on the Move-Hub (2).

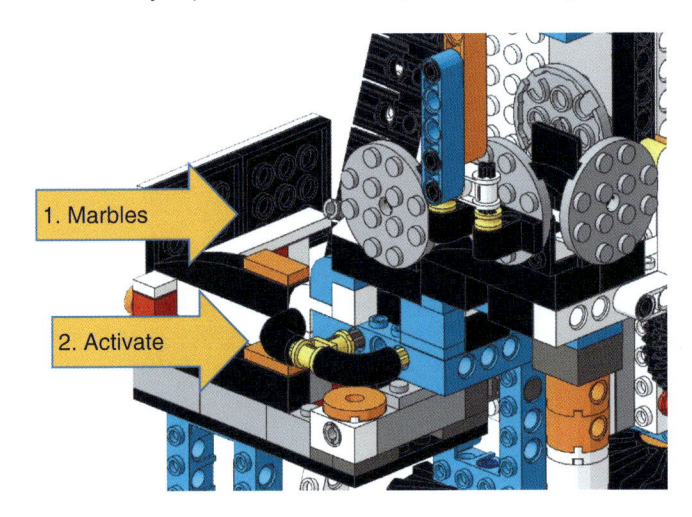

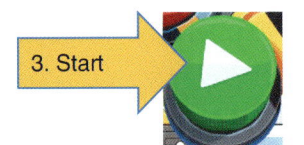

You must start the program via the central start button in the upper right corner of the program screen (3). Motor B then drives the conveyor belt till the marble falls down the marble run. As soon as the sensor detects the marble, motor B is stopped, a sound is played, and the external motor pushes the marble onto the catapult. The catapult is tilted up and down by Motor A and the marble lands in front of the conveyor belt again.

The program expects a white marble (e.g. Lego soccer ball). If the marbles have a different color, the sensor color must be changed accordingly (e.g. red for a Lego basketball).
If the marble is not detected by the sensor you might have to adjust the starting angle of the turnstile by a few degrees towards the marble.

Attention: If the marbles are derailed from the guiding rails, the diameter of the marbles might not be suitable (ideal diameter is 14 mm) or the guide rails are not adjusted correctly.

Ball-Booster

Play

Although the program is simple, there are some opportunities to play with its parameters. The sensor can react differently to colors or it can react to any color other than the blue plates in the background. Instead of stopping, the conveyor could keep on running slowly while the catapult is operating. To be able to do these changes, you first need to understand all programming blocks used in this program.

The program begins with a starting block:

Motor B is started at jump label 1. This way the motor starts at the same time as the infinite loop. Furthermore, jump label 1 can also be addressed from inside the loop. The speed of motor B is to be entered as a negative value.

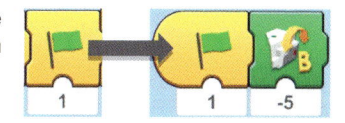

All other programming blocks are within the infinite loop. The loop runs till the program is stopped by the user.

The first block within the loop lets the program wait till the sensor detects the specified color. The programming block containing the "=" generally checks if both sides of the equation have the same value. Only then the program stops waiting and continues with the next block.

To detect white as well as red marbles you can use an OR term to connect the results of two equations. In this example the program continues when white or red is detected.

Alternatively, the equation can be reversed so the program continues when the sensor does not see blue (the plate in the background), anymore. Replace the "=" equation by the one shown in the example.

The following block stops the movement of motor B. You can delete this block if the conveyor should keep running during the catapult movement. This might jam the marble run in case you fill too many marbles into the hopper.

To let the conveyor run slowly during catapult movement, the stop block can also be replaced by another motor B block with a lower speed value.

At jump label 2 a sound (Vernie 21) is played. At the same time, the external motor turns the turnstile. Jump labels are particularly useful to execute two programming blocks in parallel.
The turnstile is turned a little more than the theoretically required 90° to make sure that the marble is pushed onto the catapult. After the 130° turn the turnstile is turned back by 40° so it is in its starting position again.
The marble should now be on the catapult.

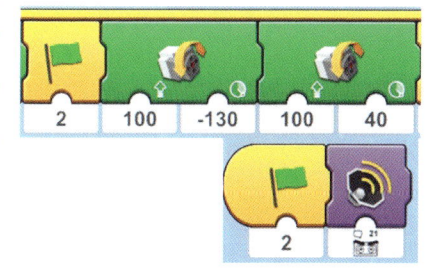

Ball-Booster

Again, jump label 3 executes some blocks in parallel. Here, the program waits for 0,2 seconds while motor A moves the catapult. At the end of the movement, a sound (Dragon 25) is played and the catapult is moved back down.

The speed and turning angle of motor A is to be adjusted to the weight of the marble. Shown values are good for Lego balls. The speed and success of the throw is also dependent on the condition of the batteries.

The last block in the loop jumps to label 1, to again set motor B (the conveyor) to its initial speed.

Some of the proposed changes are integrated in the program version shown below.

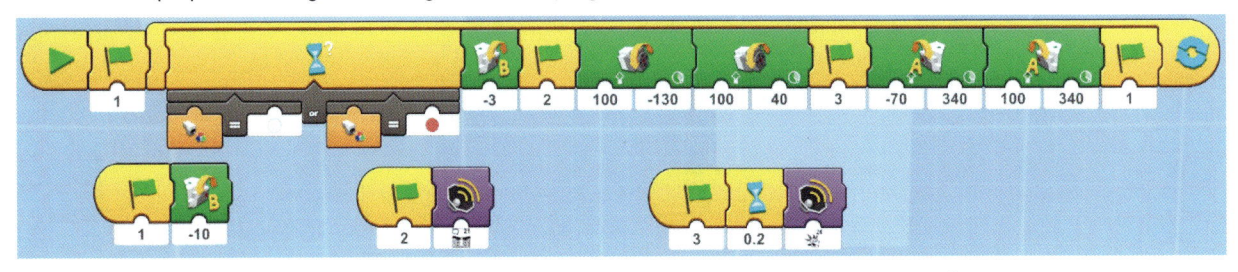

Bob-It-Booster

Bob-It-Booster – The Party-Game

This model is inspired by the successful game "Bob-It". It is a speedy game to test your motor skills and concentration.

Build

The built is very simple and only few of the bricks in the Boost-set are used.

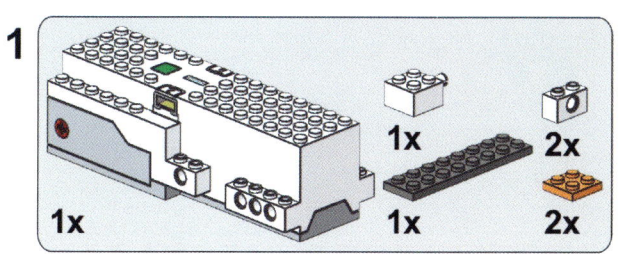

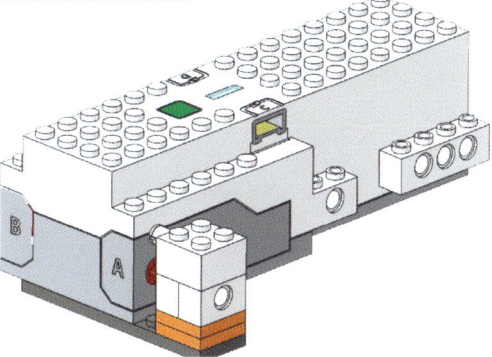

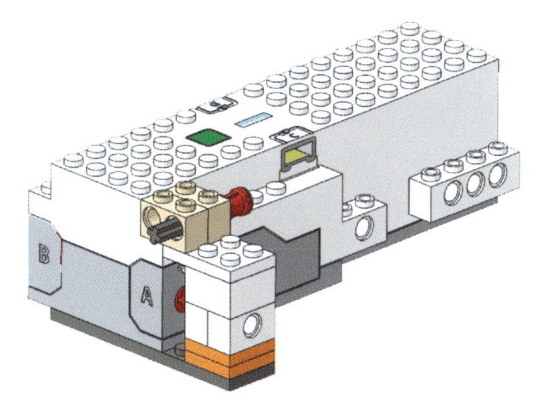

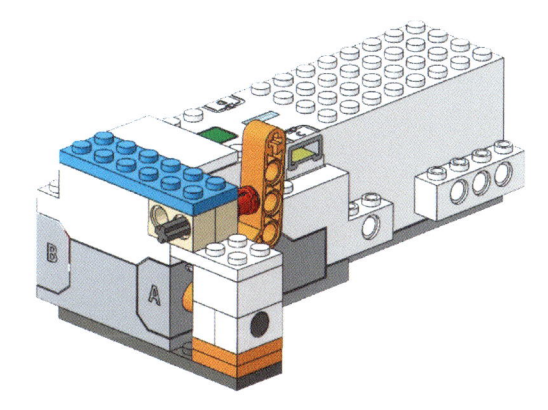

1
1x   1x   2x
     1x   2x

2
1x   2x   4
1x   1x

3
     4
1x   1x
1x   1x

Bob-It-Booster

4
1x 1x 2x 1x 1x

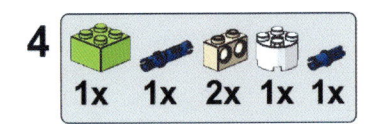

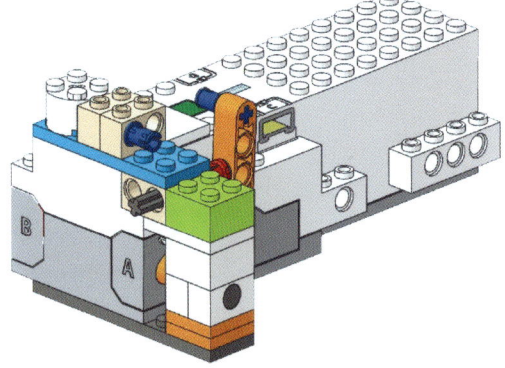

5
2x

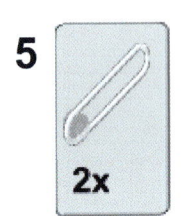

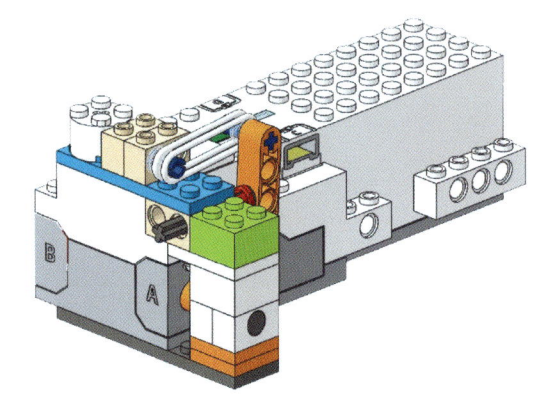

6
1x 2x
1x 1x

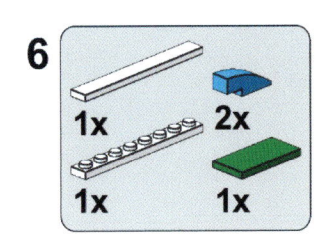

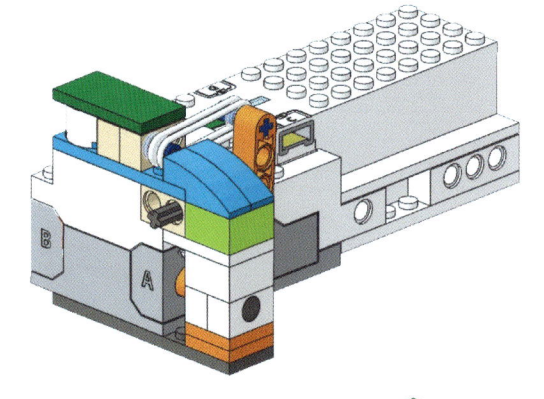

7
1x 2x
1x 2x 1x 1x

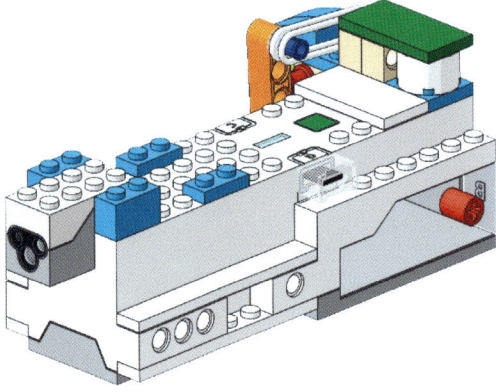

46

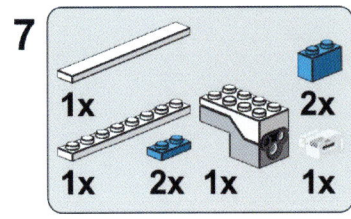

Bob-It-Booster

BUILD

8 2x / 1x

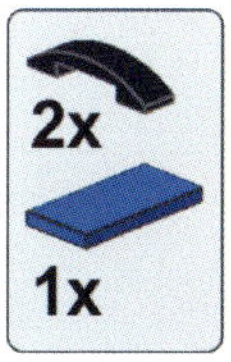

Fold cable multiply and squeeze under here

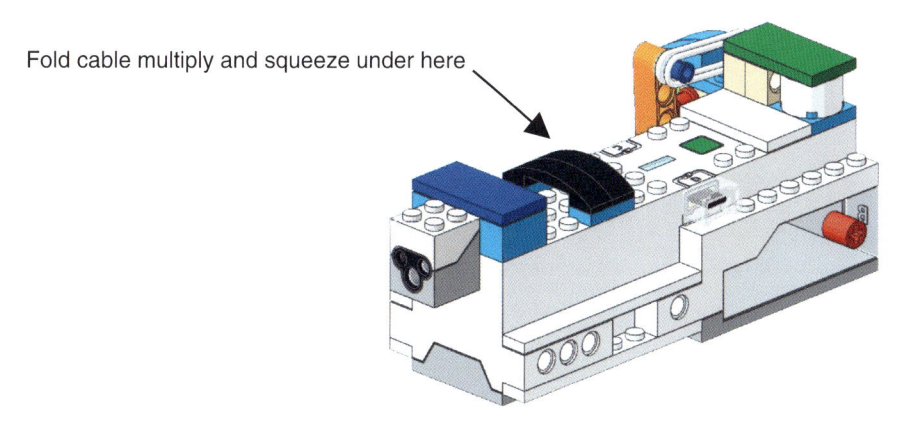

9 1x

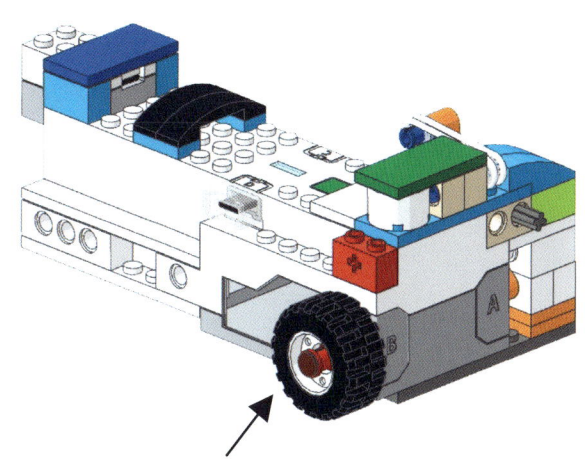

1: 1x 1x
2: 1x 1x

Bob-It-Booster

Code

The game needs to play five voice commands. First, these commands must be recorded and stored within five programming blocks.

Command:	Wave	Turn	Shake	Push	Game Over
Block:					

Your voice commands can be recorded in the Boost-App:

1. Click on the microphone to enter the voice recorder menu
2. Select the „+" to open the recorder

1. Select menu

2. Open recorder

3. Start the recording via the red dot
4. After speaking the command, stop the recording via the square symbol.
5. Change the appearance via the block symbol
6. Add sound effects if desired (e.g. a hamster voice)
7. Save your recording via the green button

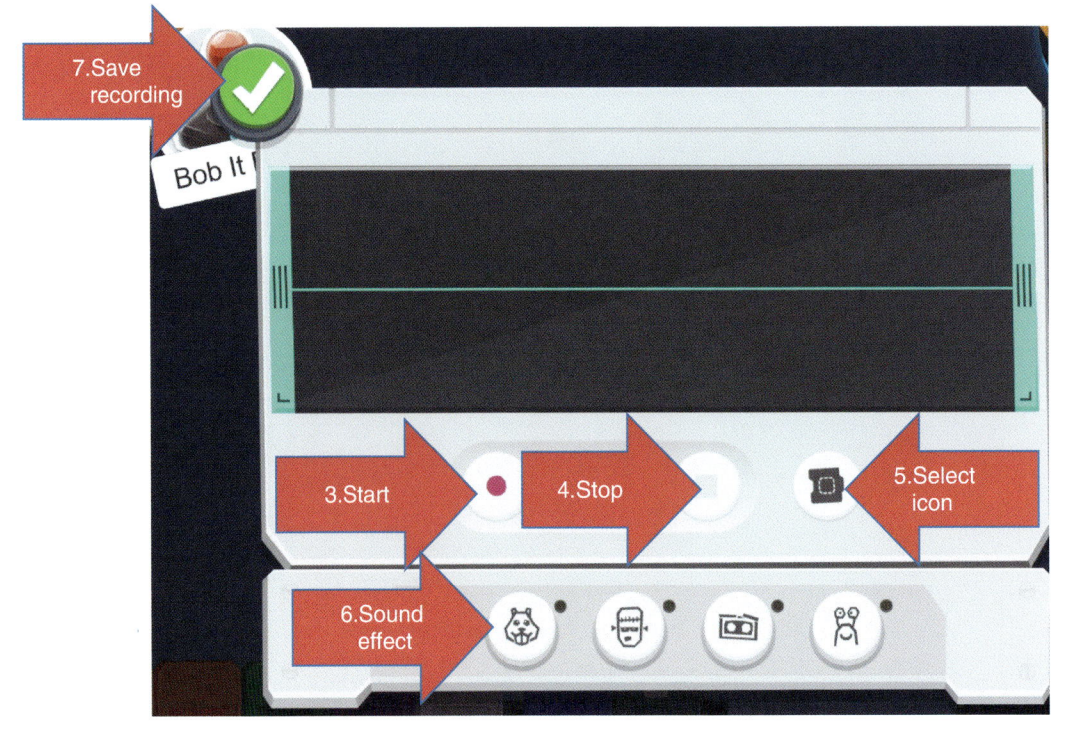

7. Save recording

3. Start

4. Stop

5. Select icon

6. Sound effect

48

Bob-It-Booster

As with the Ball-Booster the program must be created in an empty program window in which you also create the five voice commands.

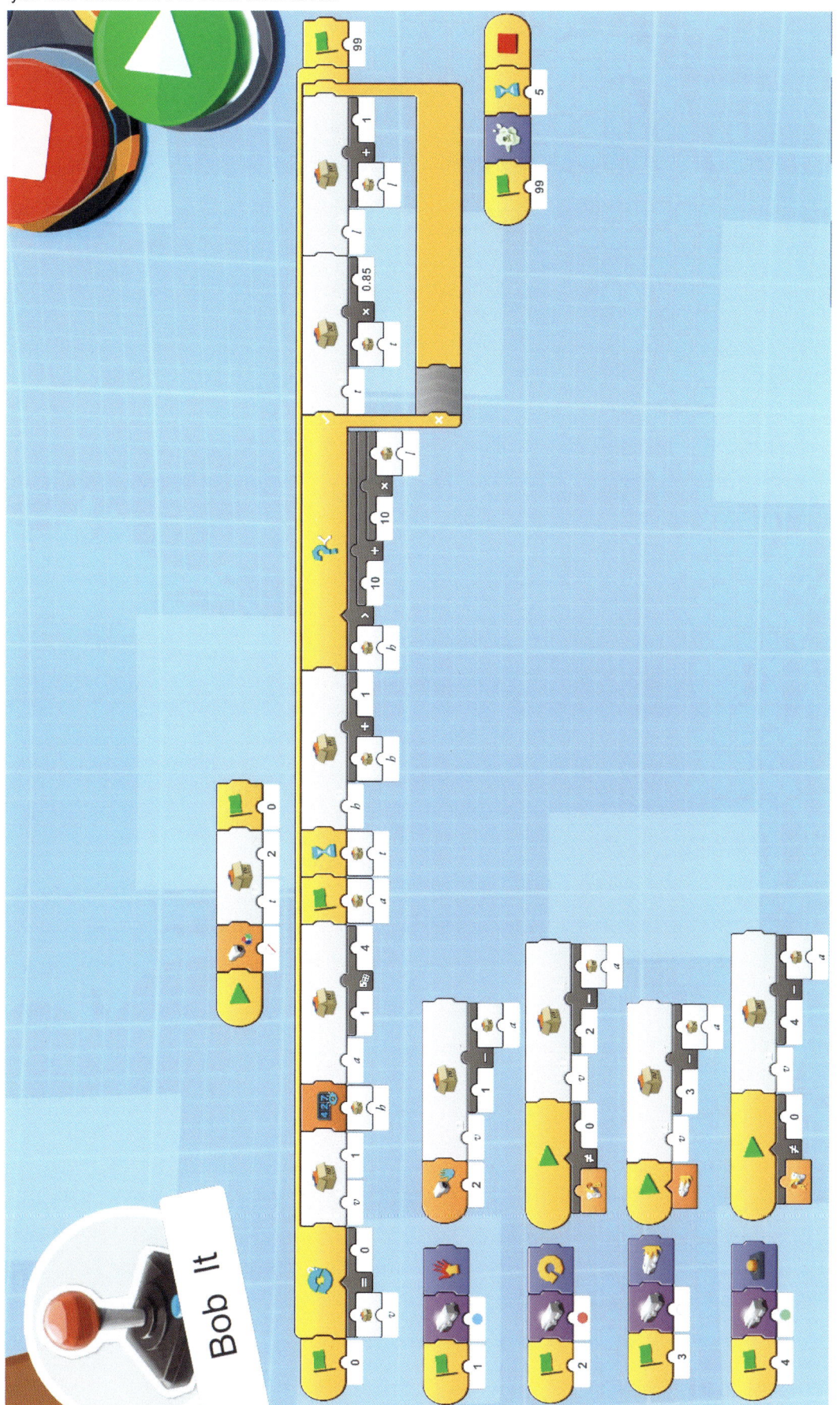

Bob-It-Booster

Start the program via the central start button in the upper right corner. One of the voice commands is played. The player must quickly perform an action according to the command:

Wave - Wave closely in front of the sensor

Turn - Turn the wheel

Shake - Shake the Move-Hub.

Push - Push the rod to turn the bent Technic beam.

The number of the performed actions is displayed by a counter on the screen. The time available to perform each action is shortened with an increasing number of actions performed successfully. Is one action not performed within the time limit, the "Game Over" command is played, and the program ends. The final score is displayed for a few seconds.
Attention: Make sure the sensor points away from your body when starting the program. Otherwise, the sensor might detect parts of your body and interpret it as a „wave" action which might end the program immediately.

Play

Although the building is simple, the logic of the program is quite complex. Let us look at each programming block in the program to understand what it does.

At the start of the program the light of the sensor is turned off and the variable t is set to 2. Variables are used to store information to be referenced and manipulated in a computer program. With variables, a computer can remember certain values. Here, in variable t the time available for the players reaction is stored (2 seconds).

Jump label 0 is just used to make the program shorter on the screen, the block for setting variable t can alternatively also be connected directly to the conditional loop block.

Different from the loop we used for the marble run, this loop does not run infinitely. It is a conditional loop which runs as long as v is equal to 0. At the start of a program, all variables have the value 0. Hence, the loop will be executed. The first block within the loop sets v to 1. If v is not set back to 0 (e.g. by the correct action of the player) within the loop, the loop will not execute again.

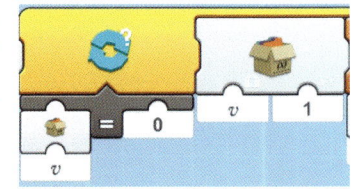

The current score will be displayed. The score is stored in variable h. Variable h will also be 0 at the start of the program, so 0 is displayed.

A random value between 1 and 4 will be stored in variable a. This value determines which voice command is played and which action is expected from the player. The next block jumps to the label with the number stored in variable a. Before continuing, the program waits for the number of seconds stored in variable t. During this time the blocks at the jump label are executed.

Bob-It-Booster

At jump label 1 to 4 the LED light of the Move-Hub is set, and the voice command is played.

There is a colored 4x2 tile to identify the "Push" and "Wave" action on the Move-Hub. Above the "Turn"-wheel a red brick is placed. The "Shake" command is identified by the white body of the Move-Hub.

The colors enable to react with the correct action even before the voice command is fully played. This is useful as soon as the game speed has increased to a very fast level.

After the voice command, the program awaits an action from the player.

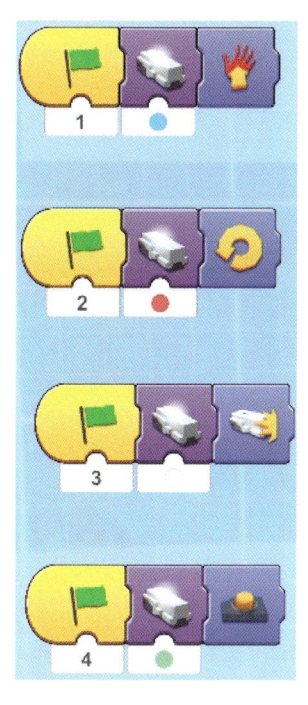

This sequence of blocks starts as soon as the player waves in front of the sensor. The sensitivity of the sensor is reduced to a low level of 2 to prevent it from detecting other far away movements as a "Wave".
In the one programming block within this sequence the variable v is set to a new value. This value is calculated as a subtraction of 1 minus variable a. Variable a is our random value to identify the expected action. Only if a is 1, the subtraction will result in variable v being equal to 0. Only when variable v is 0, the main loop will continue to be executed for the next action. Otherwise the program will end.

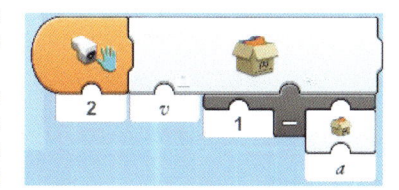

This sequence is executed as soon as the user turns the wheel on motor B. When the speed of the wheel is not 0 a rotation of the wheel is detected. Again, a new value in variable v is stored. The value is calculated as 2 minus variable a. When the voice command was "turn", variable v will only be set to 0 if the user has turned the wheel.

When the bump-sensor is detecting movements the variable a is subtracted form 3 and the result is stored in variable v.

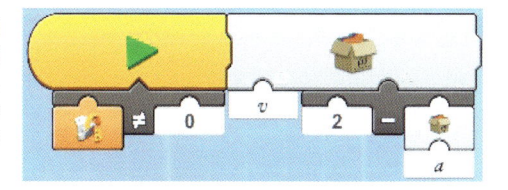

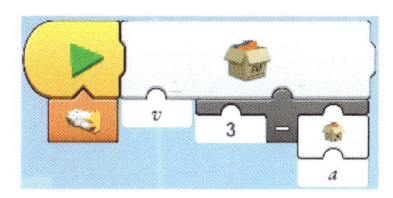

A push on the Technic-rod results in a slight turn of Motor A. This turn is enough to execute this sequence and results in v being the subtraction of 4 and variable v.

Bob-It-Booster

The remaining quite complex part of the program is only for calculation of the score and to gradually increase the speed at certain score levels.

Variable h is increased by 1. To do so, the value of h+1 is stored in variable h.

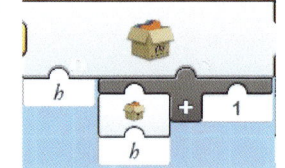

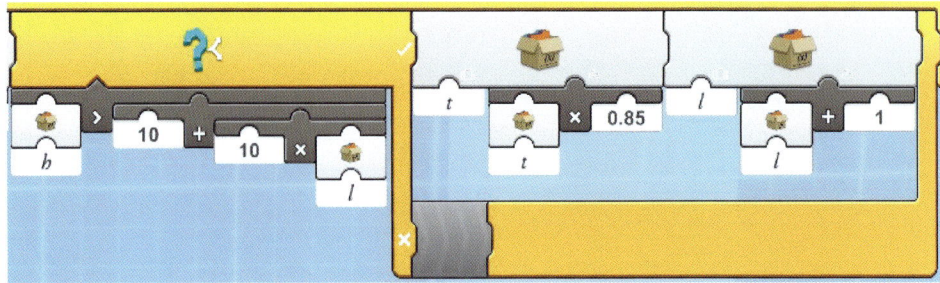

The last big "?"-block within the loop is an „if-statement". This block checks if the speed should be increased.

The "if"-block can execute two different sequences of blocks. It checks if the score in variable h is larger then 10 + 10 imes variable l. As l is 0 at the start of the program, the calculation results in 10. As long as h is lower than 10 the "If"-block will execute the lower sequence which does not contain any programming block. So, the speed is not changed.

Every 10 loop cycles, the "if"-block will execute the upper sequence. Here the variable t is multiplied by 0.85. The time available for a player action is reduced by 15%. The speed level is stored in variable l. Every speed change also results in an increase of variable l by 1.

Is the player not fast enough to execute the required action then variable v will stay at 1. Has the player executed the wrong command, variable v will also not be 0. In both cases, the loop will not be executed again but the blocks behind the loop are executed. Jump label 99 only serves the purpose to shorten the appearance of the progra. Alternatively, you can attach the "Game Over" command and the following blocks directly to the loop block. The "Game Over" command is played, and the player has 5 seconds to view the final score before the program and all related sequences are stopped.

Most of the complexity is caused by the display of the score and the speed increase. The game can also be played without these features. Below a simpler program version without score and speed increase is shown. For a better understanding of the concept of the program it might help to start with this version.

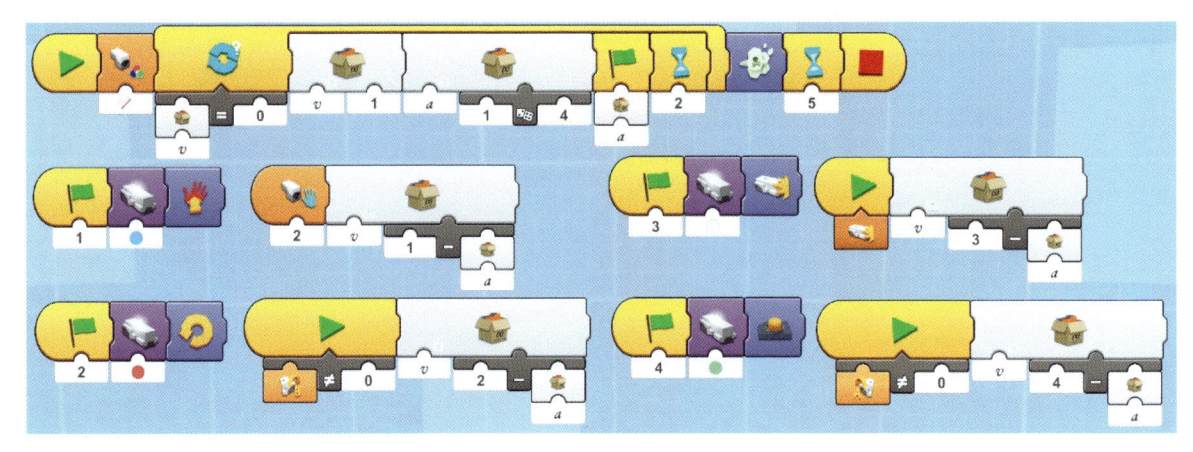

Weight-Booster

Weight-Booster – The Balance

For a long time, I was thinking about what to do with the tilt sensor of the Boost-Set. A mechanical beam balance seems to be a decent application to learn about simple mechanics and the center of gravity.

Build

Compared to the other models in this book the balance is a bit more fragile but still simple to build.

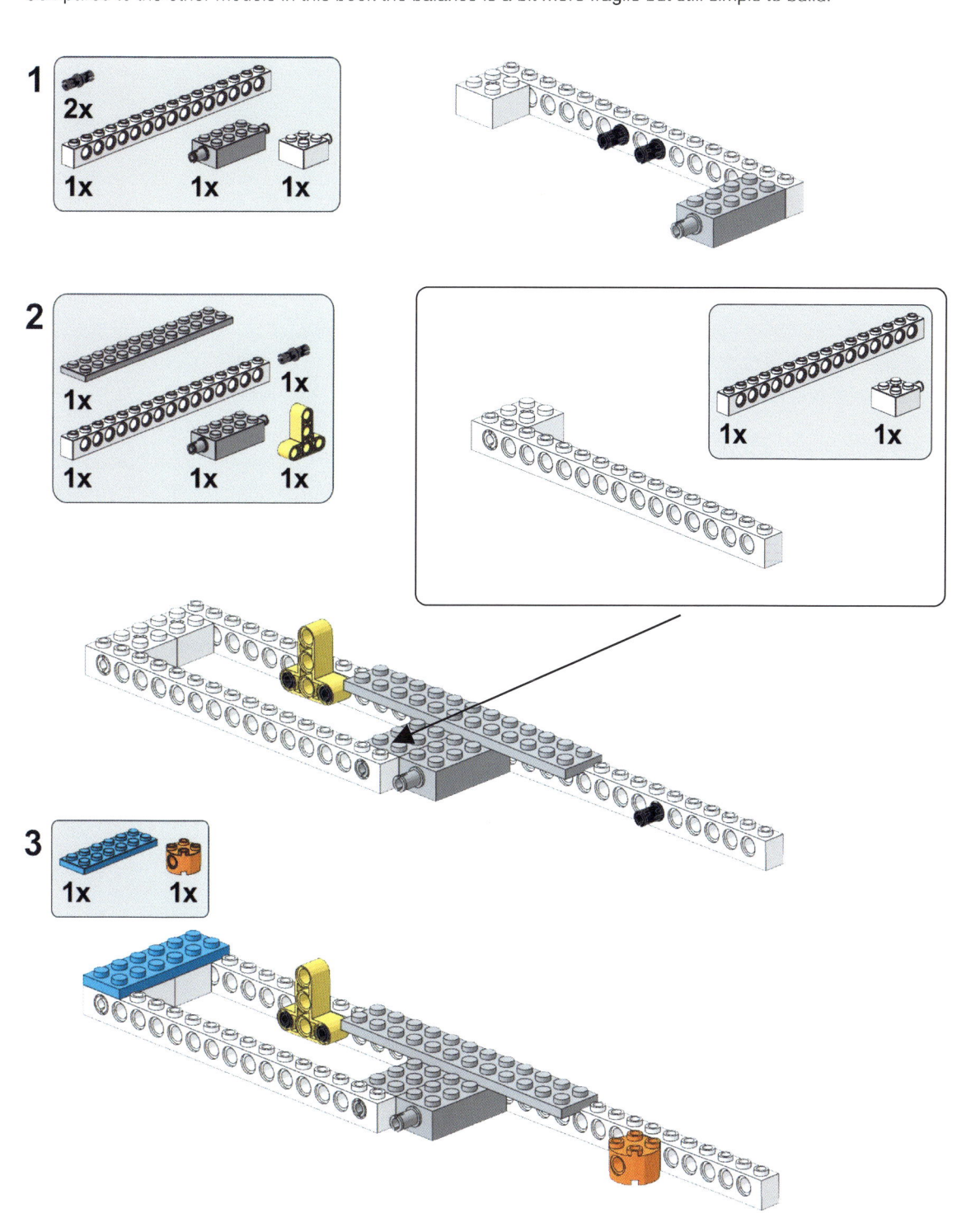

1 2x, 1x, 1x, 1x

2 1x, 1x, 1x, 1x, 1x, 1x

3 1x, 1x

53

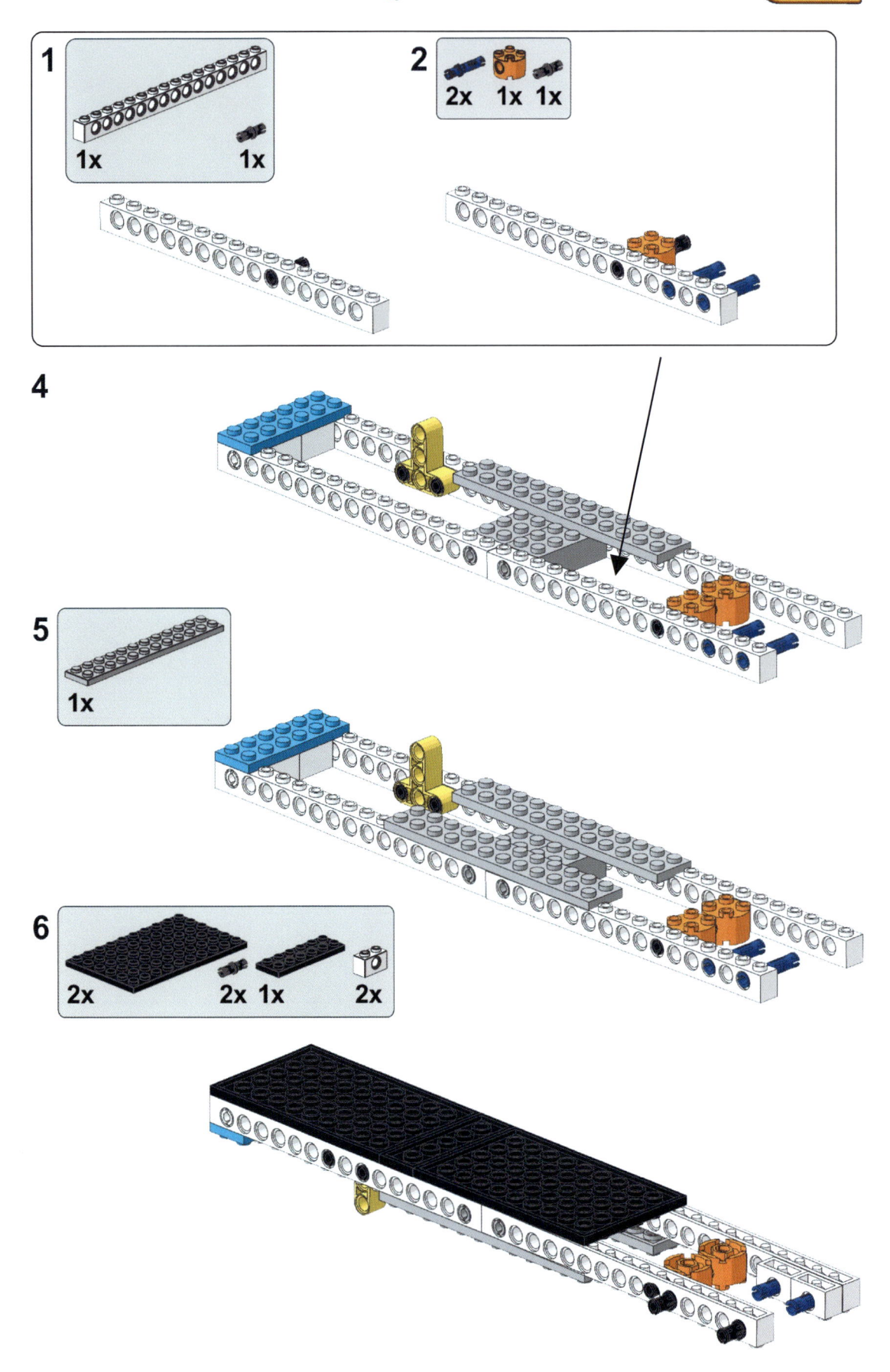

Weight-Booster

1 1x 1x

2 2x 1x 1x

4

5 1x

6 2x 2x 1x 2x

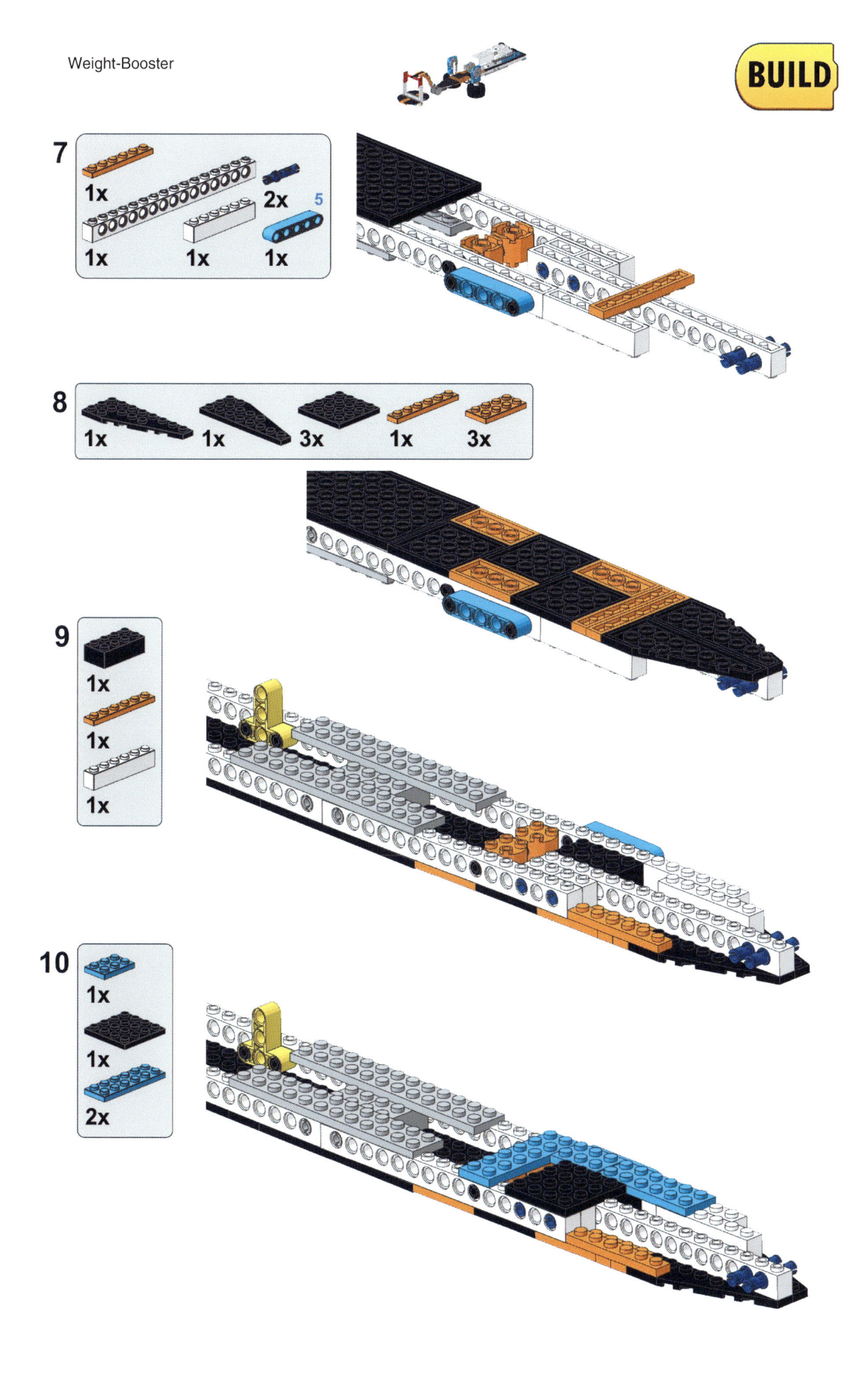

Weight-Booster

7
1x, 2x, 1x, 1x, 1x

8
1x, 1x, 3x, 1x, 3x

9
1x, 1x, 1x

10
1x, 1x, 2x

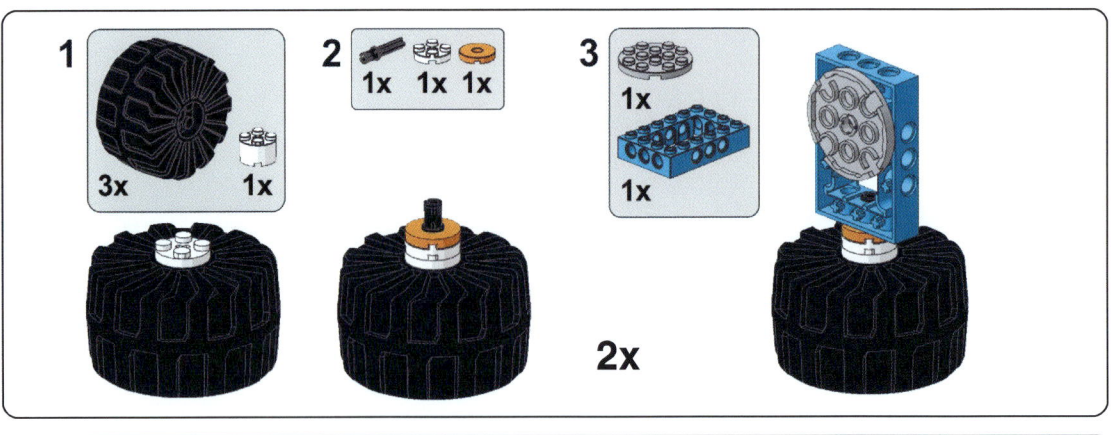

Weight-Booster

BUILD

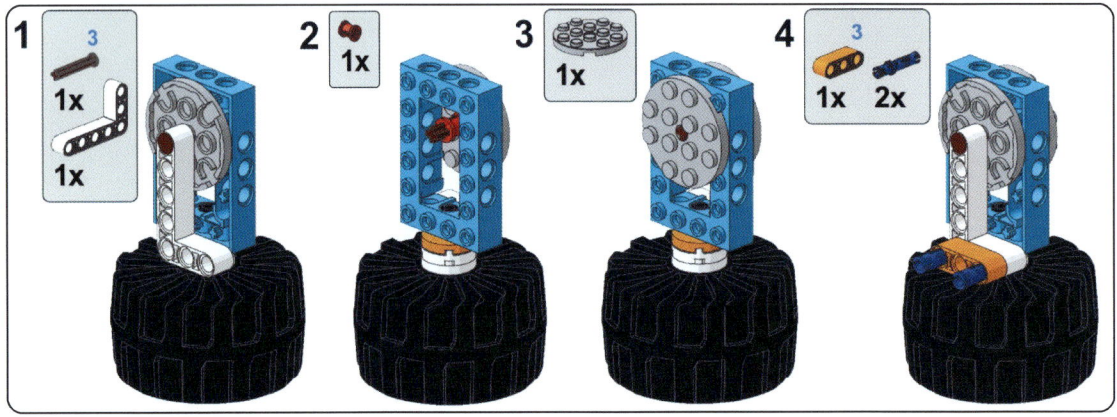

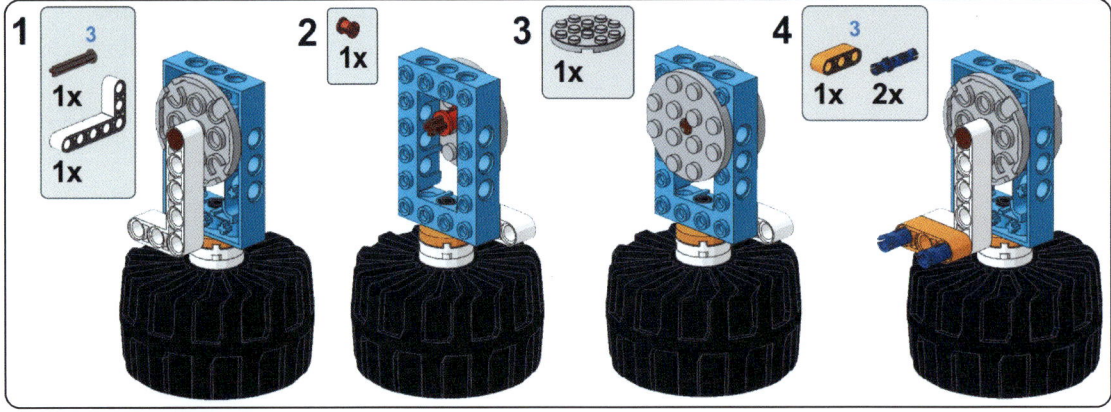

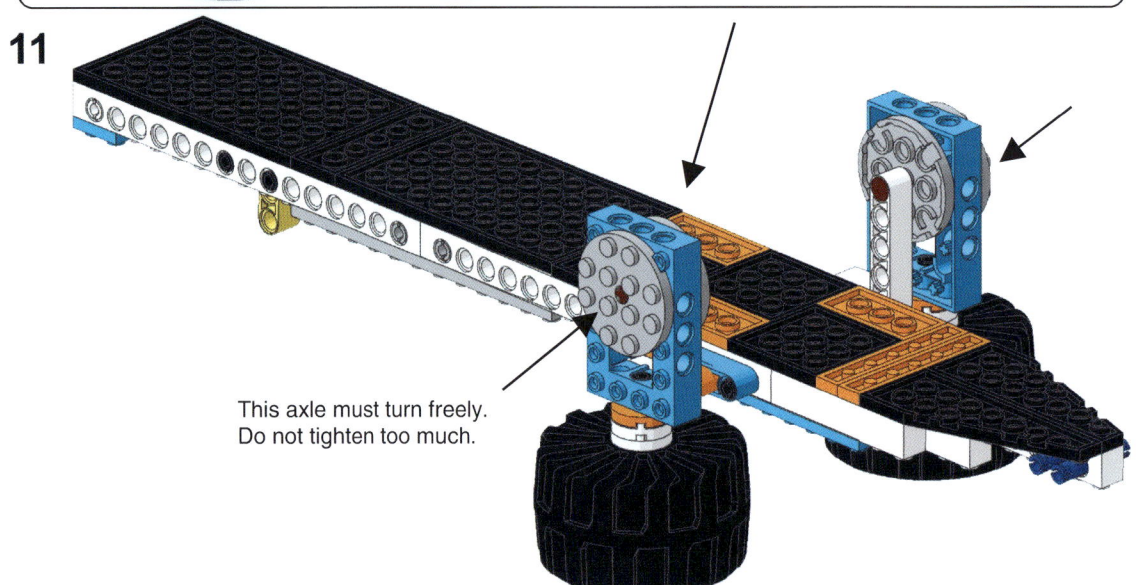

This axle must turn freely.
Do not tighten too much.

Weight-Booster

BUILD

12

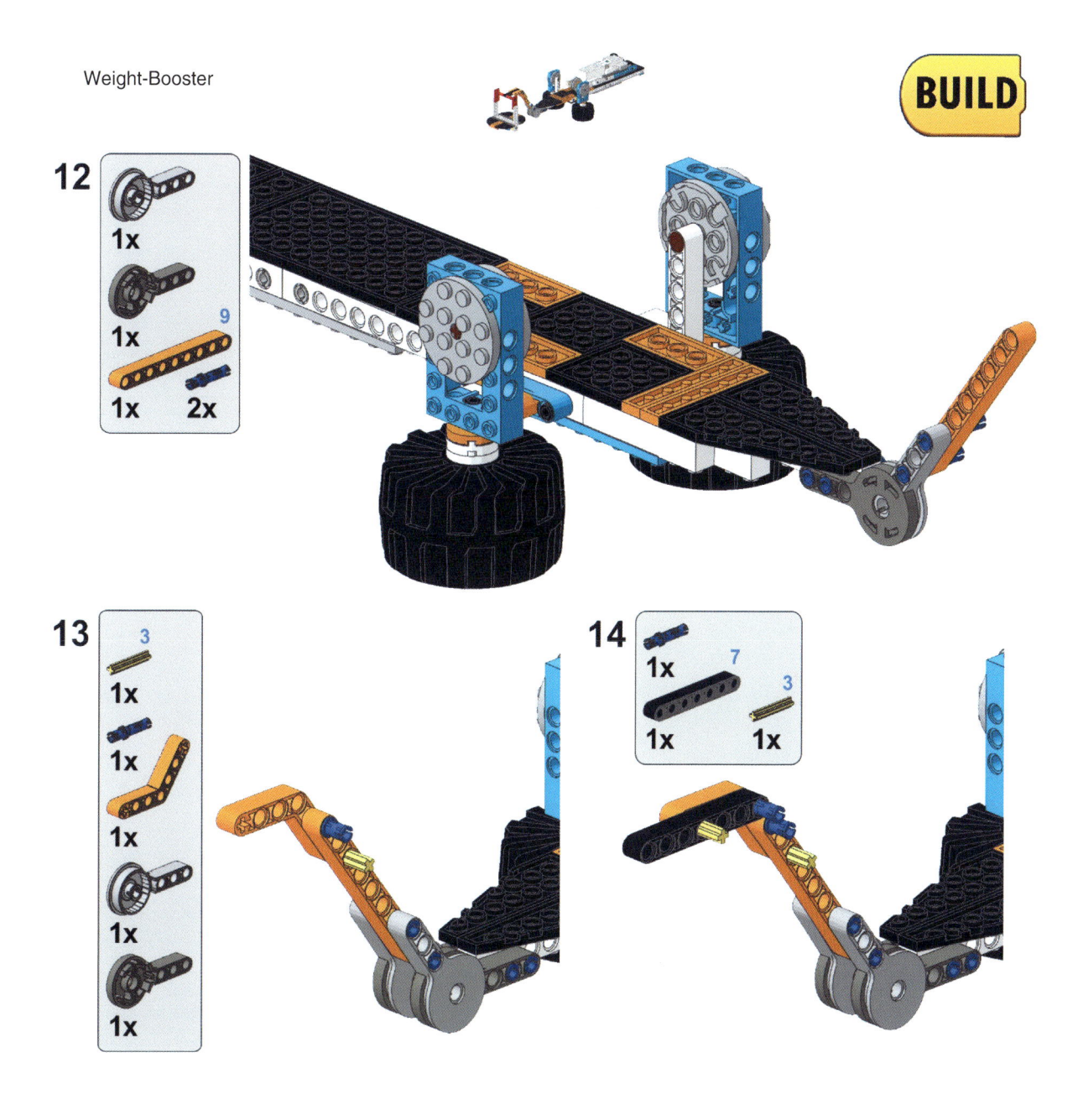

13

14

15

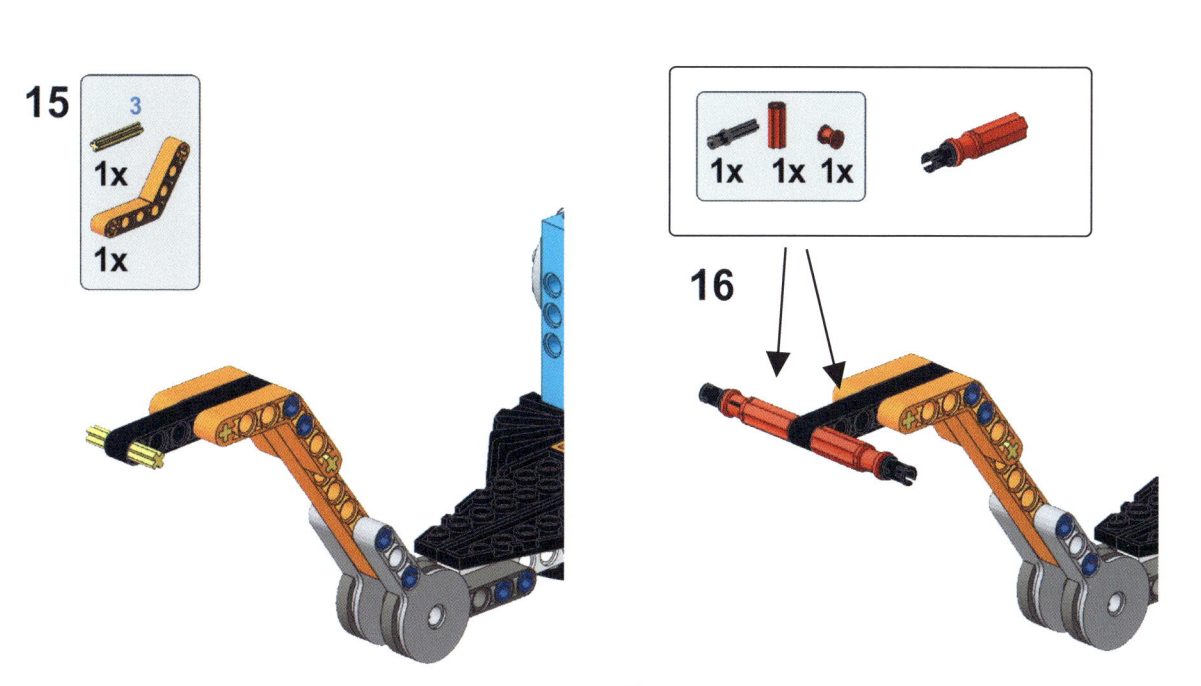

16

Weight-Booster

BUILD

1
2x
2x
1x
2x

2
3x

3
4x
2x
2x

4
4x

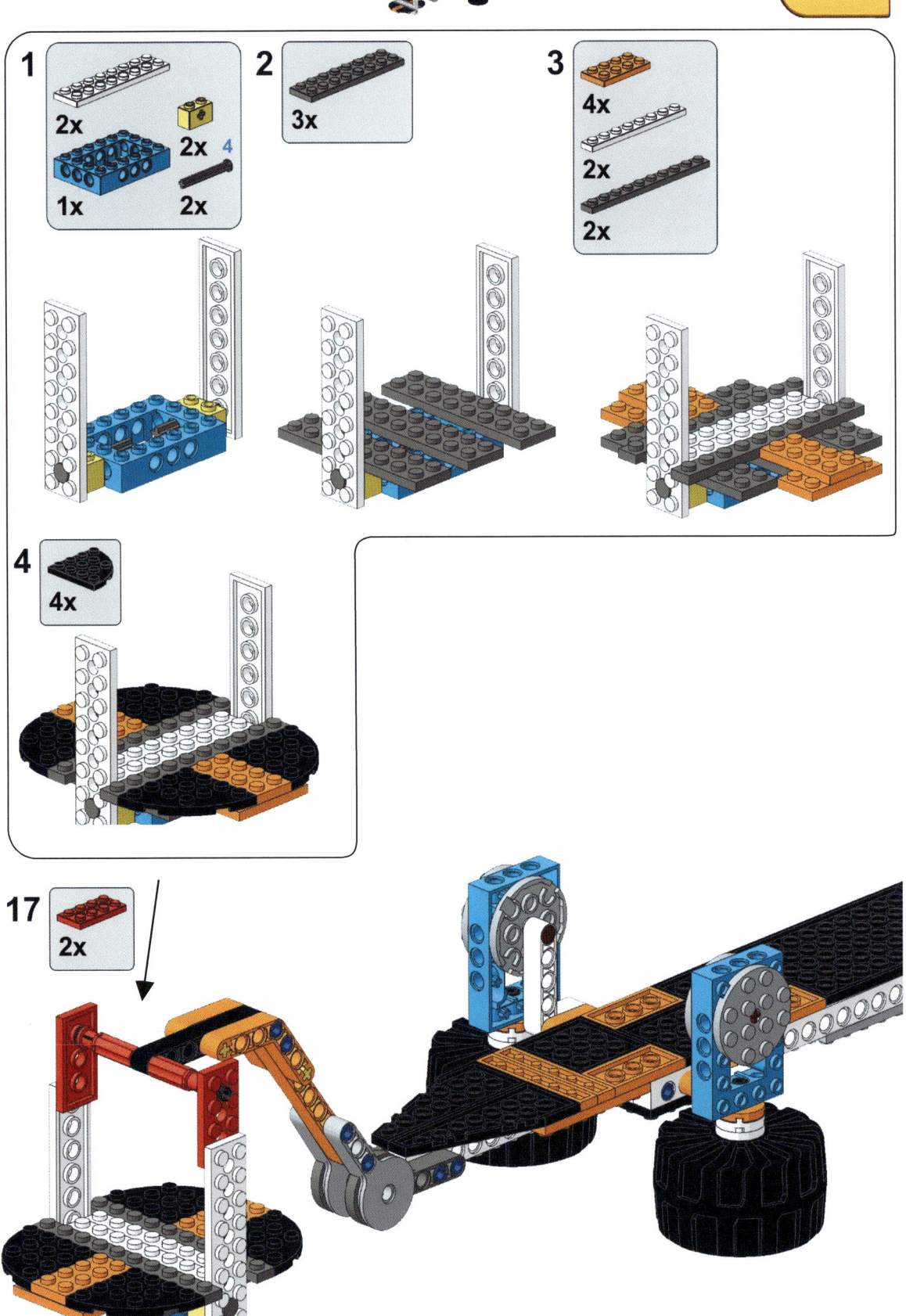

17
2x

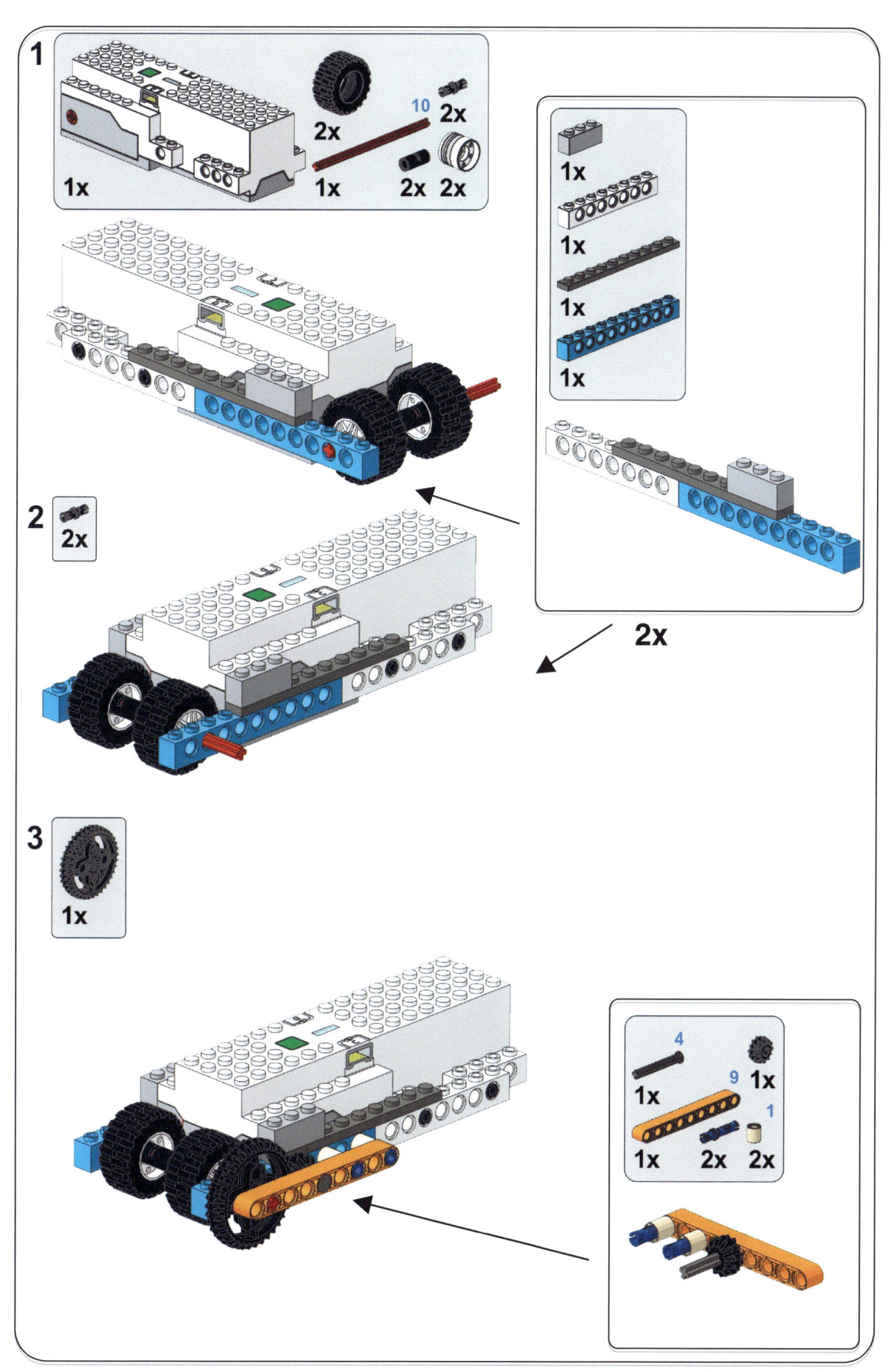

Weight-Booster

1

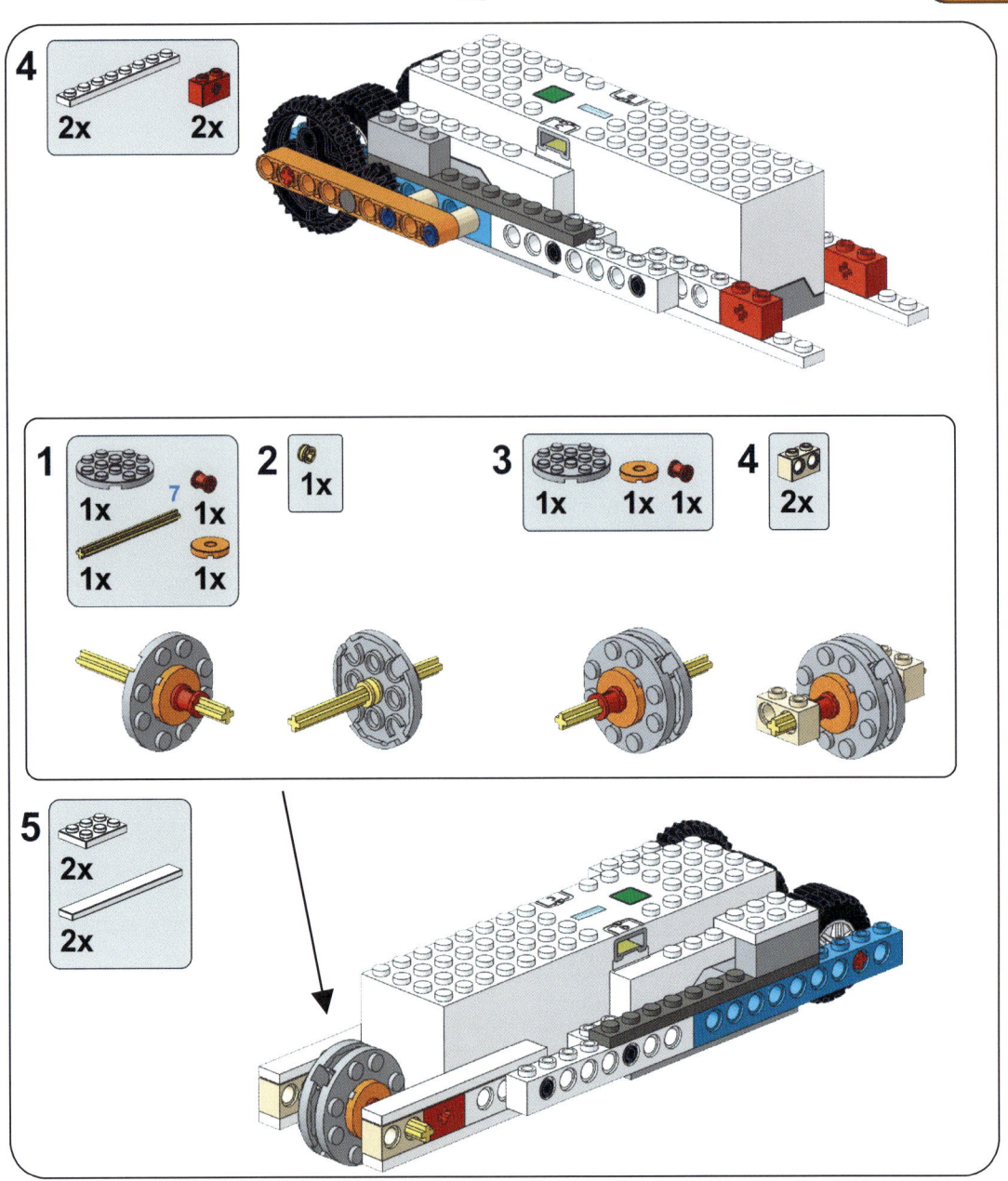

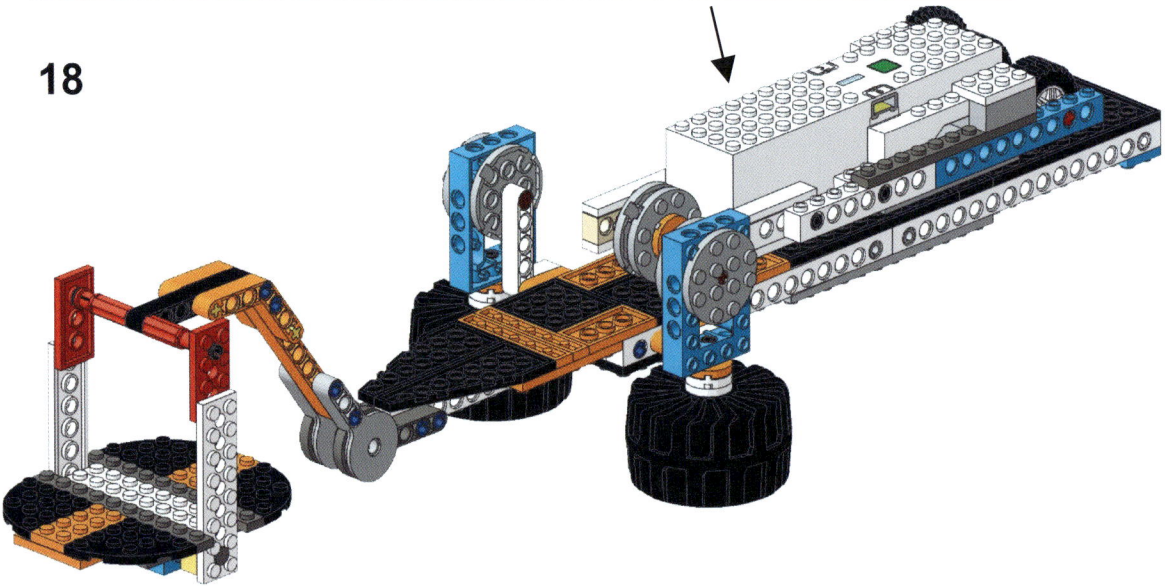

Weight-Booster

18

Weight-Booster

Code
The program is more complex than the simple movements of the Move-Hub might suggest.

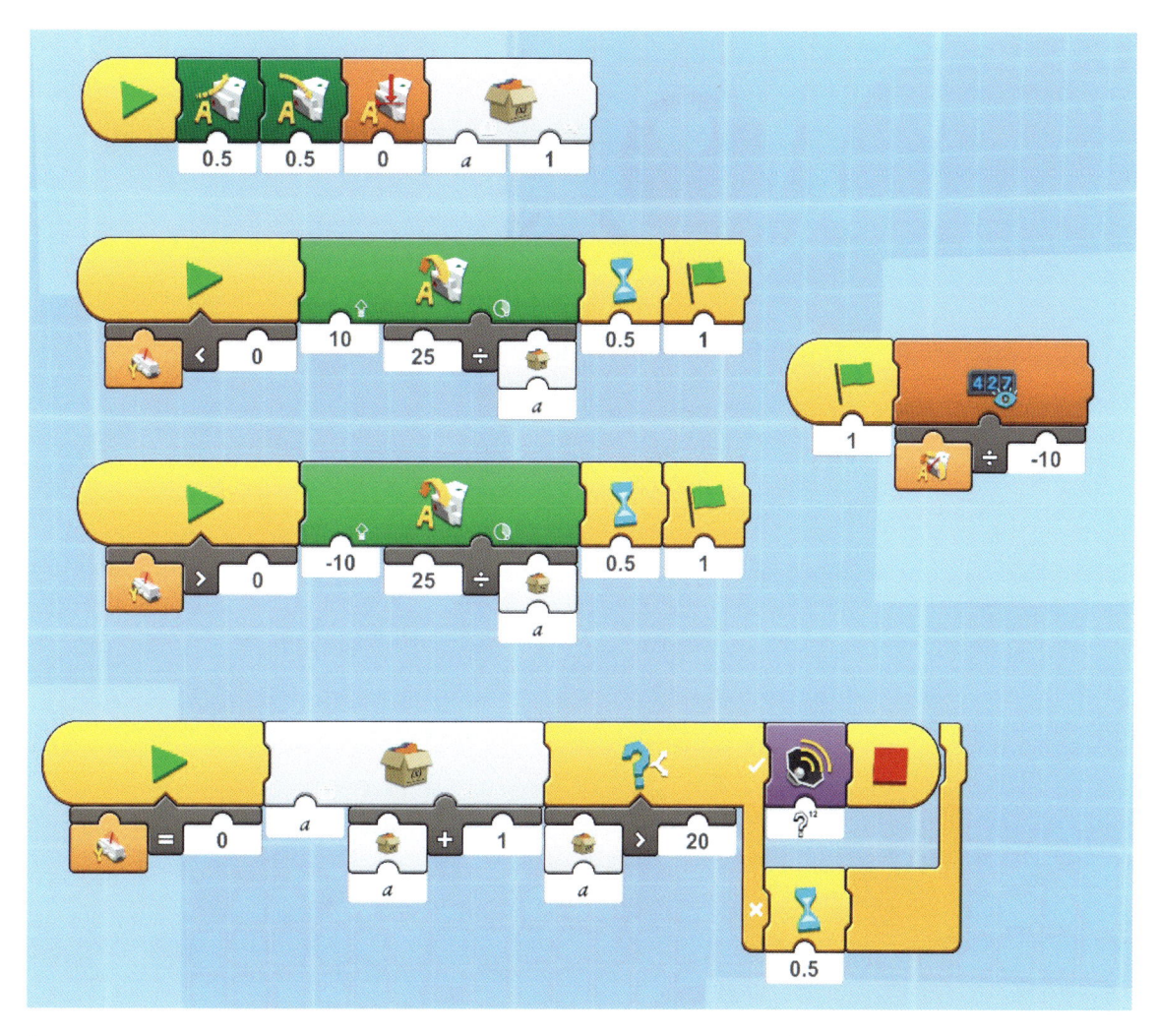

Start the program while the Move-Hub sits on the Balance and the weighing tray is empty. Click on the green central start button in the upper right corner of the screen.

The Move-Hub will move forth and back on the balance beam with decreasing distances till the beam is in balance. The display shows a value for the initial imbalance and the program ends with a sound.

Now a small weight can be placed on the tray and the program must be started again. As soon as the beam is in balance again, the weighing result is displayed.

Weight-Booster

Play

The basic setup is not very accurate. With some playful experiments you can improve the accuracy of the weighing result. To do so, you should first understand the way the program works.

First, the acceleration and deceleration values for motor A are set. These values can be changed to influence the effect of the Move-Hub movement to the reaction of the beam.

The initial position of motor A is then set to 0. So, at the end of the program, the total travel distance of the Move-Hub can be calculated.

Variable a is set to 1. This variable counts the number of direction changes of the Move-Hub. The variable is used to reduce the travel distance after each direction change.

As long as the balance beam is inclined to any side, one of the conditional start blocks is executed.

This block provides degrees of inclination of the Move-Hub. A horizontal Move-Hub results in the value 0. Hence, any value other than 0 does mean that the balance beam is not level, yet.

Because of the incline to one side, the Move-Hub moves "upwards". Motor A turns slowly with speed 10 for 25 degrees. For the first move, the division of 25 by variable a still results in 25. In subsequent moves, the value in a is increased and the division results in smaller values. The Move-Hub then moves a shorter distance.

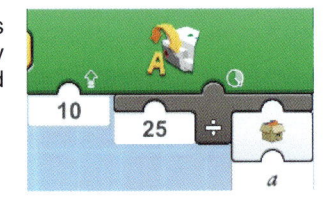

The Move-Hub waits for 0.5 seconds after each movement. This provides some time for the movement of the balance beam. This time value contributes to the accuracy of the balance. A value of 1 or 2 seconds can reduce the number of direction changes. However, the weighing process will take considerably longer. At the end of the sequence the program continues at jump label 1.

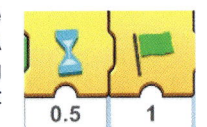

The next sequence controls the reaction to an incline to the other side. Movement direction of Motor A is therefore negative. After the waiting block the sequence also continues at jump label 1.

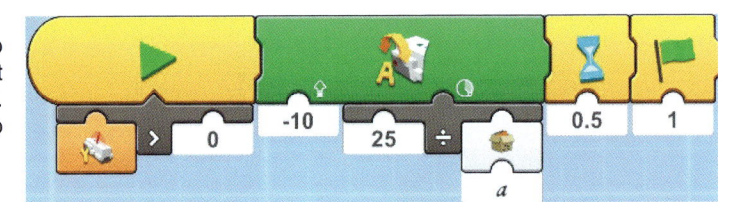

At jump label 1 the travel distance of motor A is displayed. The actual value is divided by 10 to convert the degrees of rotation in an approximate value of the weight in grams.

The required divisor may depend on several factors. Weight of your batteries, acceleration values and slippage of the wheels. An exact calculation of the required divisor value is difficult. Therefore, you can perform an experiment to improve the accuracy of the balance:

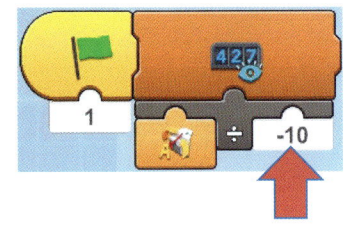

1. Enter 1 as divisor (not -10 as shown above)
2. Let the program run with an empty tray till the program stops after the beam is perfectly horizontal.
3. Put a known weight on the tray. You may want to check the weight on a digital kitchen scale.
4. Let the program run again and note the value displayed when the program ends.
5. Divide this value by the weight of your test weight and enter the result as the new divisor in place of the 1 previously entered.

Weight-Booster

The last sequence also starts with a conditional starting block. It is executed every time the beam travels though the horizontal position.

First, variable a is increased by 1. Variable a counts the number of direction changes.

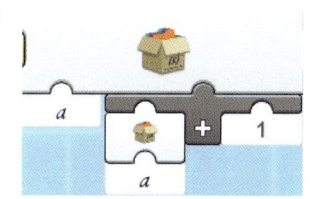

The following „if"-block checks if variable a is already higher than 20. If so, a sound is played, and the program is stopped.

Is variable a still below 20 the program waits for half a second to give the beam some time to incline to one of the sides. After that, the program will execute one of the three sequences again:
- Incline right
- Incline left
- Horizontal Position

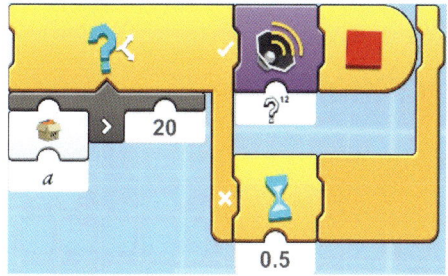

When the balance beam stays in the horizontal position before variable a reaches 20 the „horizontal" sequence will be executed till variable a is larger than 20 to finally end the program.

Boost-Writer

Boost Writer – Write, Draw and Copy bug

The built and the basic programming for this model is easy to understand. To play with the device and create own drawings is a challenge even for an expert. In addition to the programs described in this book, it is also possible to control it by a PC to simplify the definition of new drawings.

Build

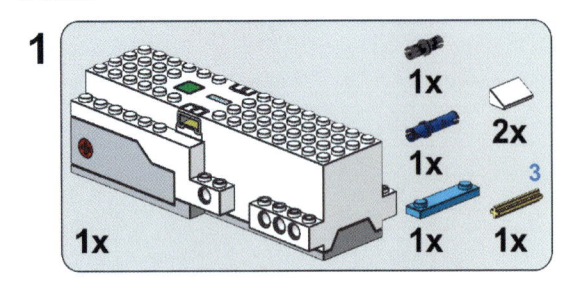

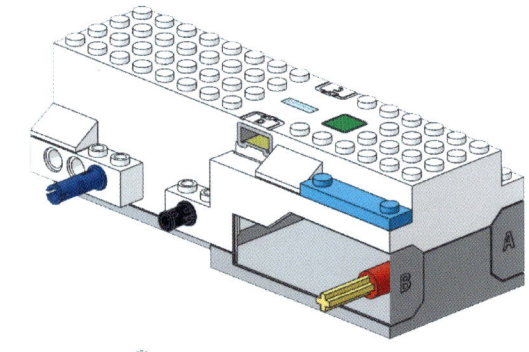

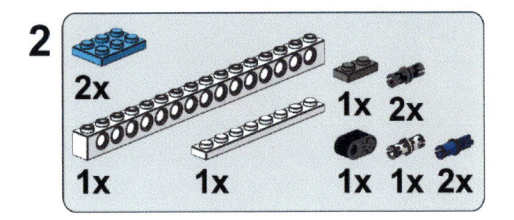

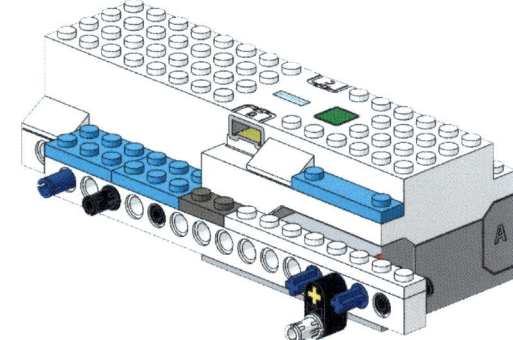

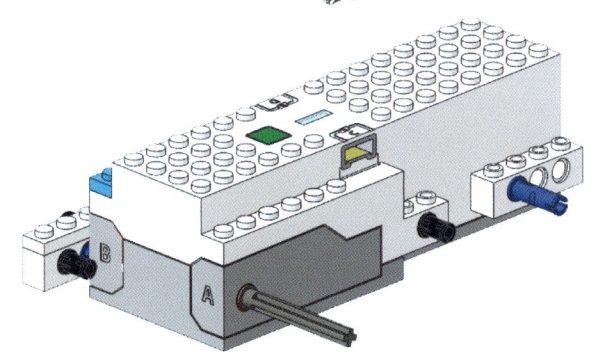

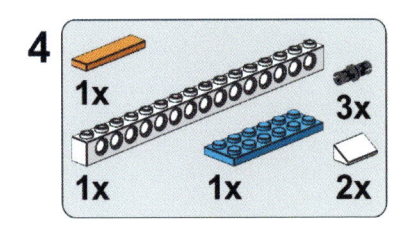

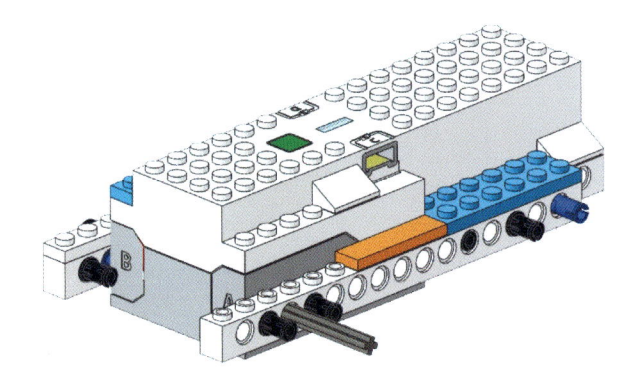

64

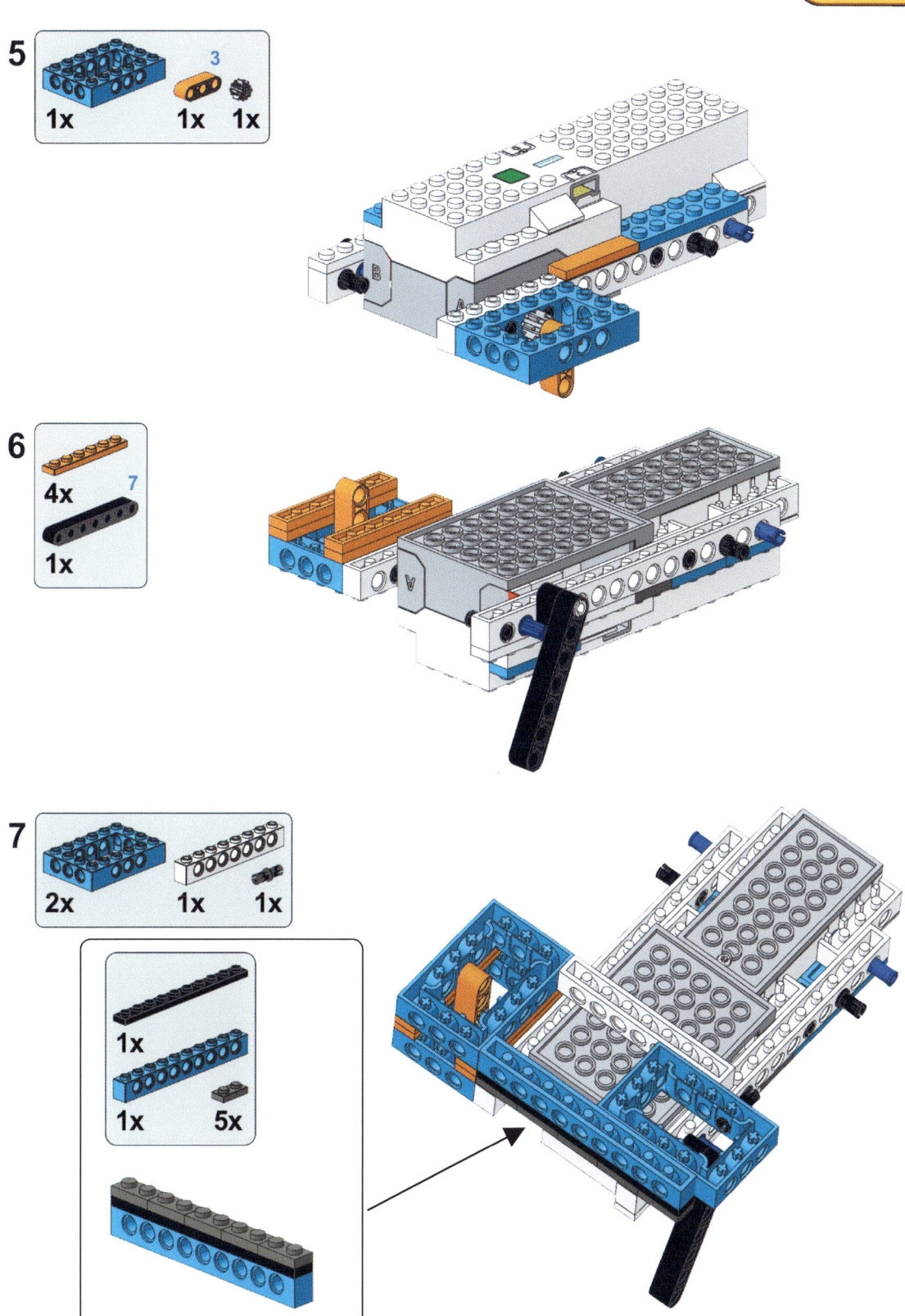

Boost-Writer

5
1x 1x 1x

6
4x 1x

7
2x 1x 1x
1x 5x

Boost-Writer

BUILD

8
1x
1x 12
1x

9
2x
2x 5
1x

10
1x

Boost-Writer

BUILD

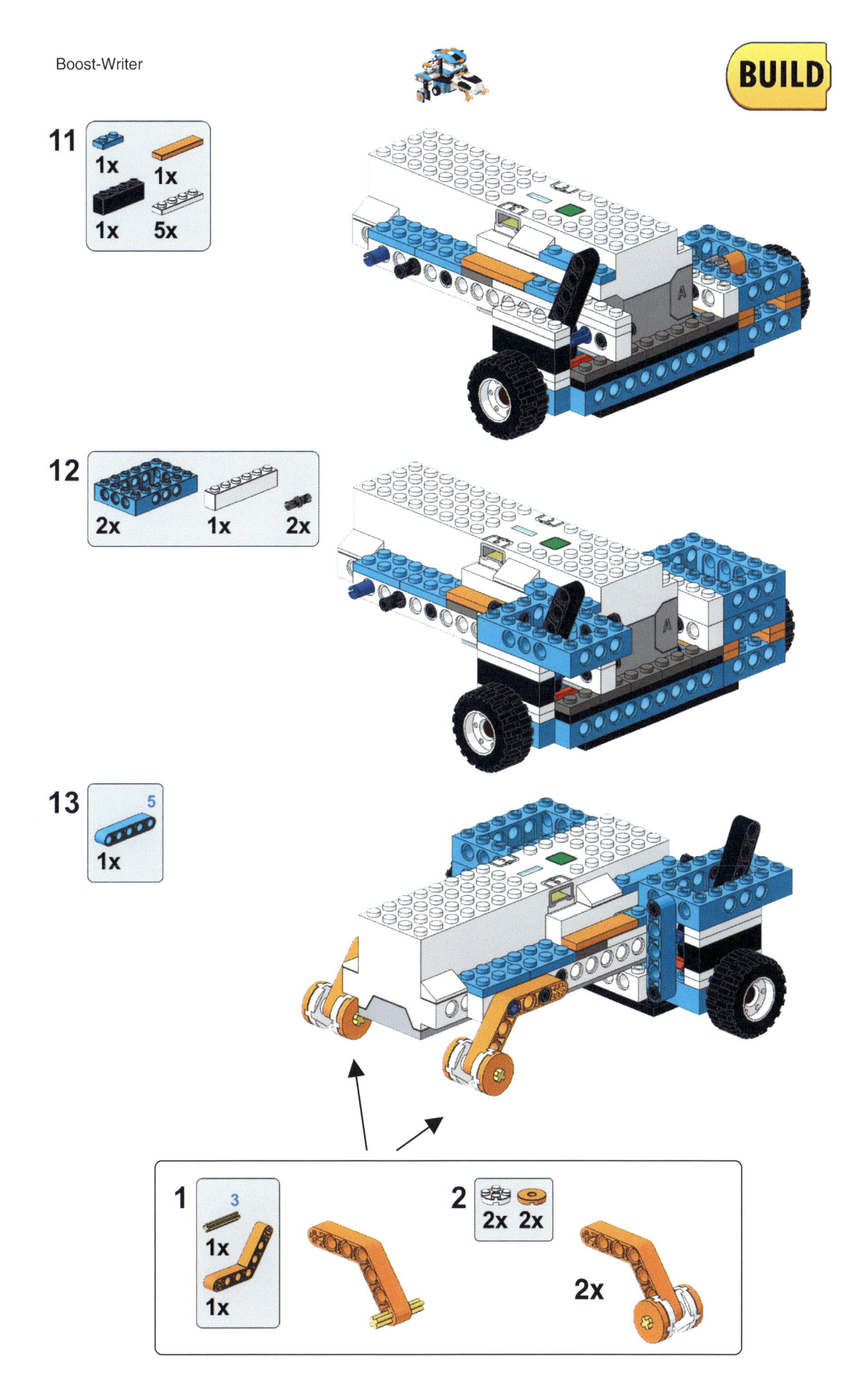

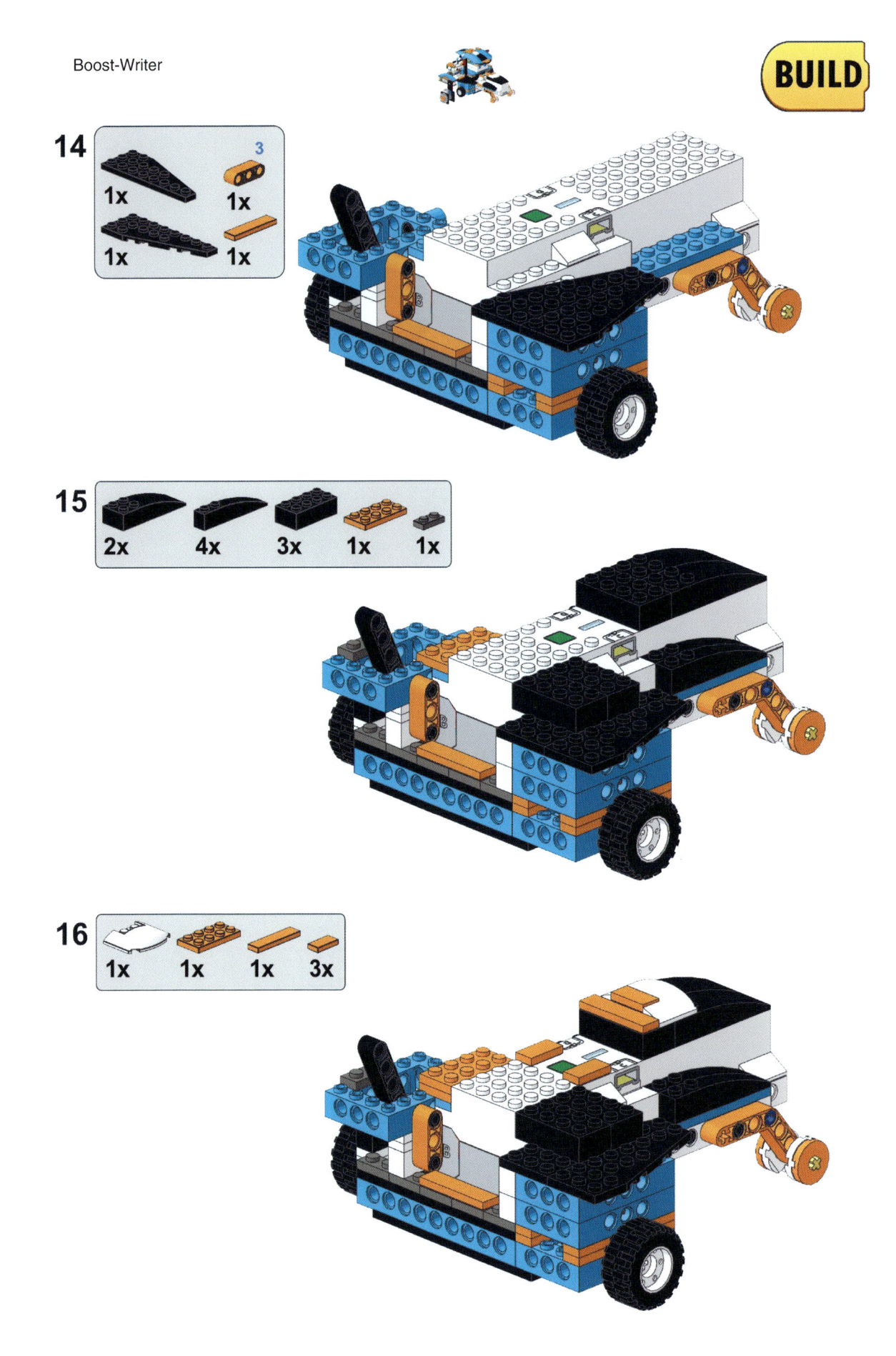

Boost-Writer

14
1x 1x
1x 1x
3

15
2x 4x 3x 1x 1x

16
1x 1x 1x 3x

68

Boost-Writer

BUILD

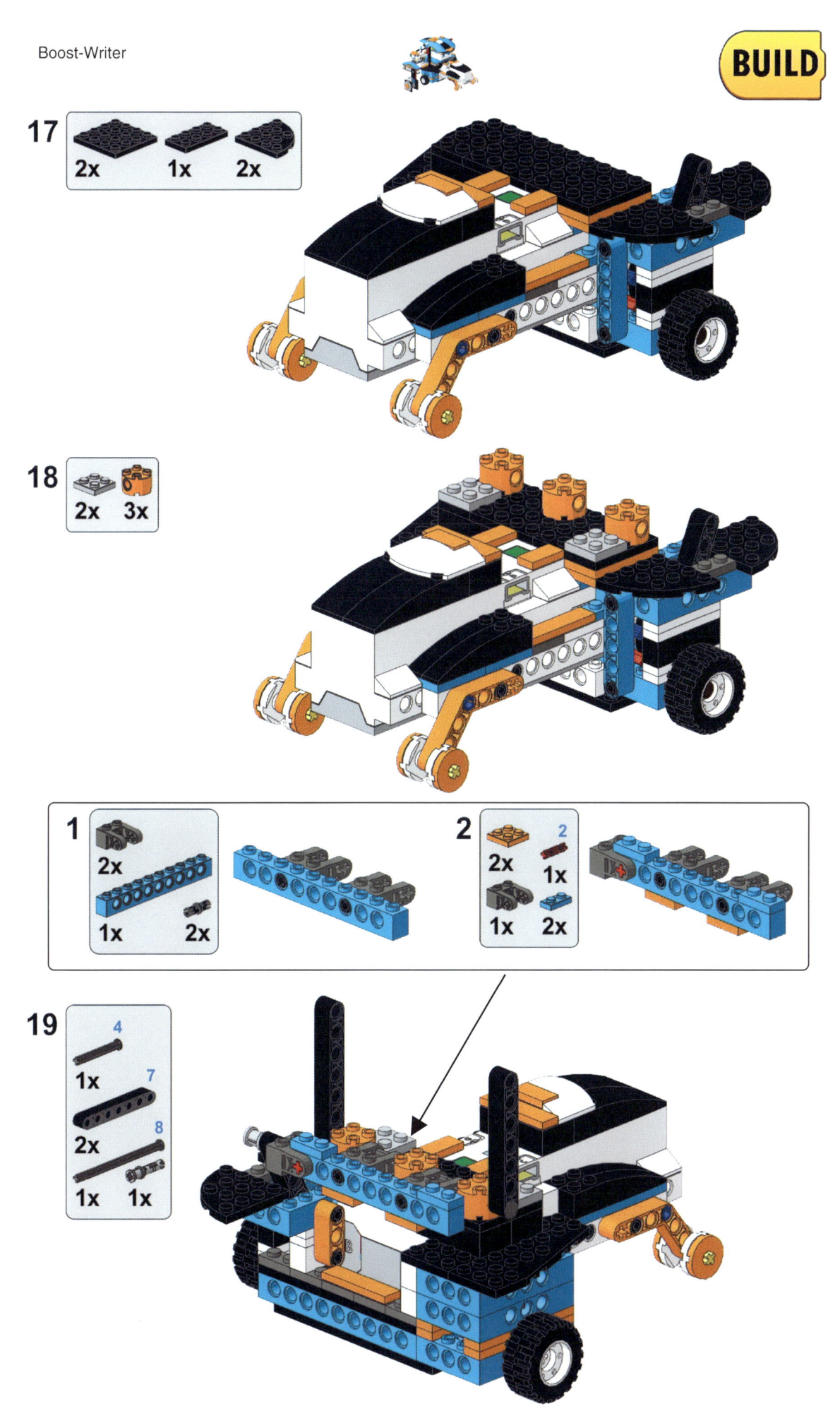

17 2x 1x 2x

18 2x 3x

1 2x 1x 2x

2 2x 1x 1x 2x

19 1x (4) 2x (7) 1x (8) 1x

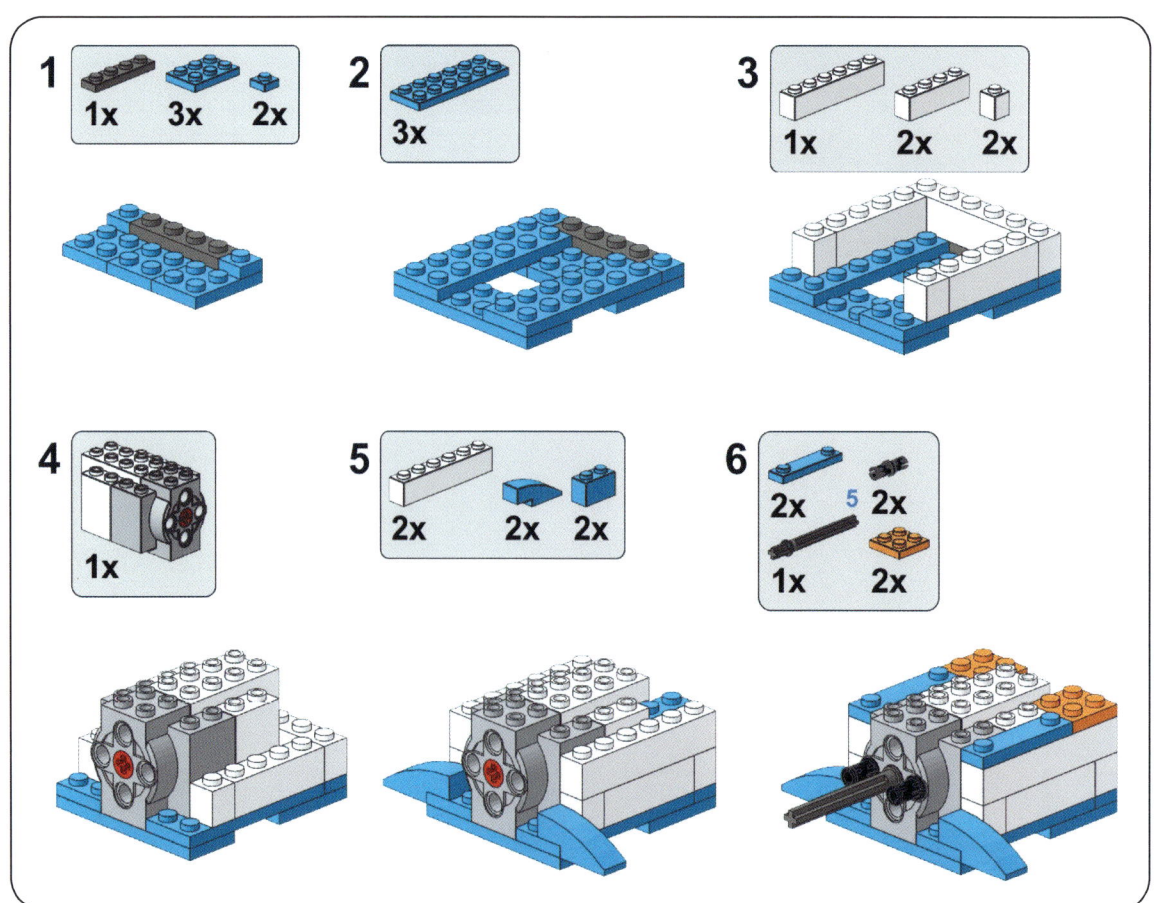

Boost-Writer

70

Boost-Writer

BUILD

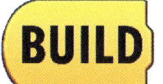

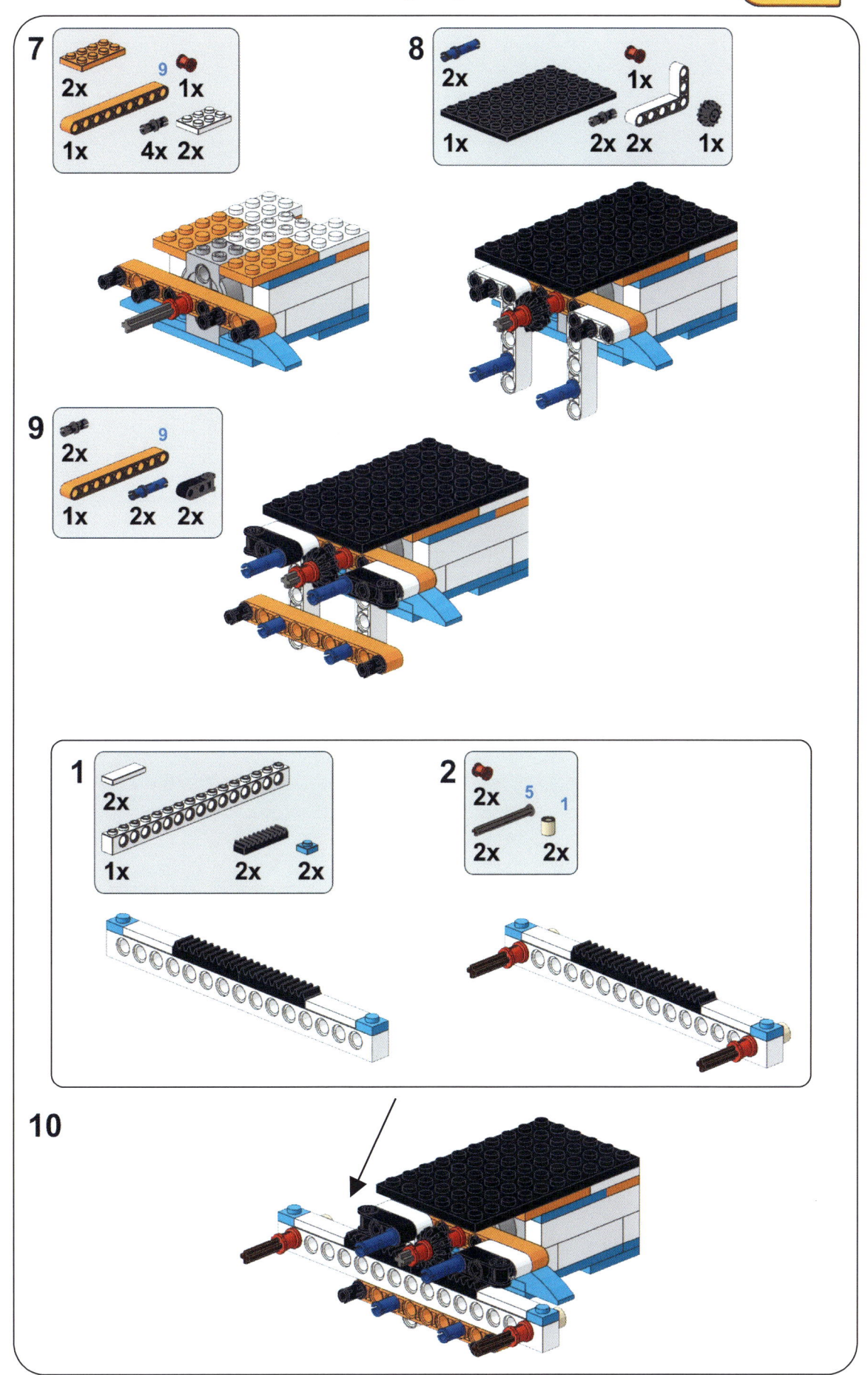

Boost-Writer

BUILD

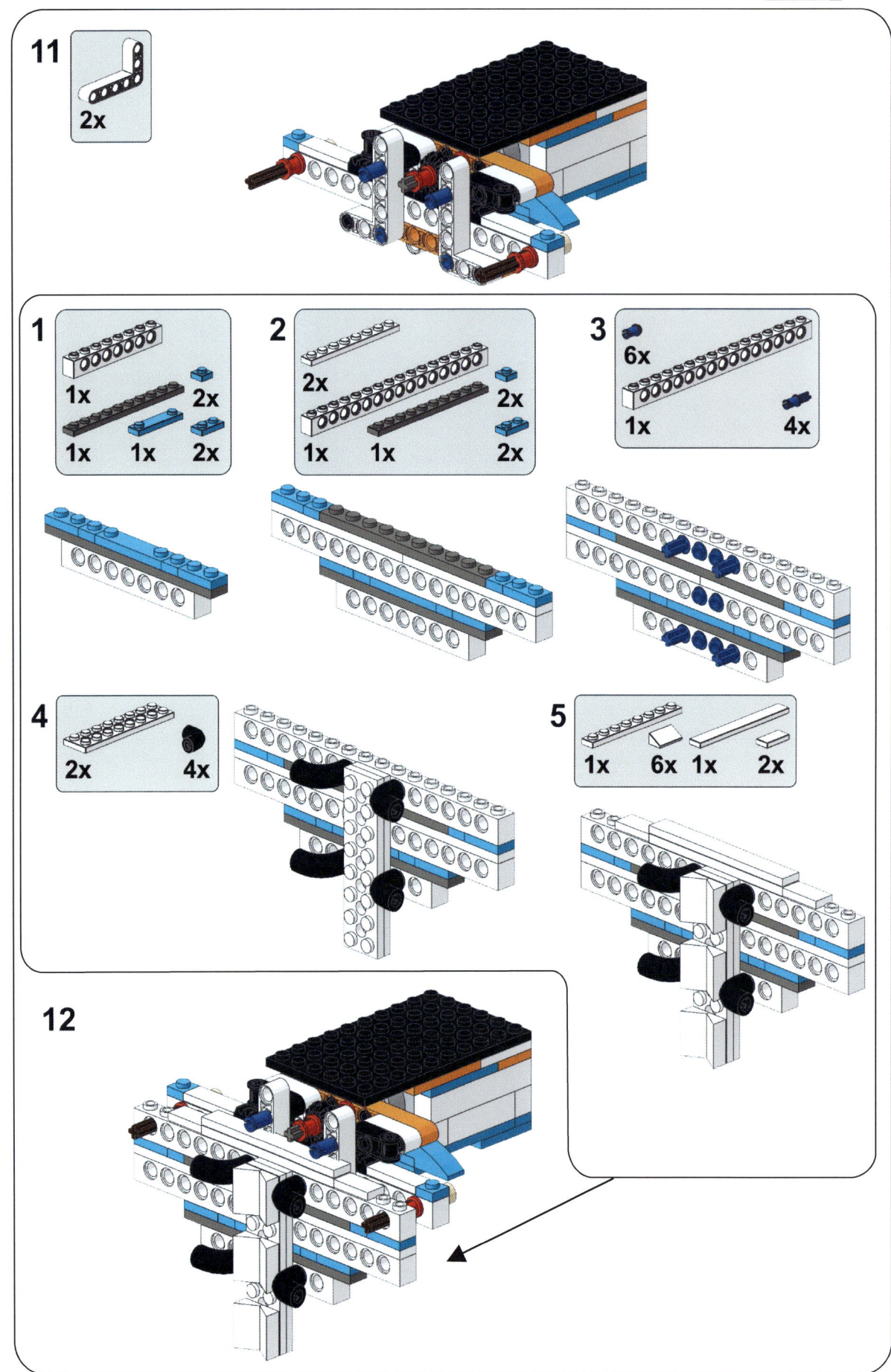

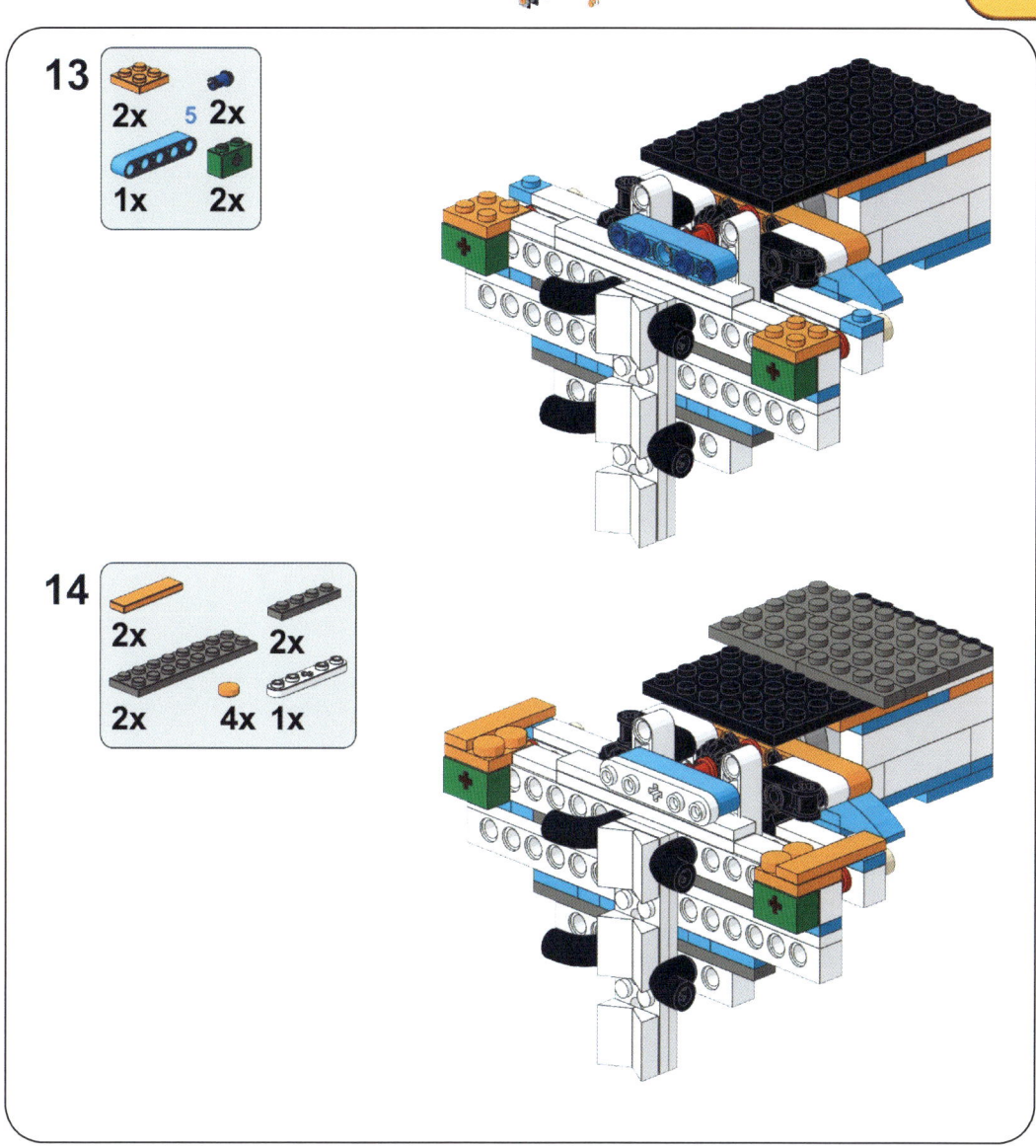

Boost-Writer

13
2x, 5, 2x
1x, 2x

14
2x, 2x
2x, 4x, 1x

22

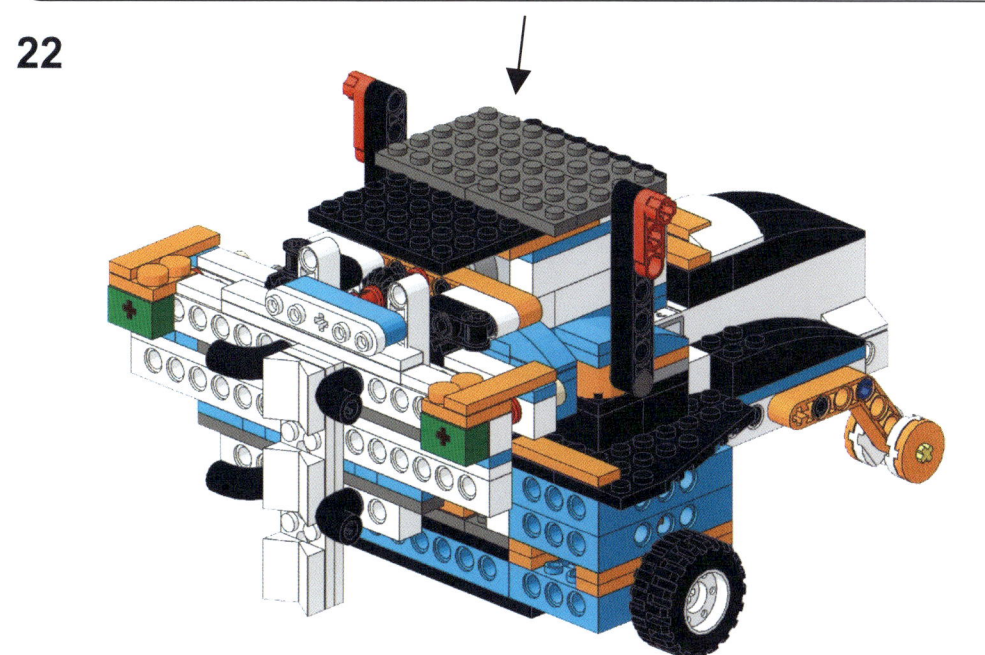

Boost-Writer

23
- 2x (red)
- 2x (yellow)
- 5
- 2x (green)
- 2x (green)

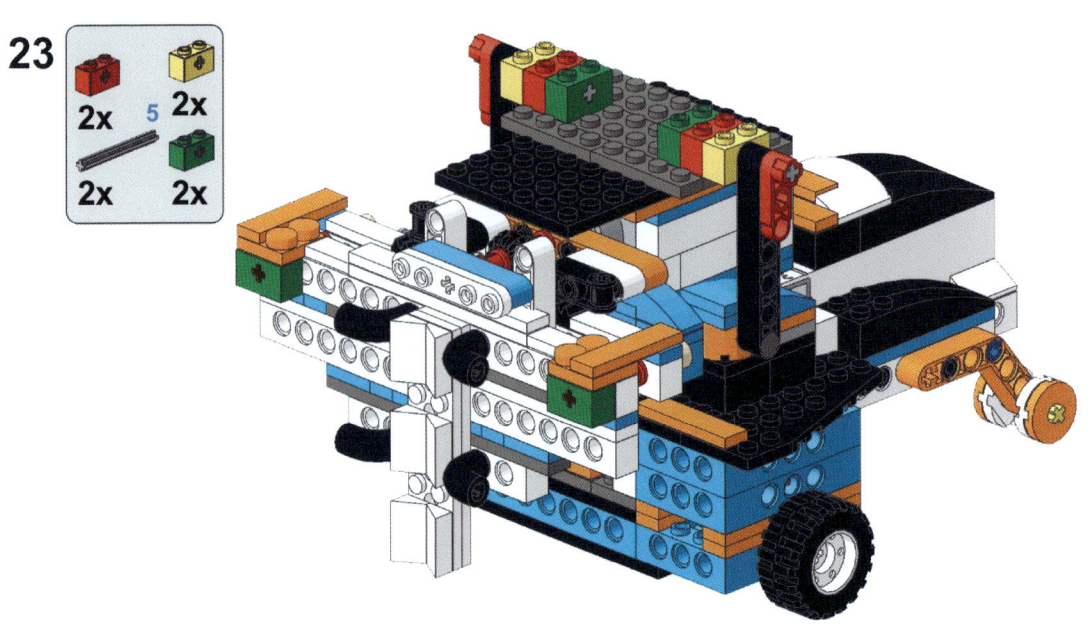

24
- 4x
- 5x

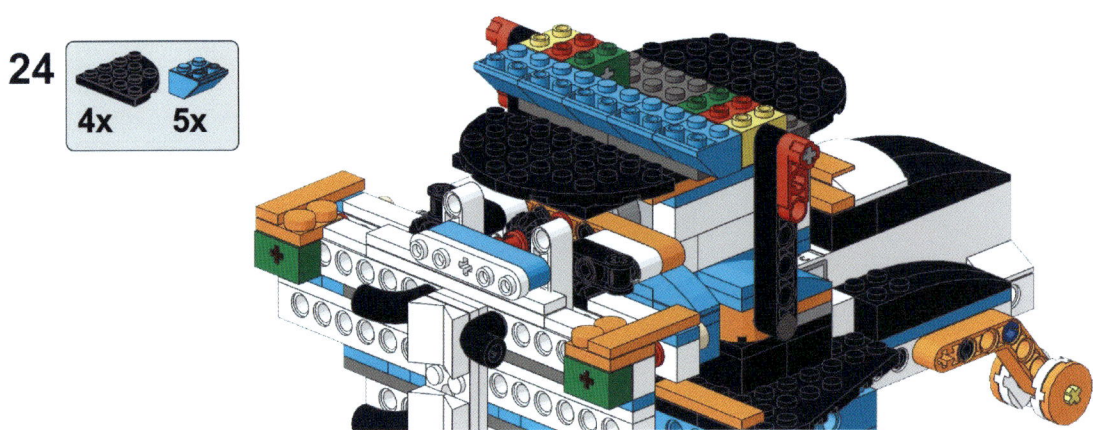

25
- 1x
- 1x
- 2x
- 2x

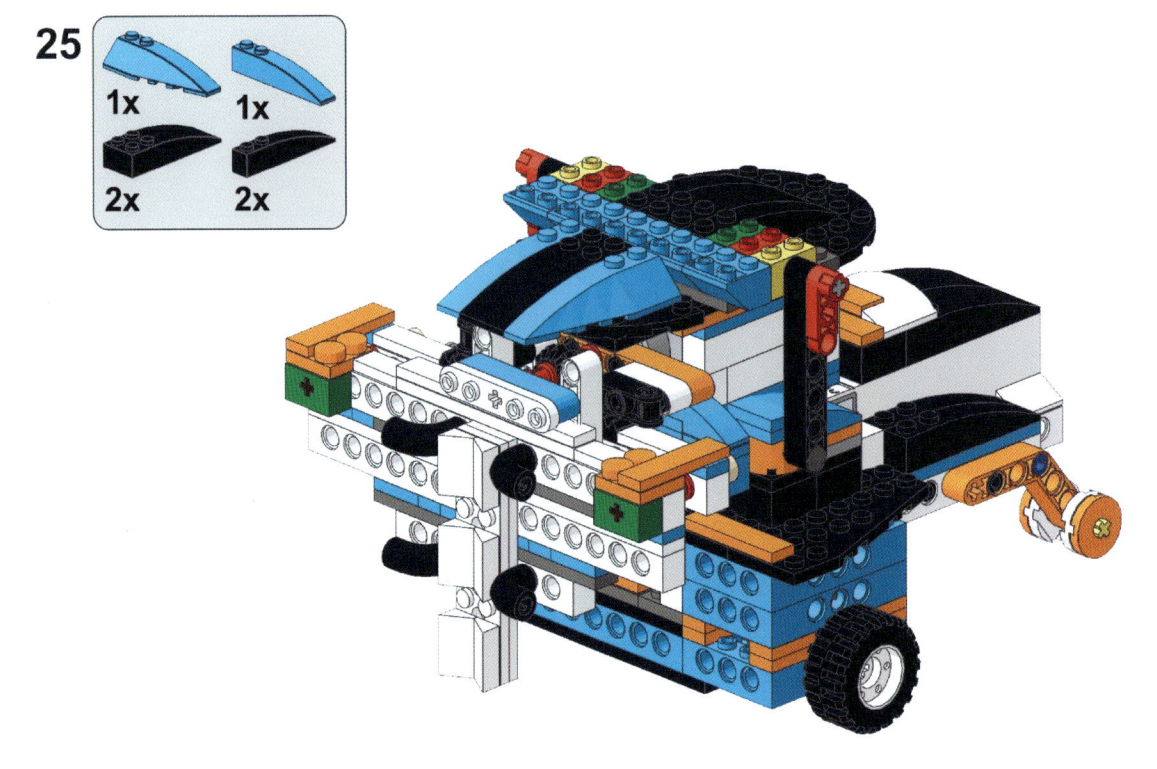

Boost-Writer

26
1x, 2x, 1x, 1x

27
2x, 2x, 2x, 4x

Brackets for rubber bands

Pen position

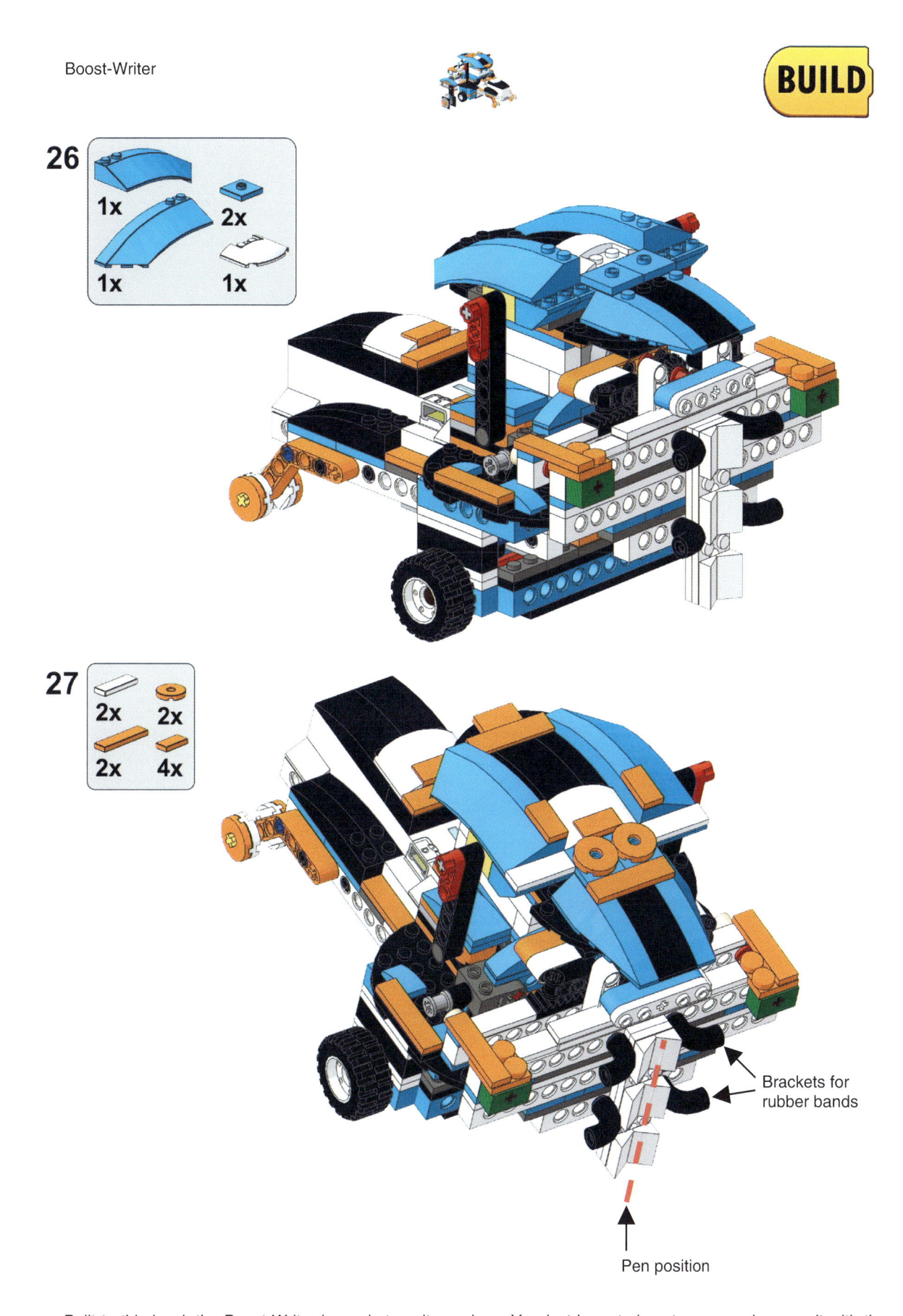

Built to this level, the Boost-Writer is ready to write or draw. You just have to insert a pen and secure it with the rubber bands.

Boost-Writer

Copy
This bracket is only needed for the copy function.

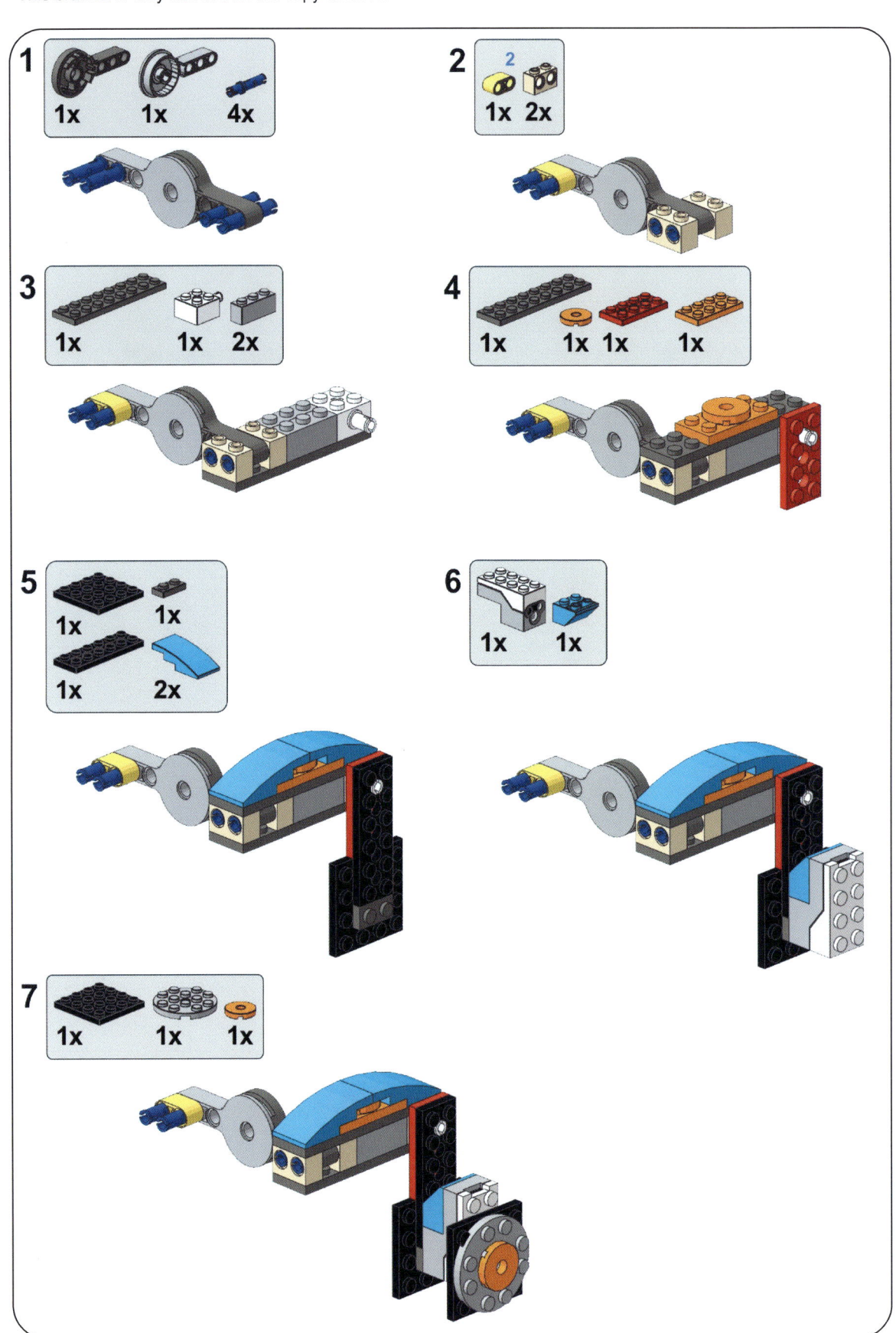

Boost-Writer

BUILD

28

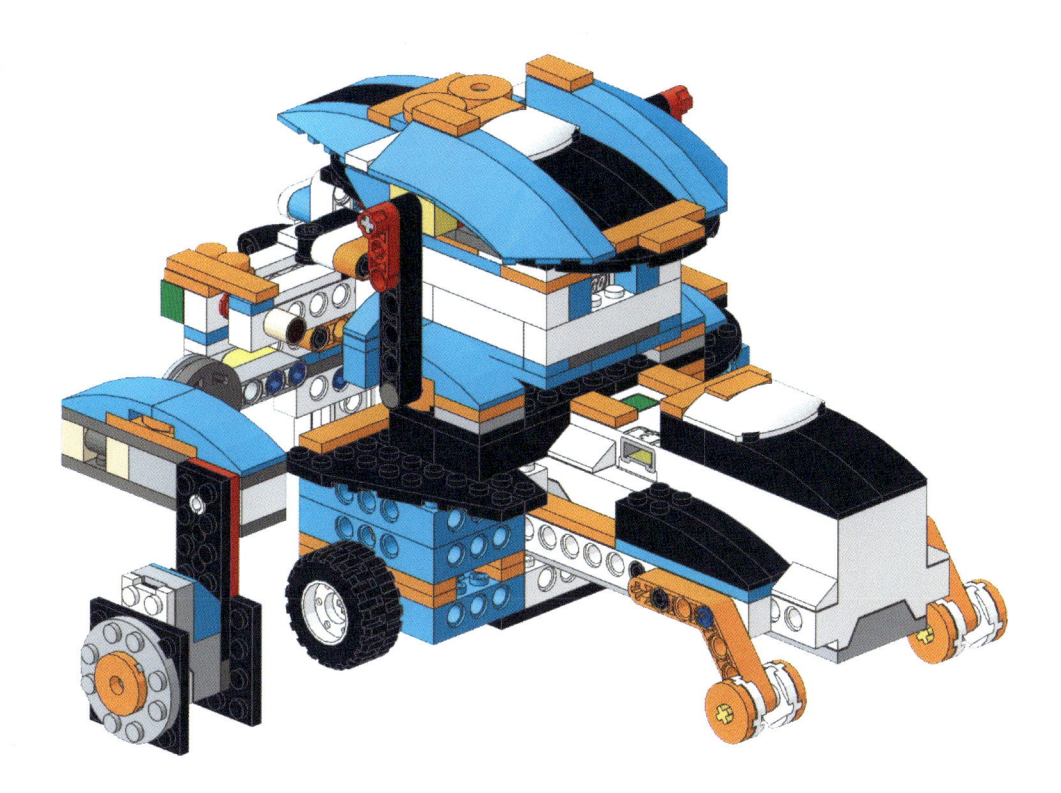

You can use the original rubber bands in the set to secure a pen into the pen bracket. The thickness of the pen and its friction on the paper do influence the results. For drawings and the Dot-Matrix mode, a medium thickness is used. For the copy function you should use a thick marker pen. In the lower position of the writing head, the tip of the pen should only slightly touch the paper. A very low pen position will result in high friction and the Writer might have difficulties to follow your drawing commands.

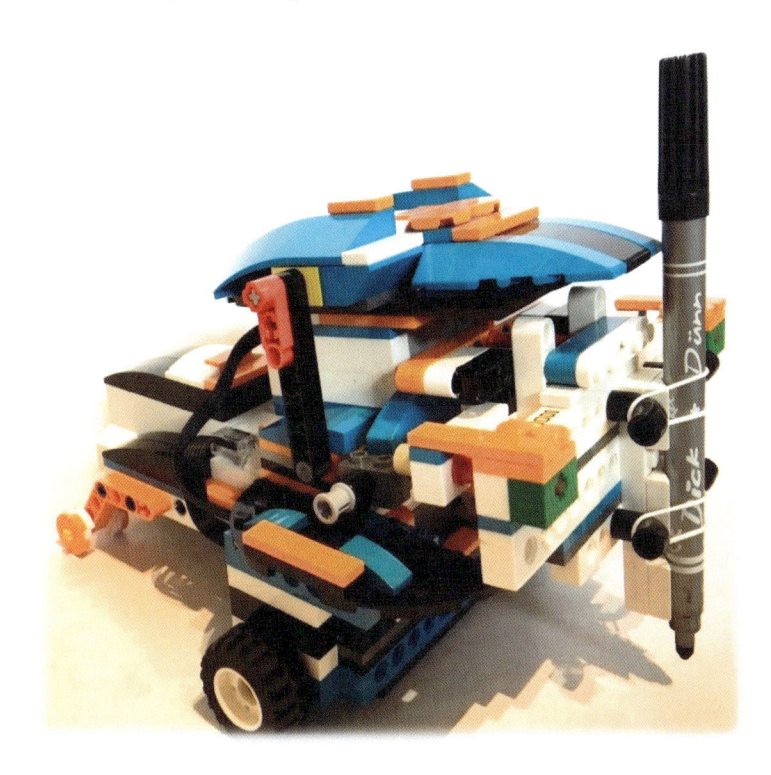

Boost-Writer

Code

There are three predetermined program types for the Boost-Writer:
- Draw – The plotter
- Write – The Dot-Matrix printer
- Copy – The copy machine

Each of the three programs is to be entered in a separate program window.

Draw

The following program generates a simple drawing. The plotter draws a small house using one continuous line. The program is created in the main programming window without the need for any subroutines.

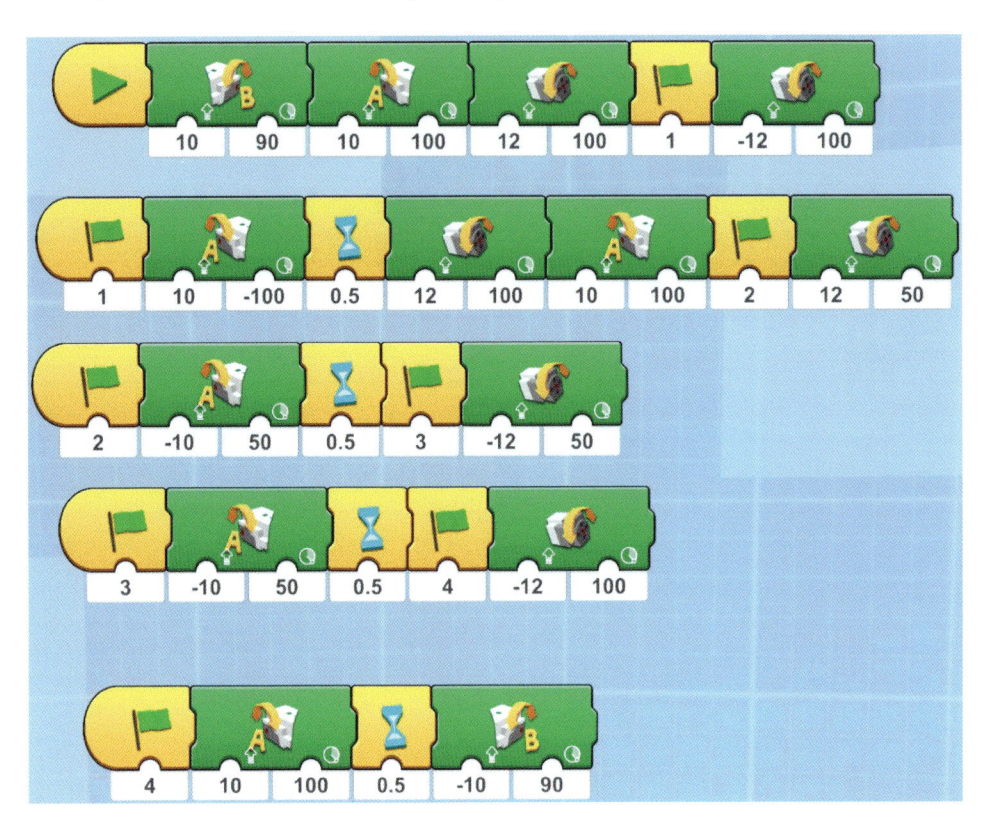

Boost-Writer

Write – Dot Matrix printing

Using the plotter technique to write letters results in a poor handwriting. Letters are easier to generate when using Dot-Matrix printing similar to the concept used by most commercial printers.

Before being able to write, the required letters must be defined. Each letter is defined in a subroutine which should be named according to that letter.

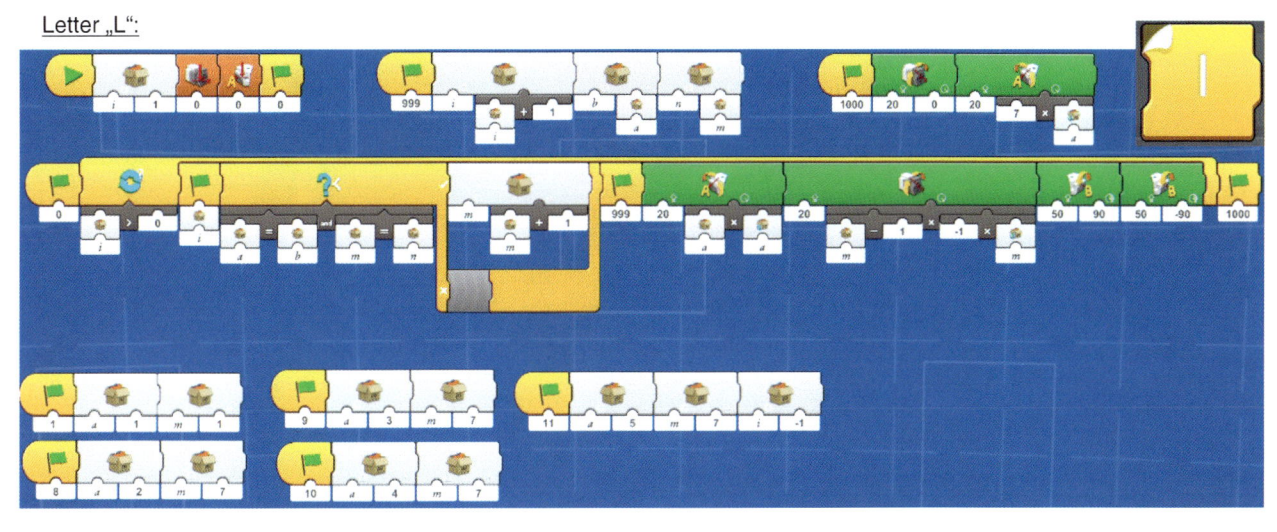

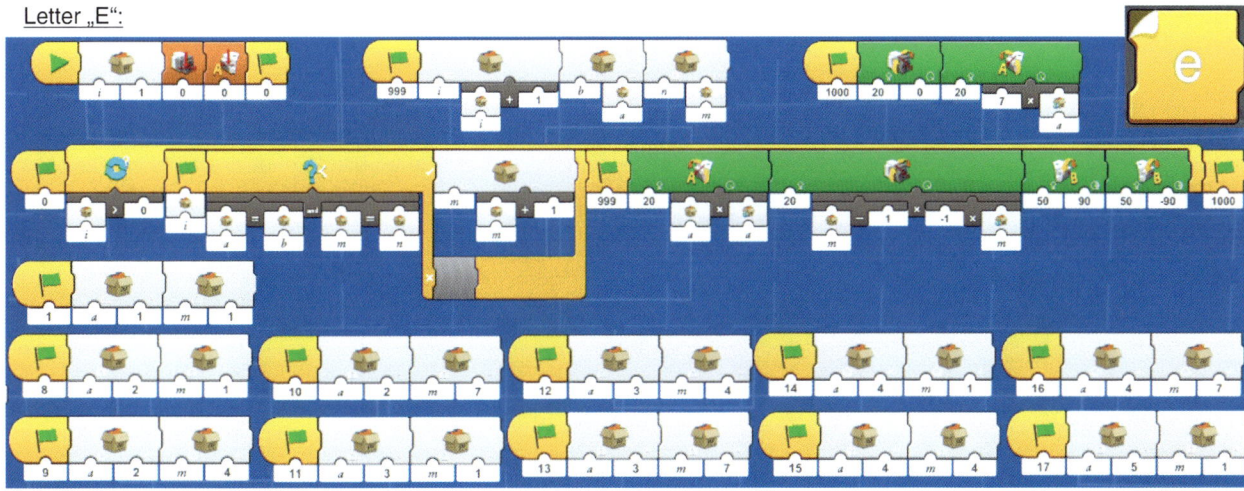

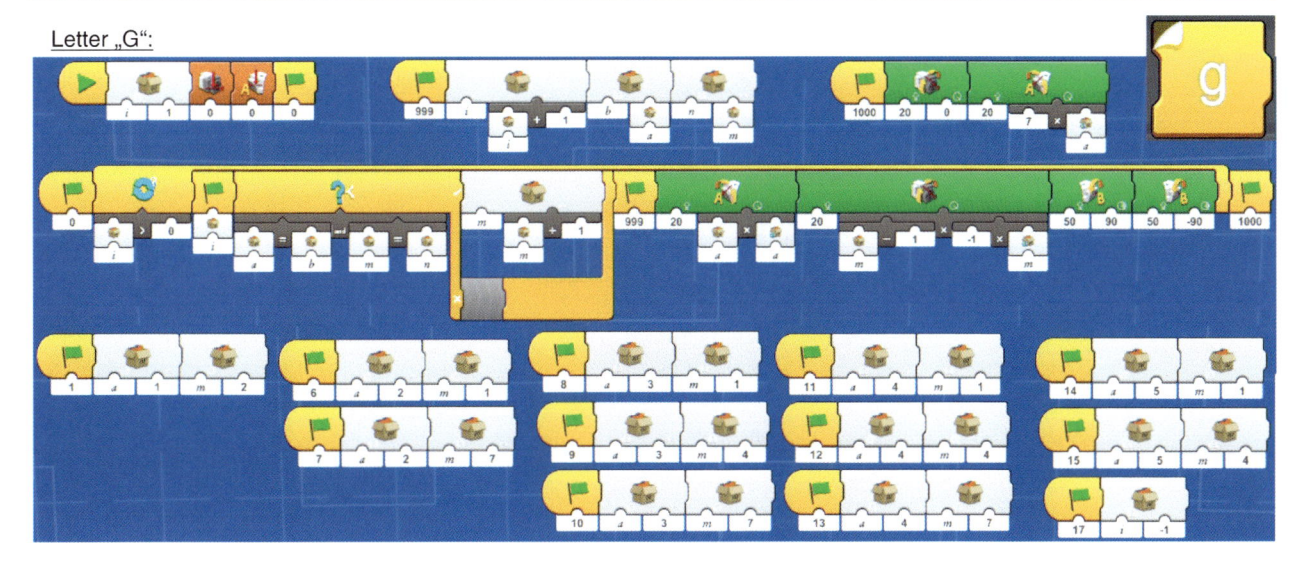

Letter „L":

Letter „E":

Letter „G":

Boost-Writer

Letter „O":

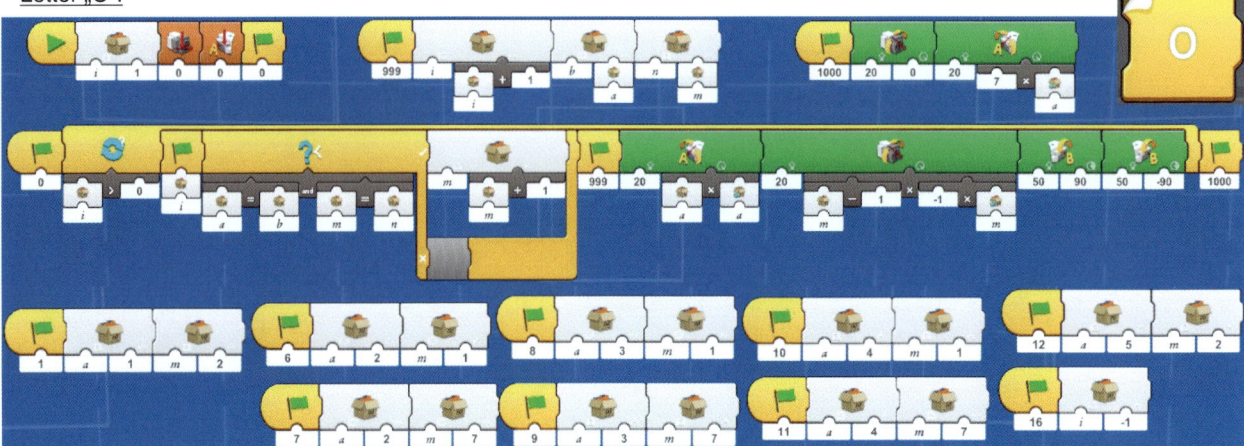

Initializing:
The initializing blocks also must be generated in their own subroutine.

As soon as all subroutines are generated the main program can be created:

Copy – The copy machine
To use the copy function, you must attach the copy bracket. You should use a thick marker pen. The program should be generated in an empty programming window. The program reacts to red ink on the source paper and transfers the shape to the destination paper.

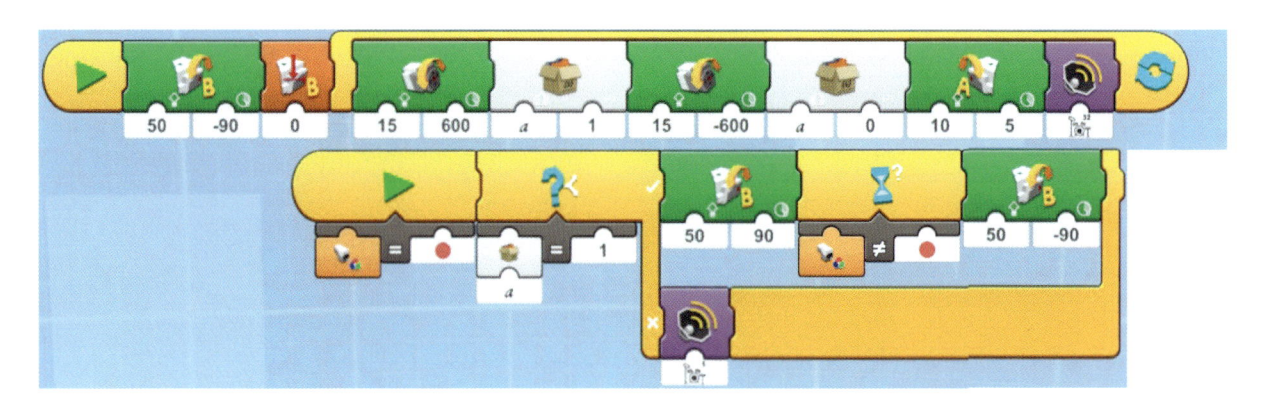

Boost-Writer

Play

Draw – The Plotter

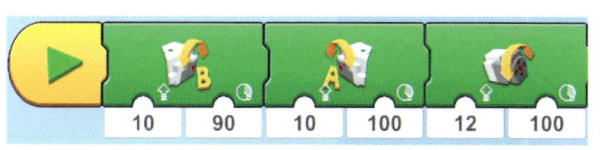

To put a line on the paper you first lower the pen. Motor B is used to move the pen up and down. At the start of the program, the pen should be in the upper position. The first programming block turns motor B by 90°. The next block turns motor A by 100°. Motor A is used to drive the vehicle. While the pen is down a line is created along the driving direction. The third block turns the external motor by 100°. A line across the driving direction is created.

Jump label 1 is used to turn motor A and the external motor at the same time. A diagonal line is created. Diagonal lines are not always homogeneous as the two motors are not synchronized. Furthermore, there is some play in the gears. The model "Egg-Booster" shows some concepts to counteract these two problems. For the writer, you can play with different speeds for the motors (e.g. 10 or 12) to compensate the different responsiveness of the motors. At the end of the movement the program waits for half a second to make sure both motors have completed their movements before starting the next line.

The following movements of motor A and the external motor by 100° each generate another two perpendicular lines.

As with jump label 1 also jump label 2 and 3 are used to move both motors at the same time and generate diagonal lines. This time the distance is reduced to 50 to generate half a roof, each.

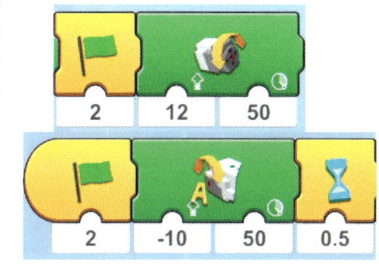

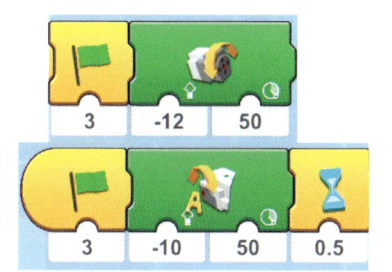

Jump label 4 generates another diagonal line across the main house. After waiting for another 0.4 seconds the pen is lifted from the paper by a turn of motor B 90° in the opposite direction.

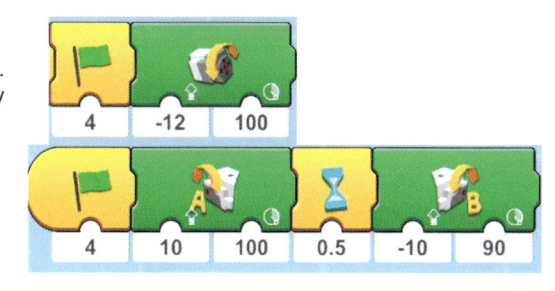

Based on this example you can generate some other line drawings.

Some guidance:
Ext. motor: across motion
Motor A: drive motion
Motor B: pen down (+90°) and pen up (-90°)

Boost-Writer

Write – Dot Matrix printer

To assure that the pen is in the upper position and to set the main variables some initializing is done at the beginning of the program.

The first block sets the power of the motor to 50%. The next block moves motor B up till it hits the upper limit. The reduction to 50% motor power is used to prevent any damage for the motor or the model. The power is set back to 100% after the turn.

The next two blocks write some values into global variables. Blocks for global variables are identified by a globe icon. In comparison to local variables which can only be used within the main program or within a subroutine, global variables can be accessed from any subroutine as well as from the main program.
In our case, global variable a is used to set the standard distance of the dots in driving direction (motor A) and global variable m is used for the dot distance across the driving direction (ext. motor). You can change the size or appearance of the font when you change these values. Larger values of a make the letters wider. Large values in m make them taller.

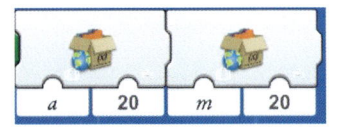

The actual code within the single letters is always the same. Only the coordinates for the dots are different. Every letter is 7 dots tall and 5 dots wide.
To avoid the need to specify a coordinate for every single dot, the program will continue to make dots under the previous one till it receives a new coordinate. Therefore, the program will generate vertical dotted lines after each new coordinate. With this method, the required number of coordinates is substantially reduced.

Right at the start variable i is set to 1. The current position of the external motor and motor A are set to 0 to remember their starting position. The program then continues at jump label 0.

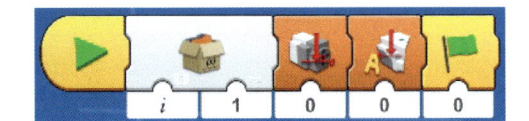

At jump label 0 a loop is executed as long as i is larger than 0. The first block in the loop jumps to the label with the value of variable i. During the first execution of the loop variable i is 1.

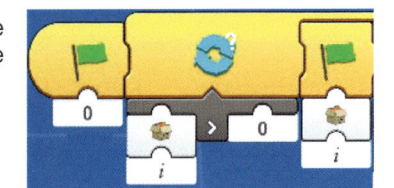

At jump label 1 the local variables a and m are set to the first coordinate. For the first dot of our "L" this is a=1 and m=1.

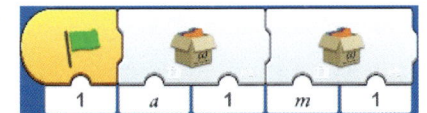

After the jump, an "if"-block checks if the coordinates have been changed by the previous jump. If not, local variable m is increased by one to make the next dot just one coordinate point below the previous one. After the "if"-block, jump label 999 is executed.

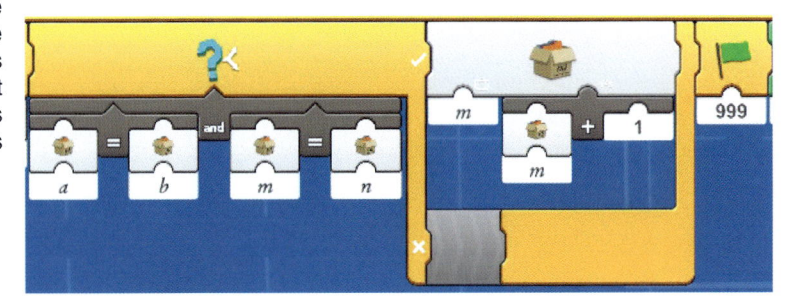

Jump label 999 is used to increase variable i by 1 and to "remember" the old coordinate a and m in the local variables b and n.

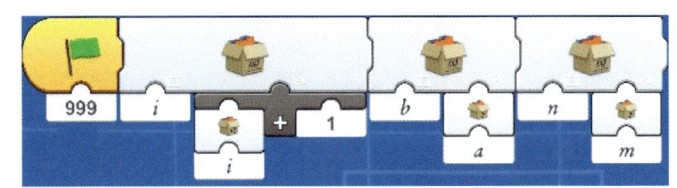

82

Boost-Writer

Next, motor A and the external motor move the pen to the given coordinate. The coordinate values are calculated as the product of local variables a and m with the global variables a and m for the distance of the dots.
The reduction of m by 1 is used to keep the same vertical position for all letters. 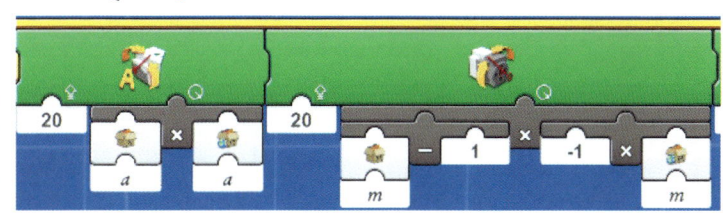
The multiplication with a negative 1 makes sure the letter is not printed upside down. To test the effect of these calculations you can try to subtract 0 instead of 1 and to multiply by a positive 1 instead of a negative 1.

After the pen is moved to the desired coordinate, the pen is lowered by motor B and immediately lifted back up again. This generates a single dot. As long as variable i still contains a positive value, the loop is executed again. The last coordinate sets variable i to a negative value. The loop will not be executed another time and the program continues at jump label 1000.

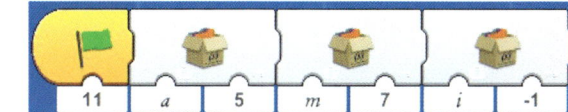

Jump label 1000 moves the pen back to the initial position to be ready for the next letter. A distance of 7 dots is kept between the letters.

An interesting variation of the main program with a changed sequence of letter and different sizes of letters prints the word „LOGO" with a large „L" and smaller "ogo".

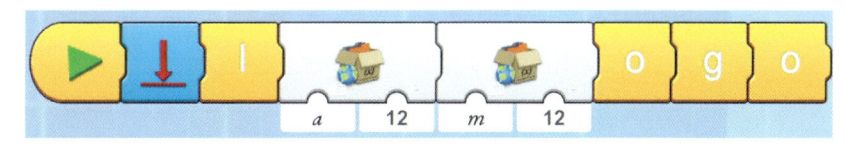

As an inspiration to program some more letter you can use the following display of the alphabet in a 5 x 7 Dot-Matrix pattern:

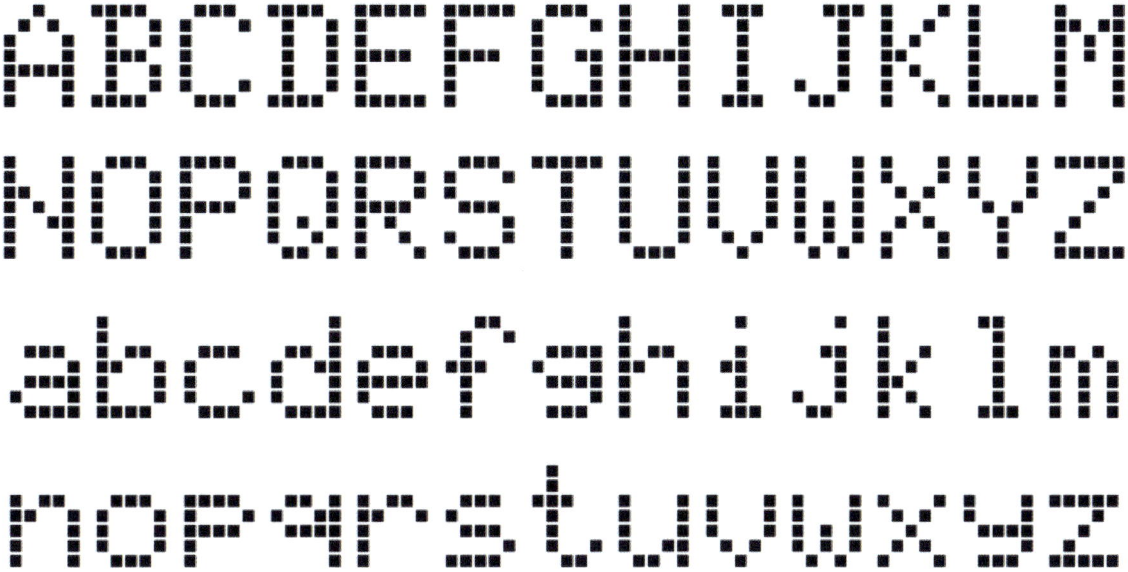

ABCDEFGHIJKLM
NOPQRSTUVWXYZ
abcdefghijklm
nopqrstuvwxyz

83

Boost-Writer

Copy – the copy machine
Motor B is moved up and the position is stored as 0.

The following infinitive loop lets the external motor go right and left by 600° (the full travel distance of the sled). In the positive direction variable a is 0, in the opposite direction it is 1.

After a full right and left movement of the external motor the Writer is moved forward by a 5° turn of motor A. A sound is played (Drum 32) before the loop is executed again.

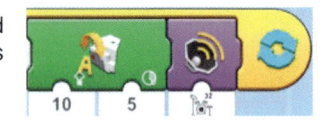

While the sled is moving, the sensor checks if it sees the predetermined color (here red). When the color is detected, an "if"-block checks if the sled is moving in a "negative" direction. If not, a sound (drum 1) is played. If the motion direction is "negative" the pen is lowered and left down as long as the color is detected. If the color is not detected anymore, the pen is lifted by motor B.

The differentiation of the movement directions is necessary to make the copier uni-directional. In a bi-directional mode the pen would be lowered in both directions. Due to the play in the gears this would lead to frayed images.

To let the sensor detect any color other than the white background paper color, the loop can be changed as follows:

Egg-Booster

Egg-Booster – Multi-colored chicken eggs

The Egg-Booster provides similar functionality as the Boost-Writer. This time the pen does not write on paper but on a chicken egg. Furthermore, the motors for positioning the pen are synchronized and the play in the vertical axis is compensated by the weight of the arm.

Build

In contrast to most „egg-bots" the egg-booster holds the egg in a vertical position. This improves pen positioning accuracy as the play in the gears is reduced. Anyway, the egg-booster is a great building and coding exercise.

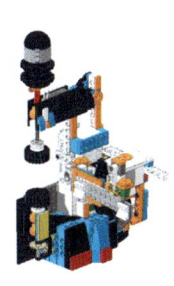

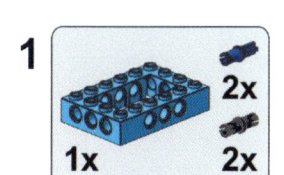

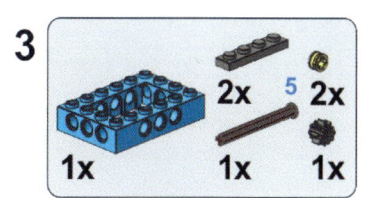

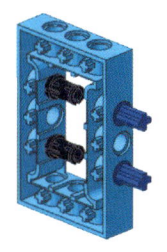

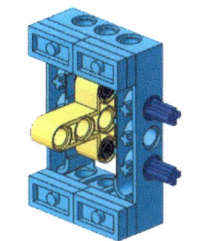

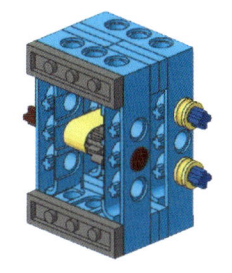

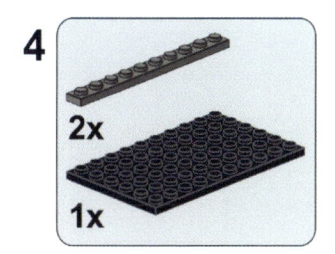

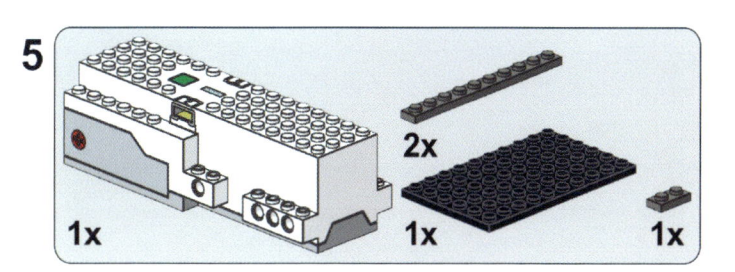

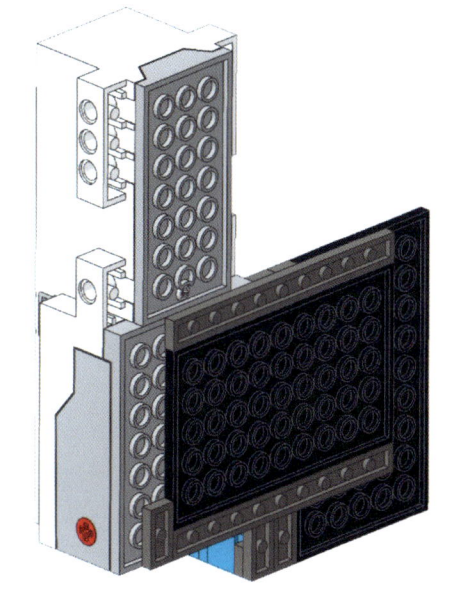

85

Egg-Booster

6
2x, 1x, 1x, 1x, 5

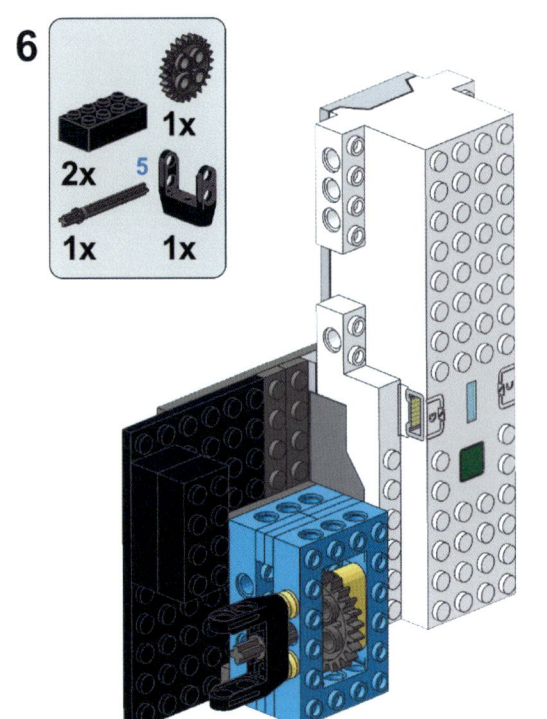

7
1x, 2x, 1x

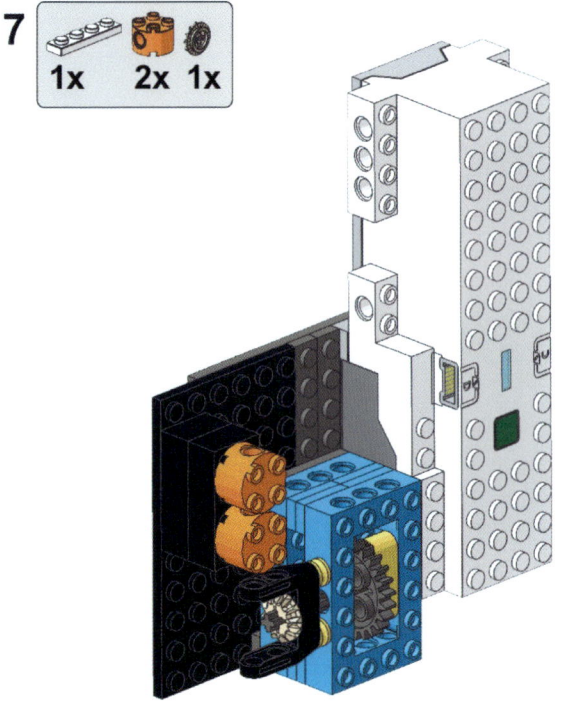

8
1x, 1x, 1x, 9 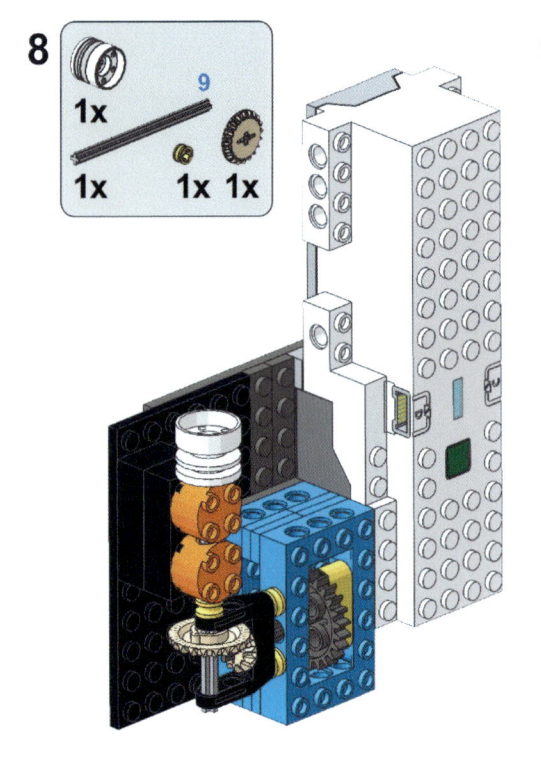

9
1x, 1x, 1x, 1x, 4x

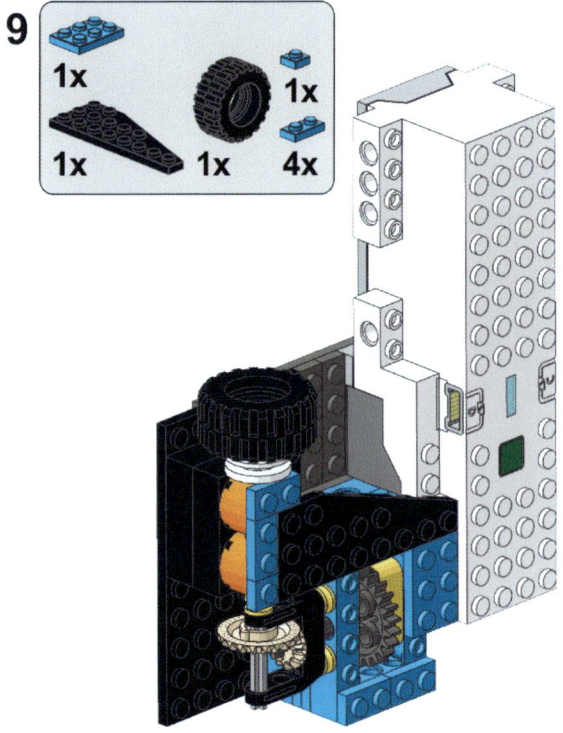

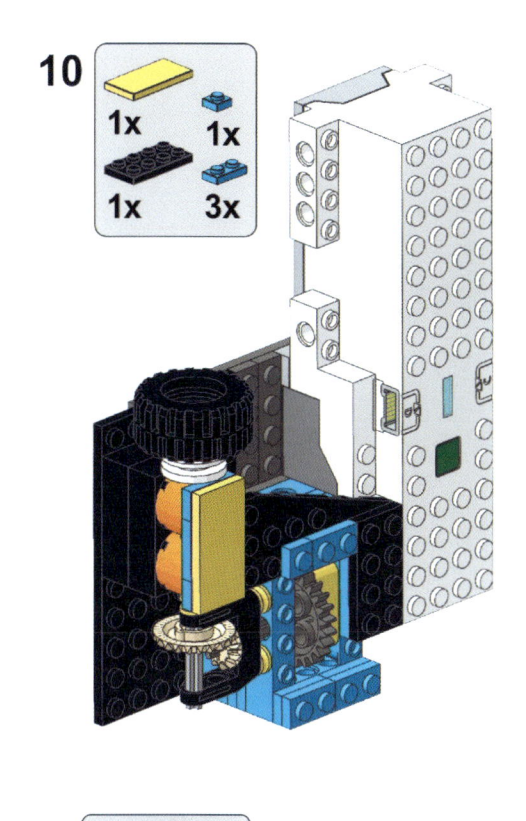

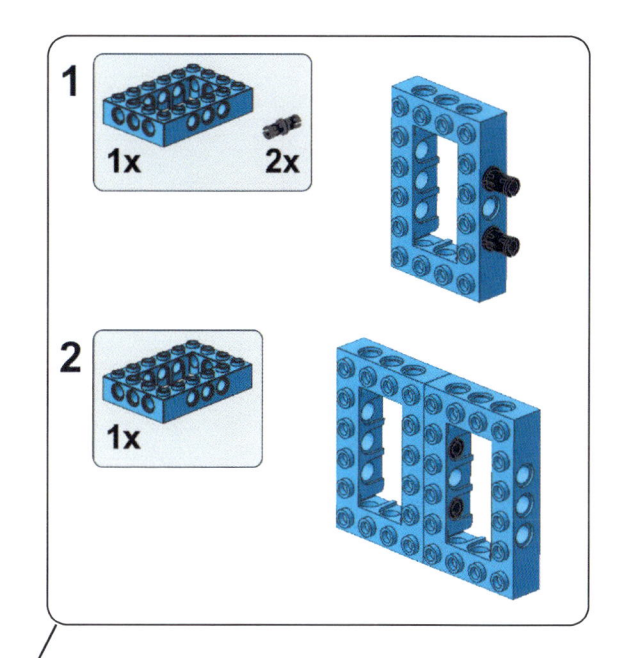

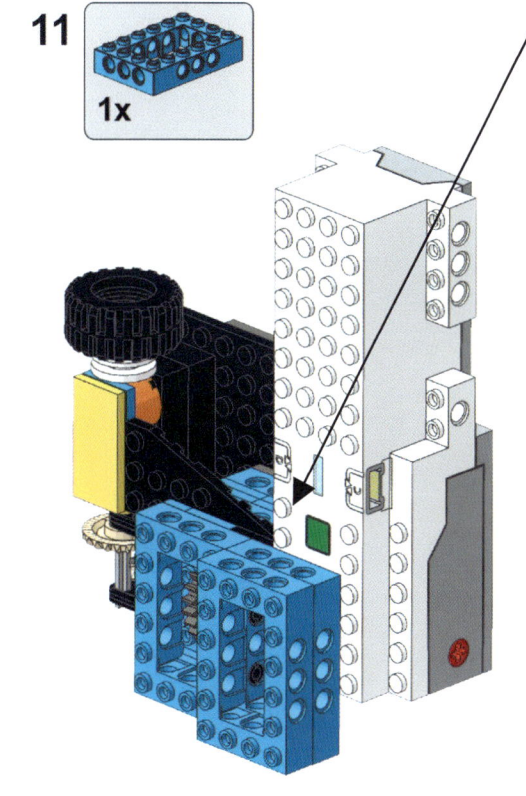

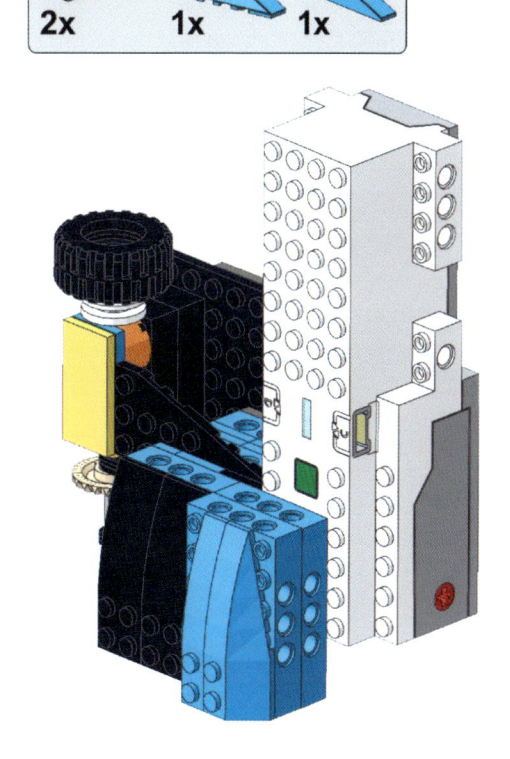

Egg-Booster

Egg-Booster

BUILD

13

14

1

2

3

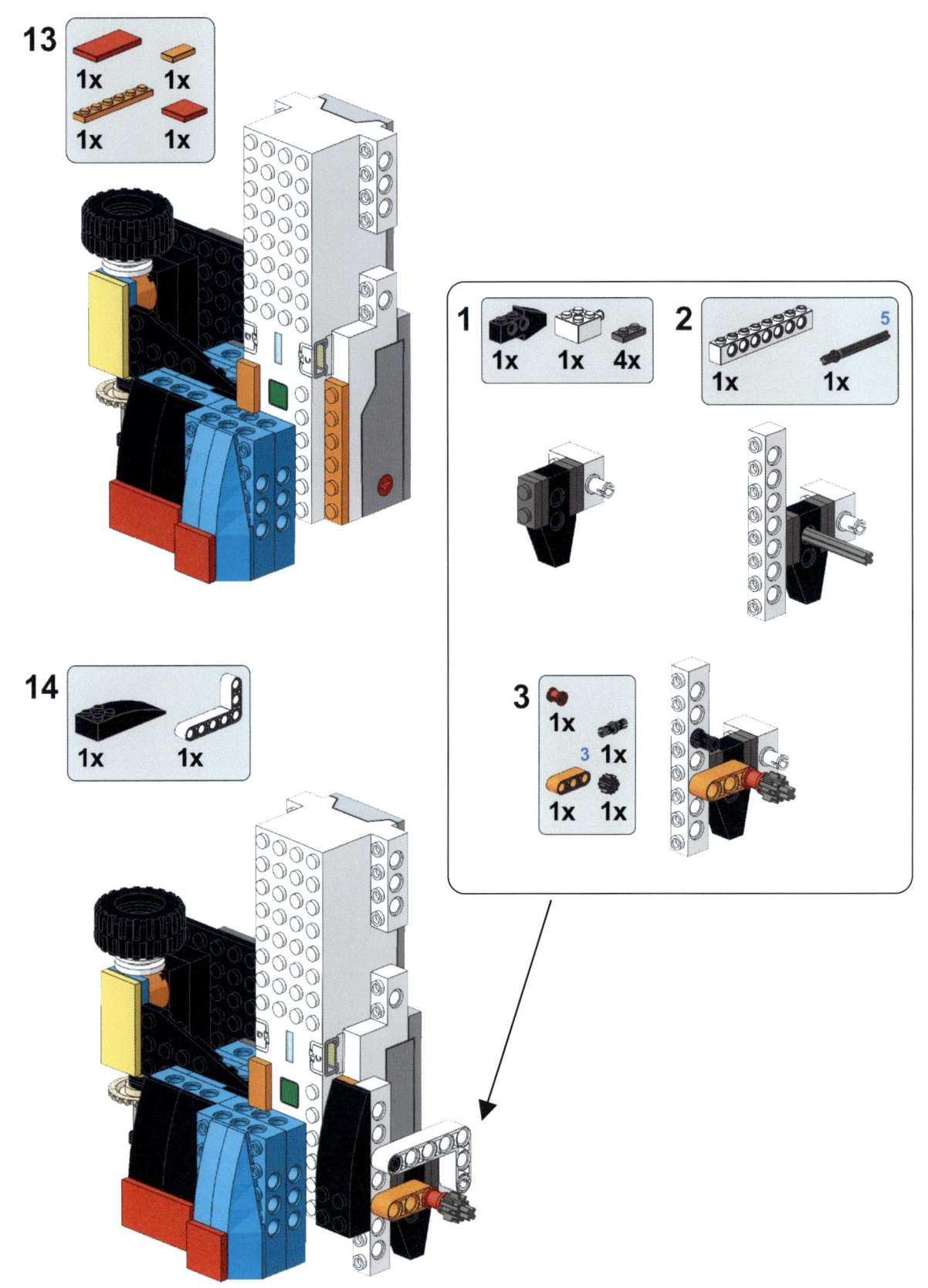

88

Egg-Booster

BUILD

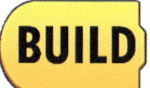

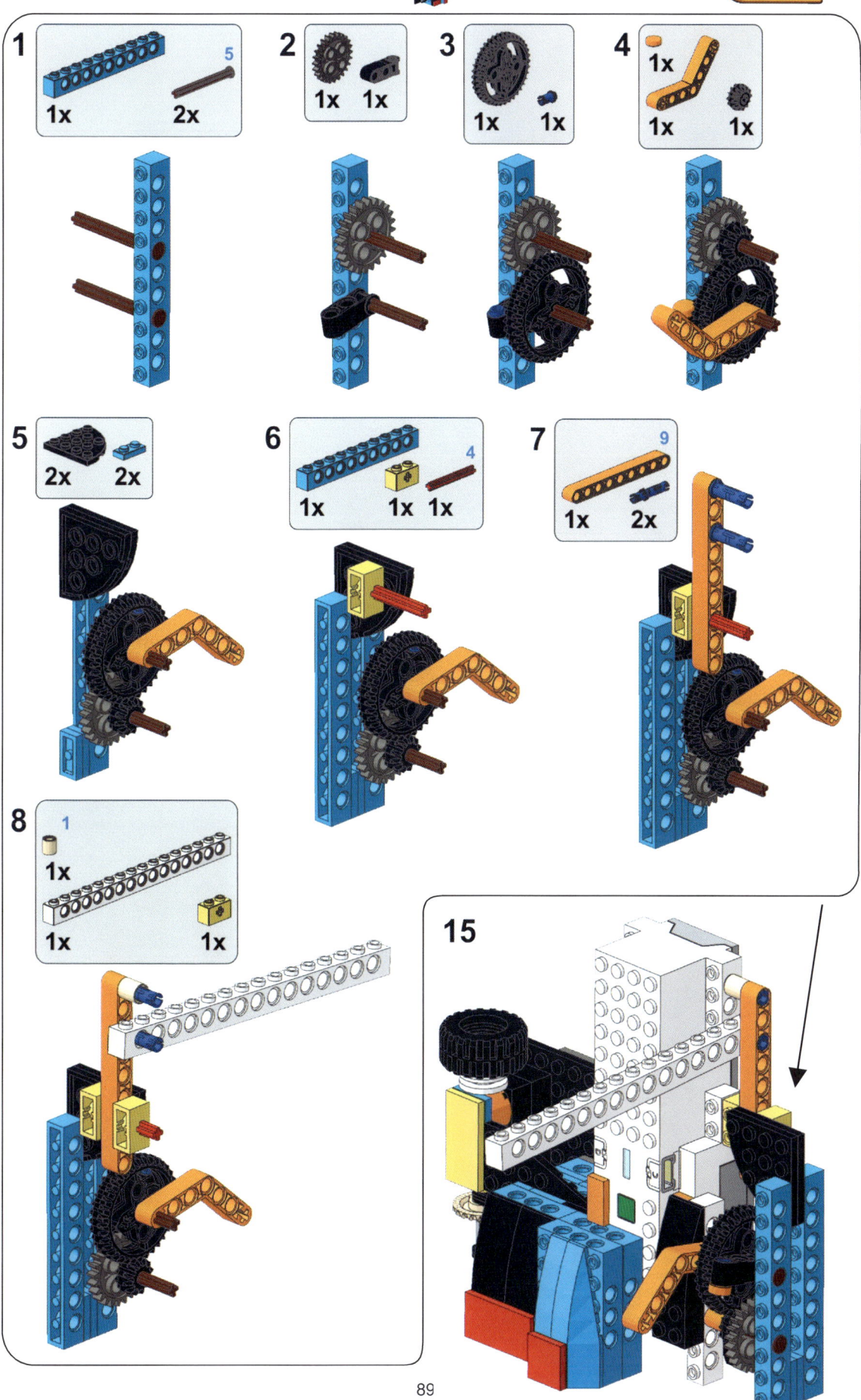

89

Egg-Booster

16
1x 1x 1x

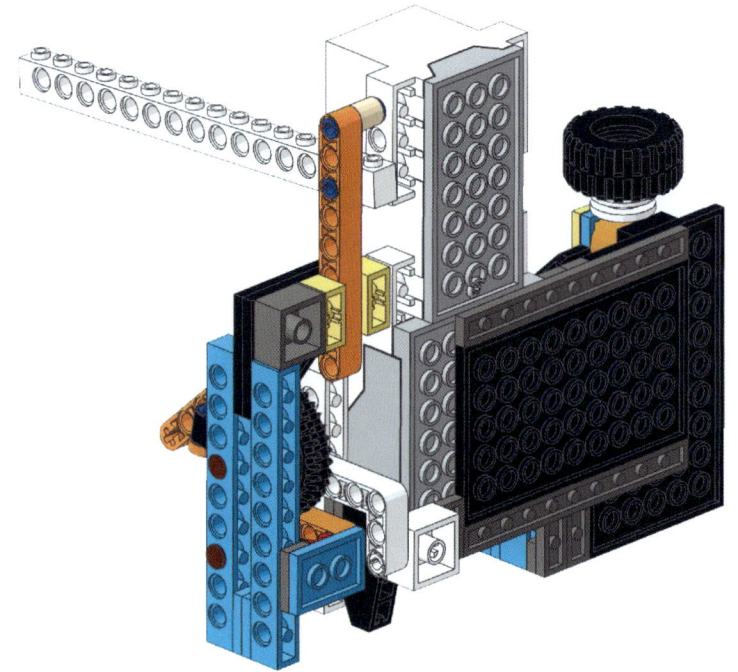

17
1x 1x 1x 1x 1x

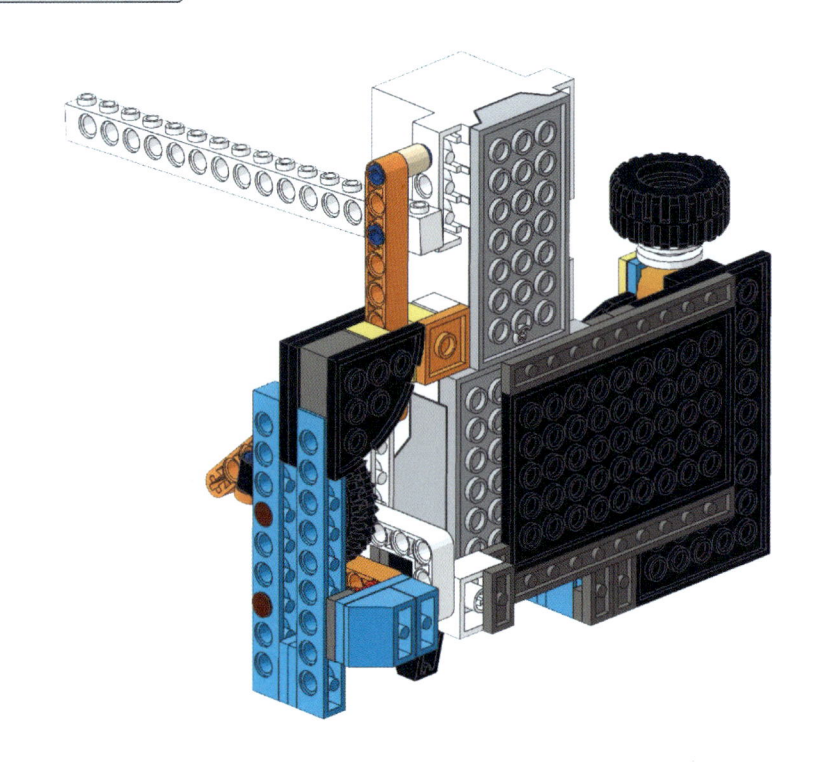

Egg-Booster

18 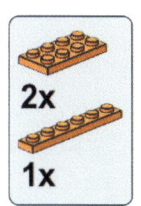 2x 1x

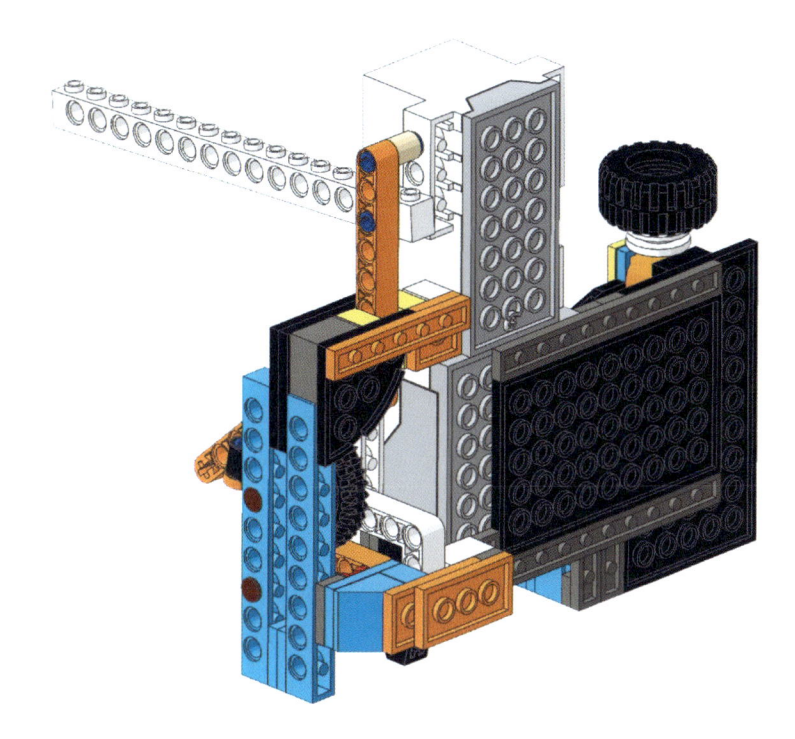

19 1x 1x 1x

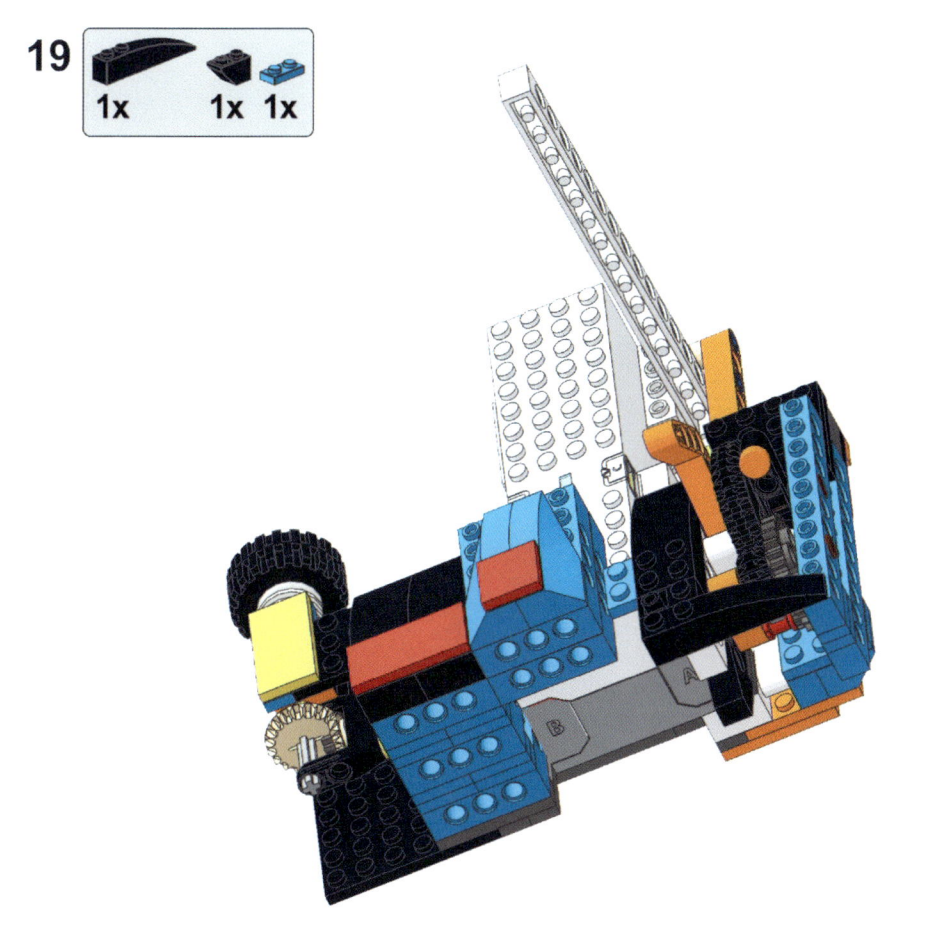

Egg-Booster

20 2x 3x 2x

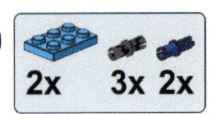

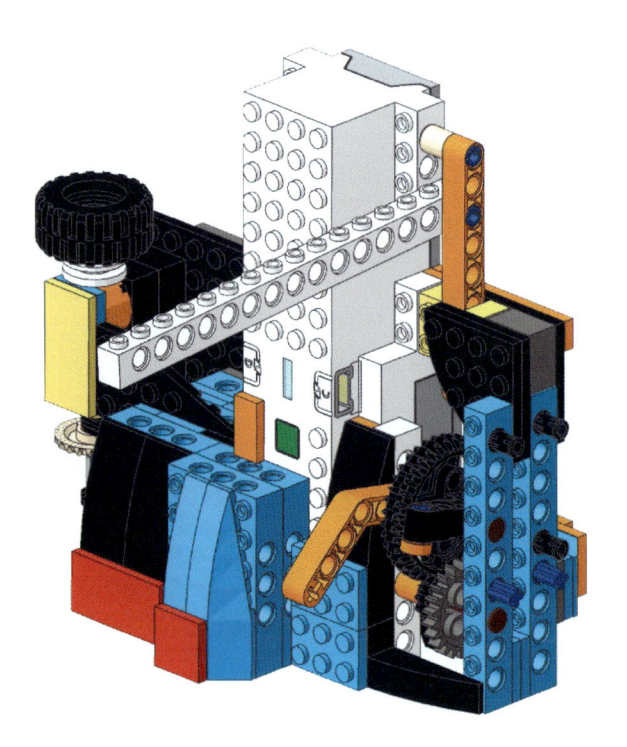

21 1x 1x 4x 1x 1x

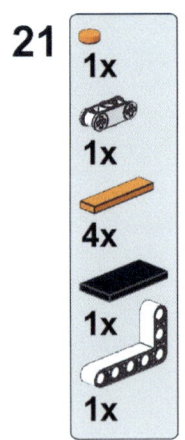

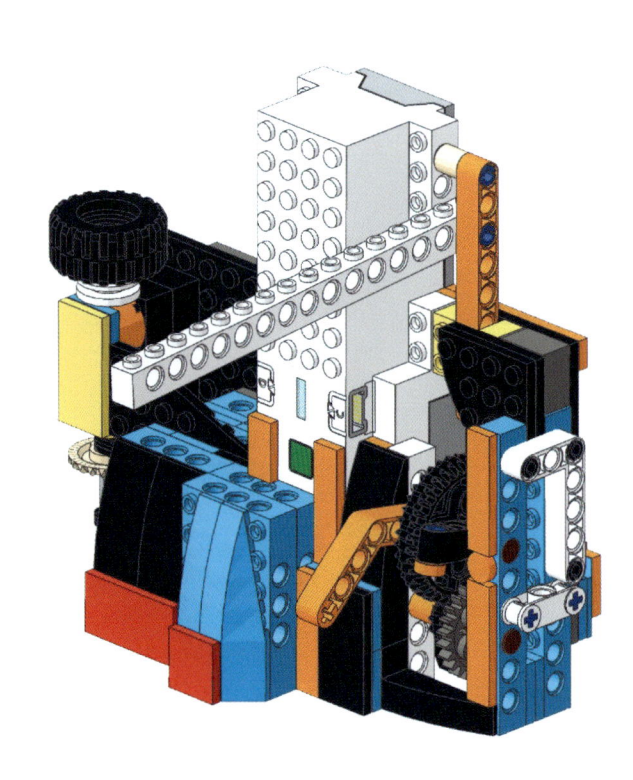

Egg-Booster

BUILD

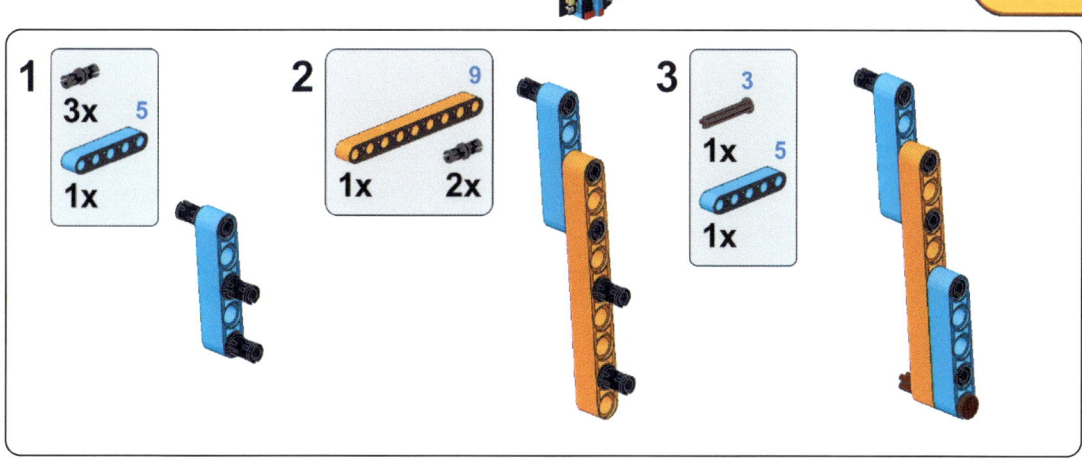

22

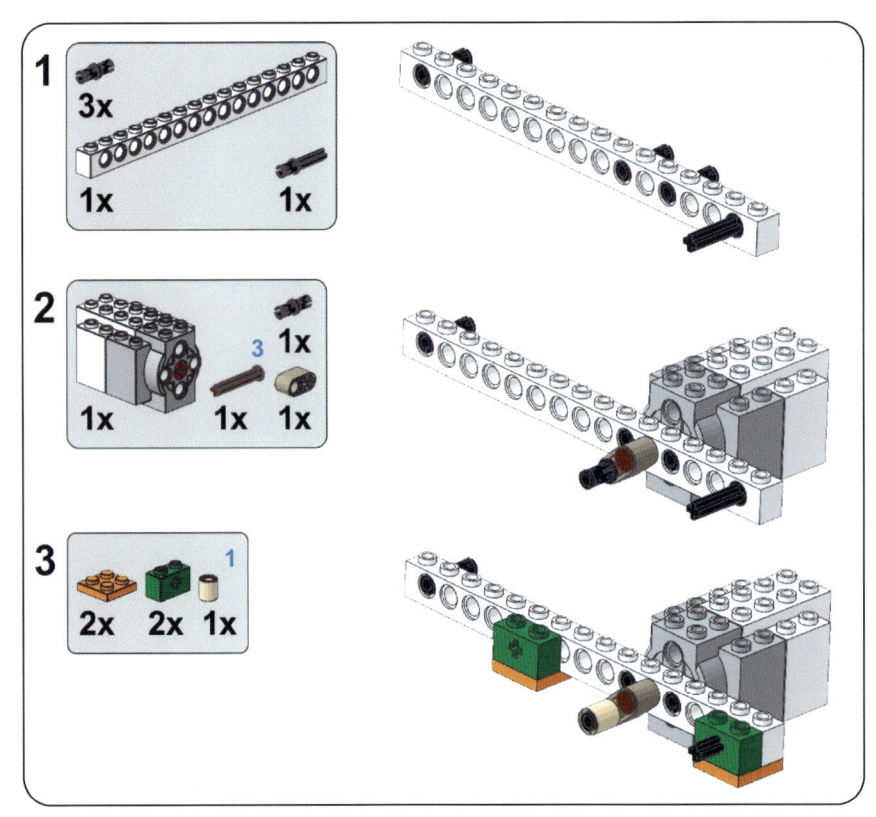

Egg-Booster

23

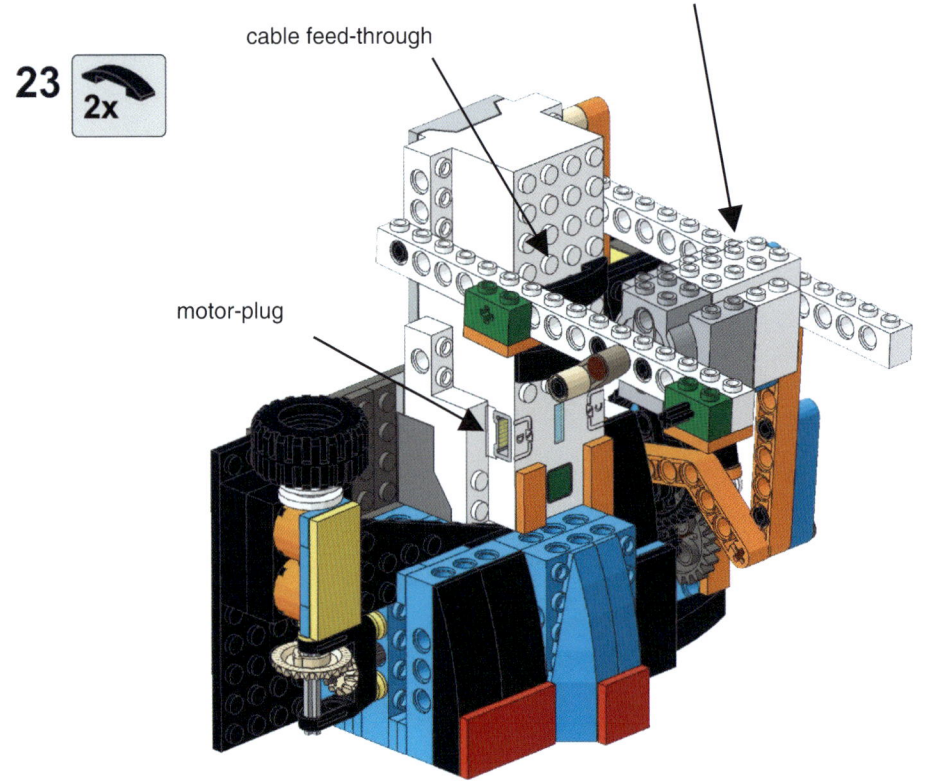

cable feed-through

motor-plug

Egg-Booster

BUILD

24 1x 1x 1x

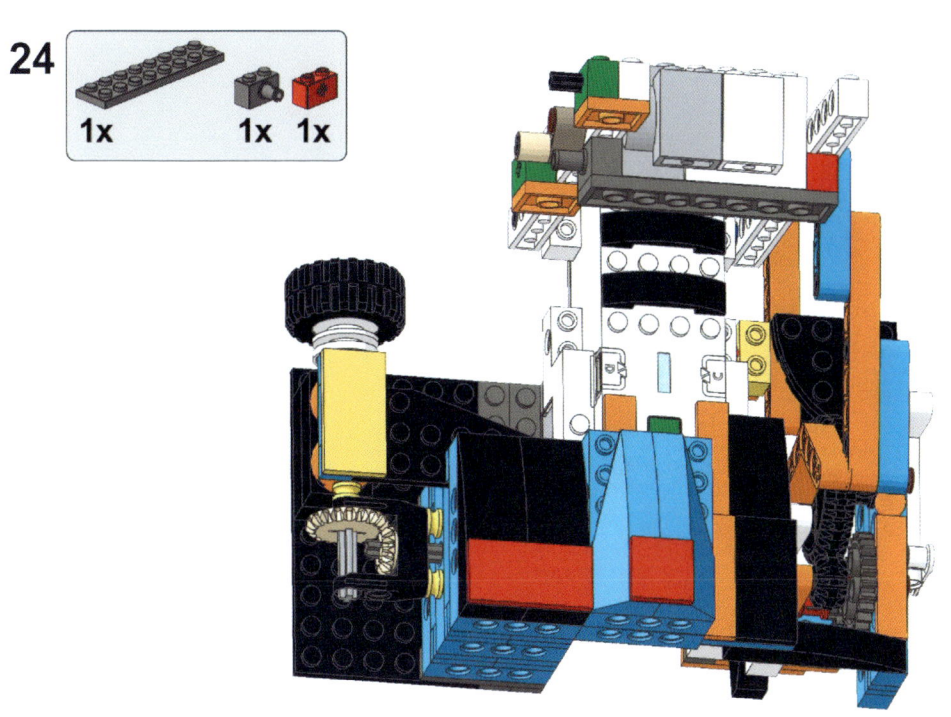

25 1x 8x

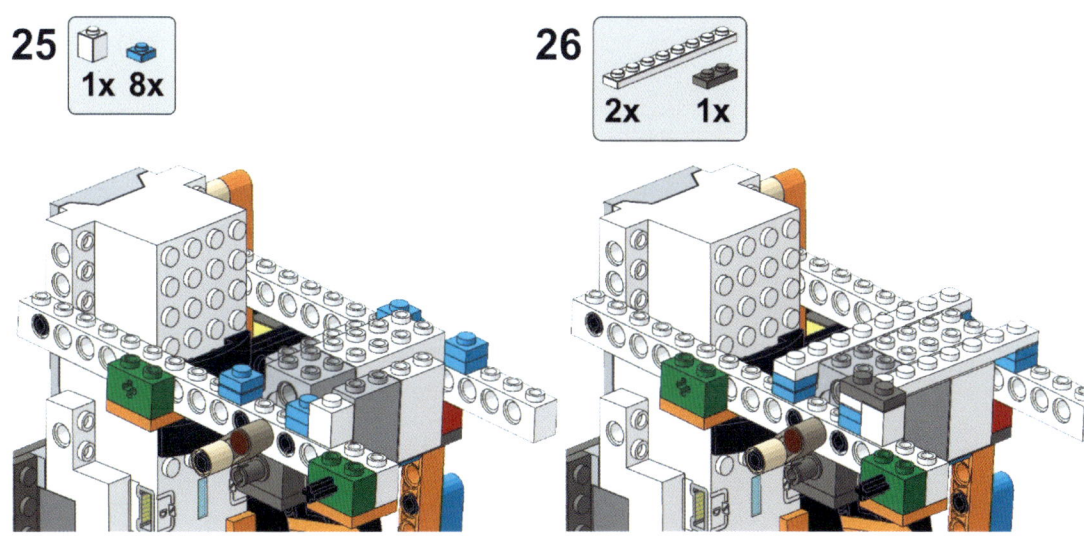

26 2x 1x

27 2x 2x 1x

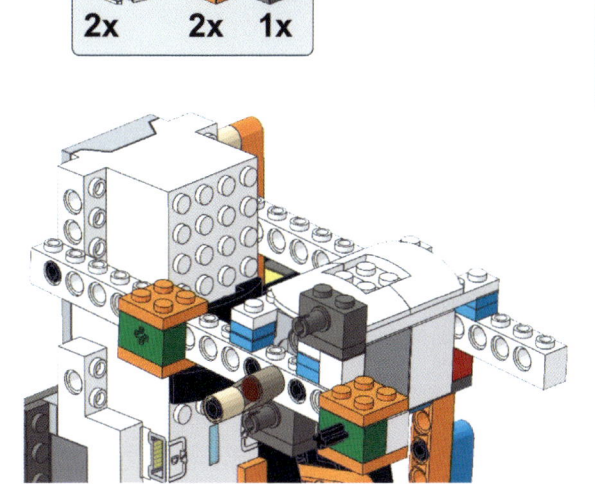

28 3x 1x 1x

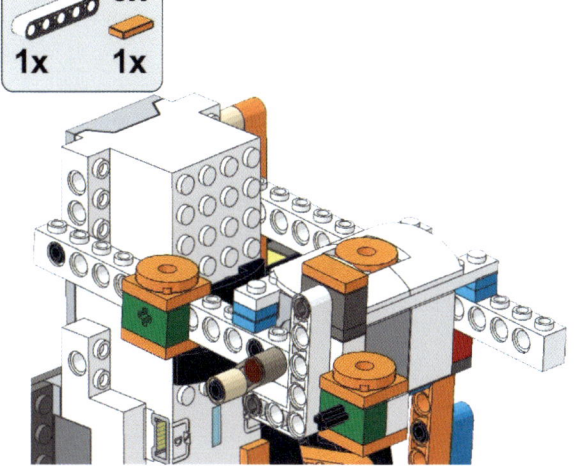

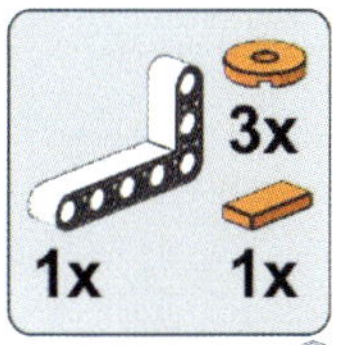

Egg-Booster

BUILD

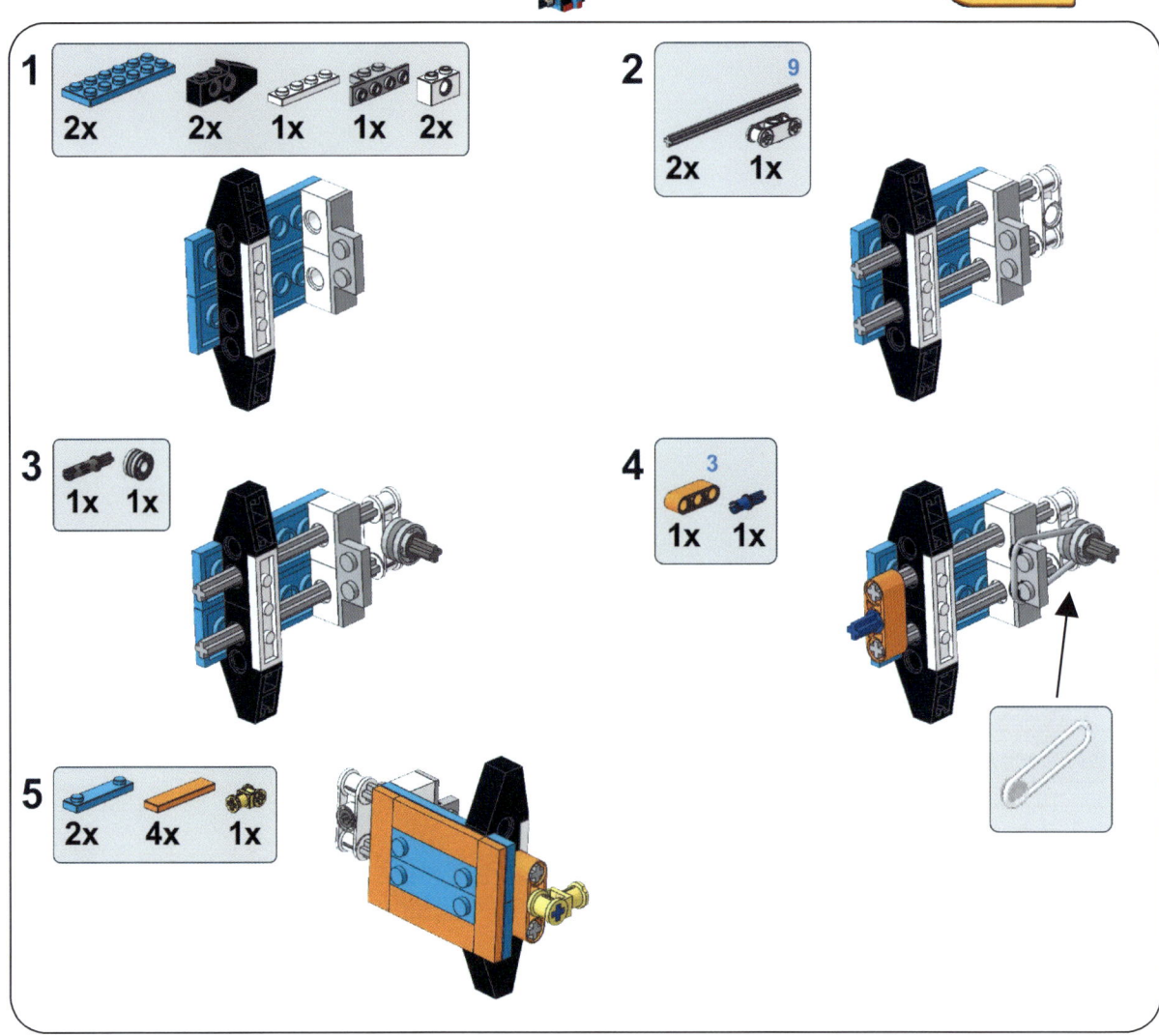

1. 2x, 2x, 1x, 1x, 2x
2. 2x, 1x (9)
3. 1x, 1x
4. 1x, 1x (3)
5. 2x, 4x, 1x

29

96

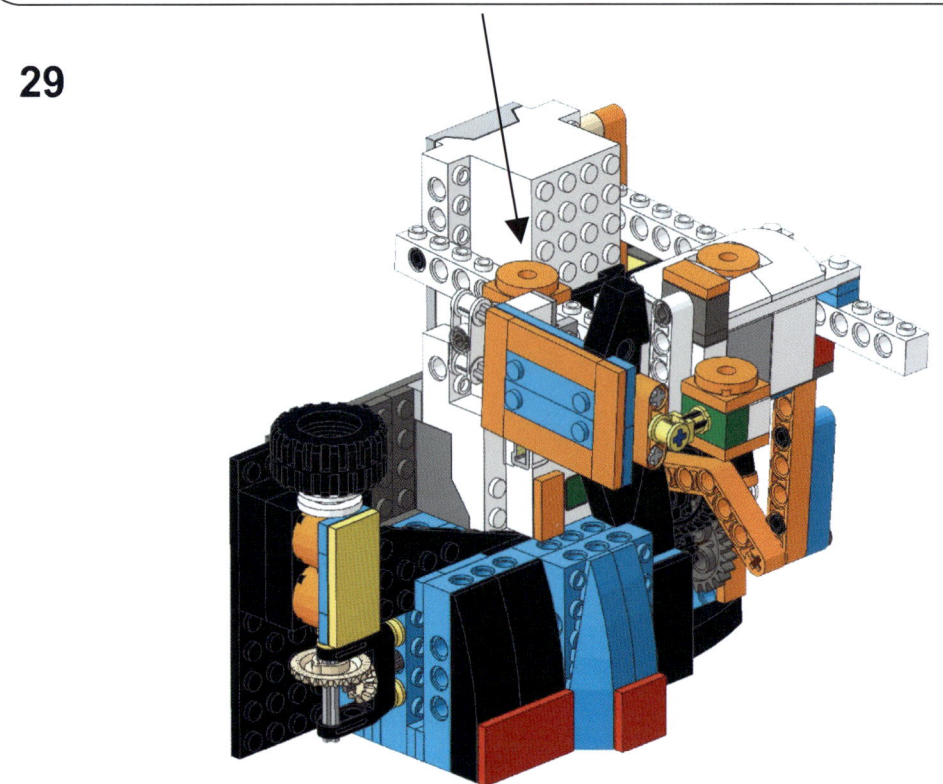

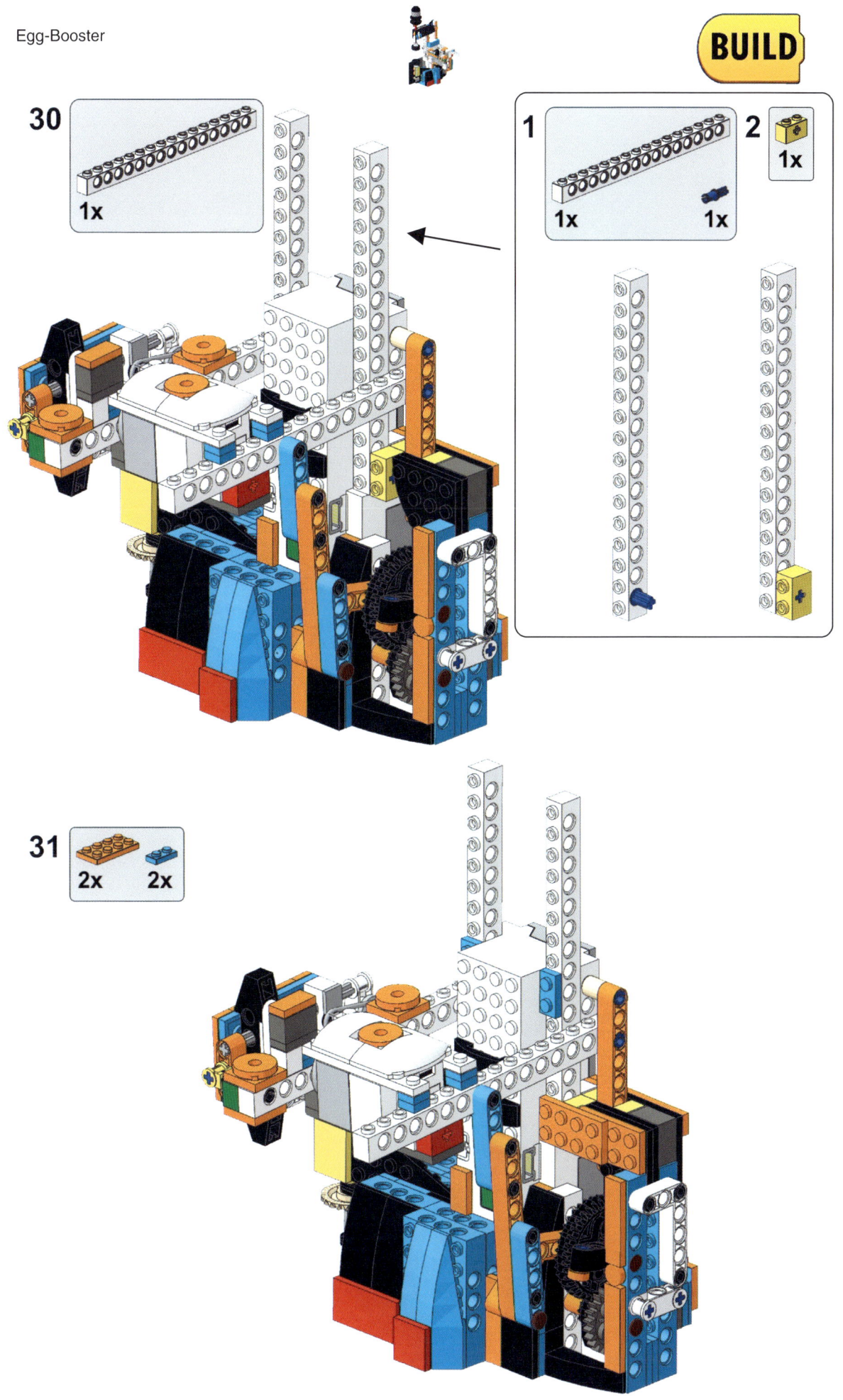

Egg-Booster

BUILD

30 1x

1 1x 1x
2 1x

31 2x 2x

Egg-Booster

32 1x 2x

33 2x 1x 2x 2x 1x 1x

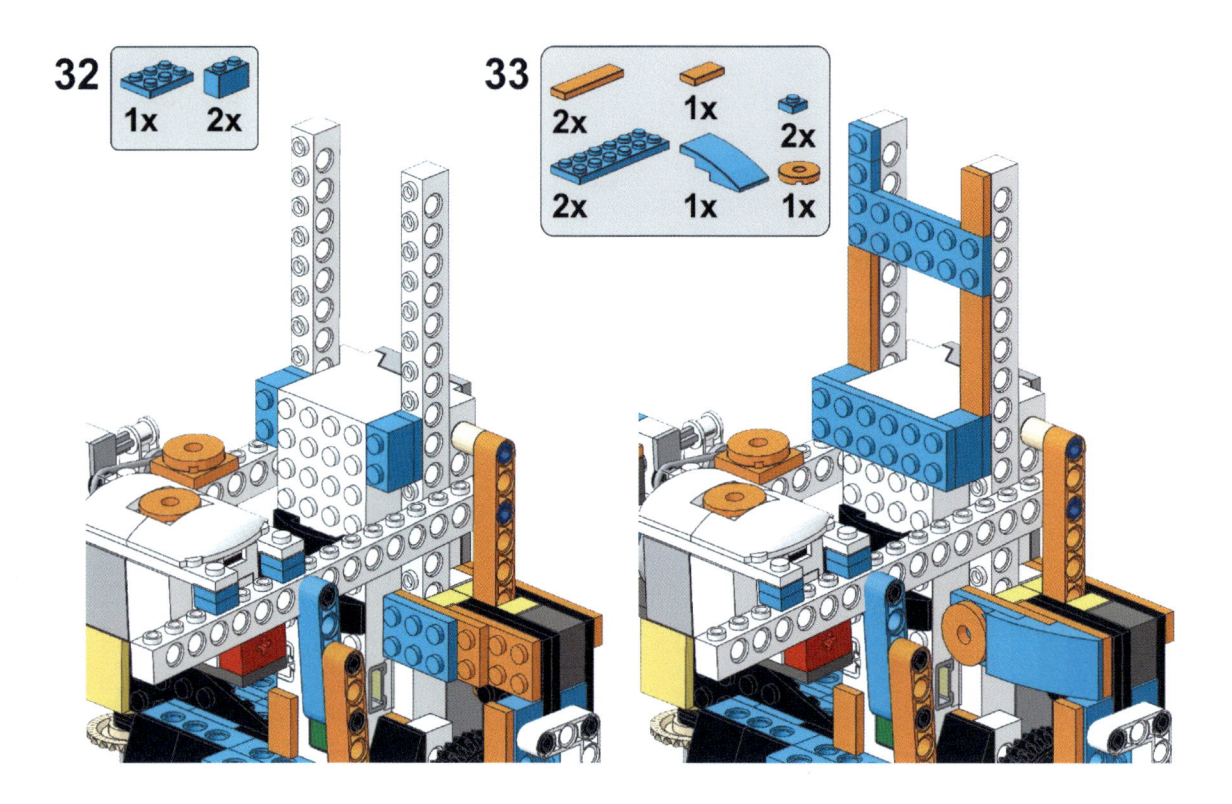

34 1x 2x 1x 1x

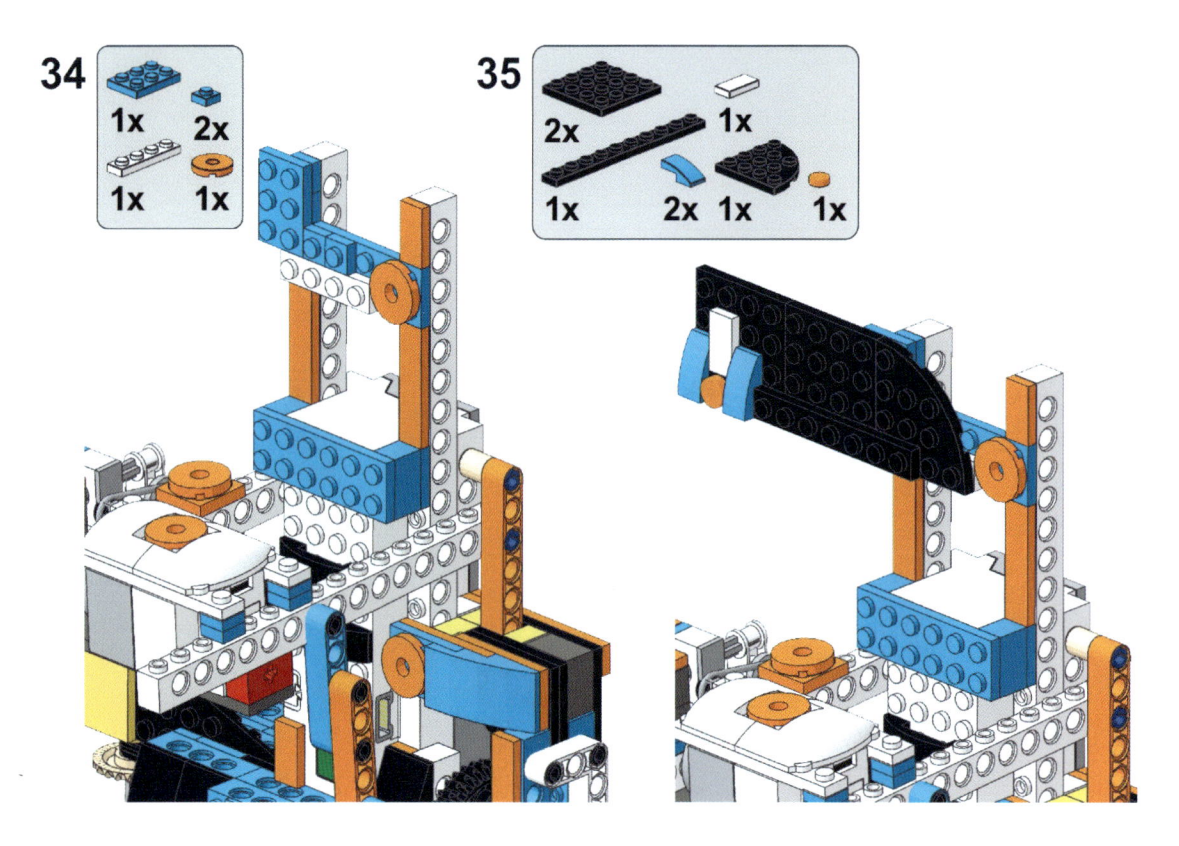

35 2x 1x 1x 2x 1x 1x

Egg-Booster

36  1x 1x

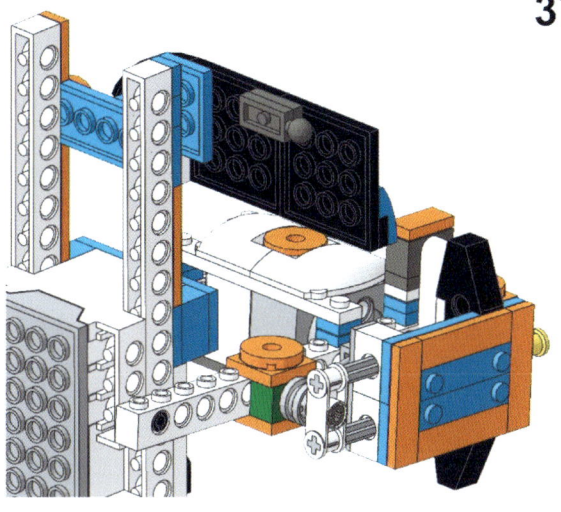

37 1x 1x 1x 1x

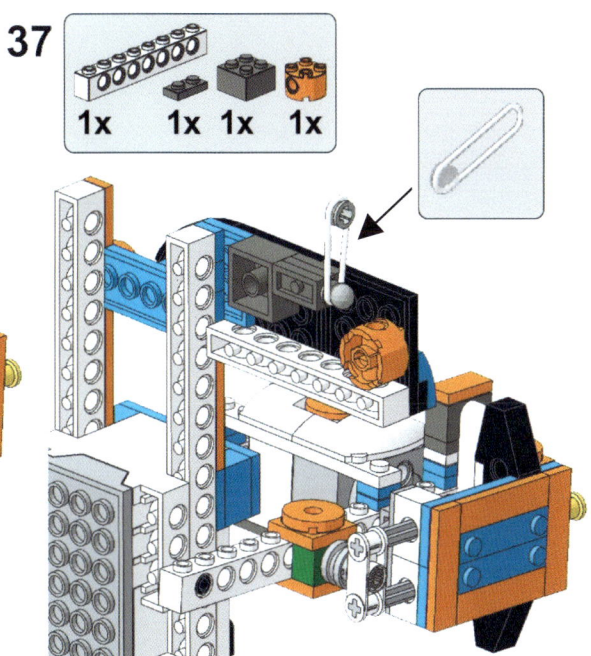

38 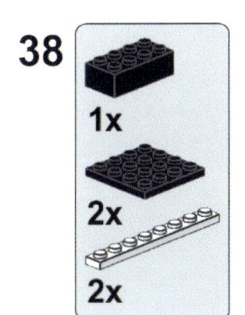 1x 2x 2x

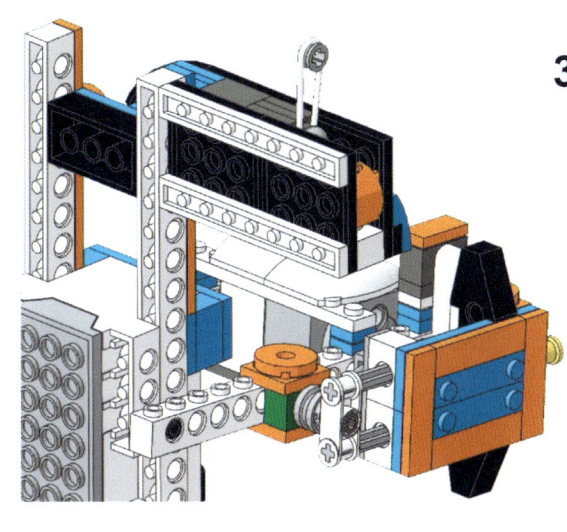

39 1x 1x 1x

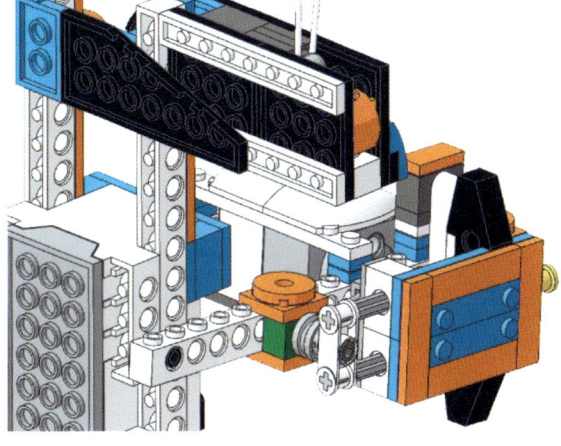

99

Egg-Booster

BUILD

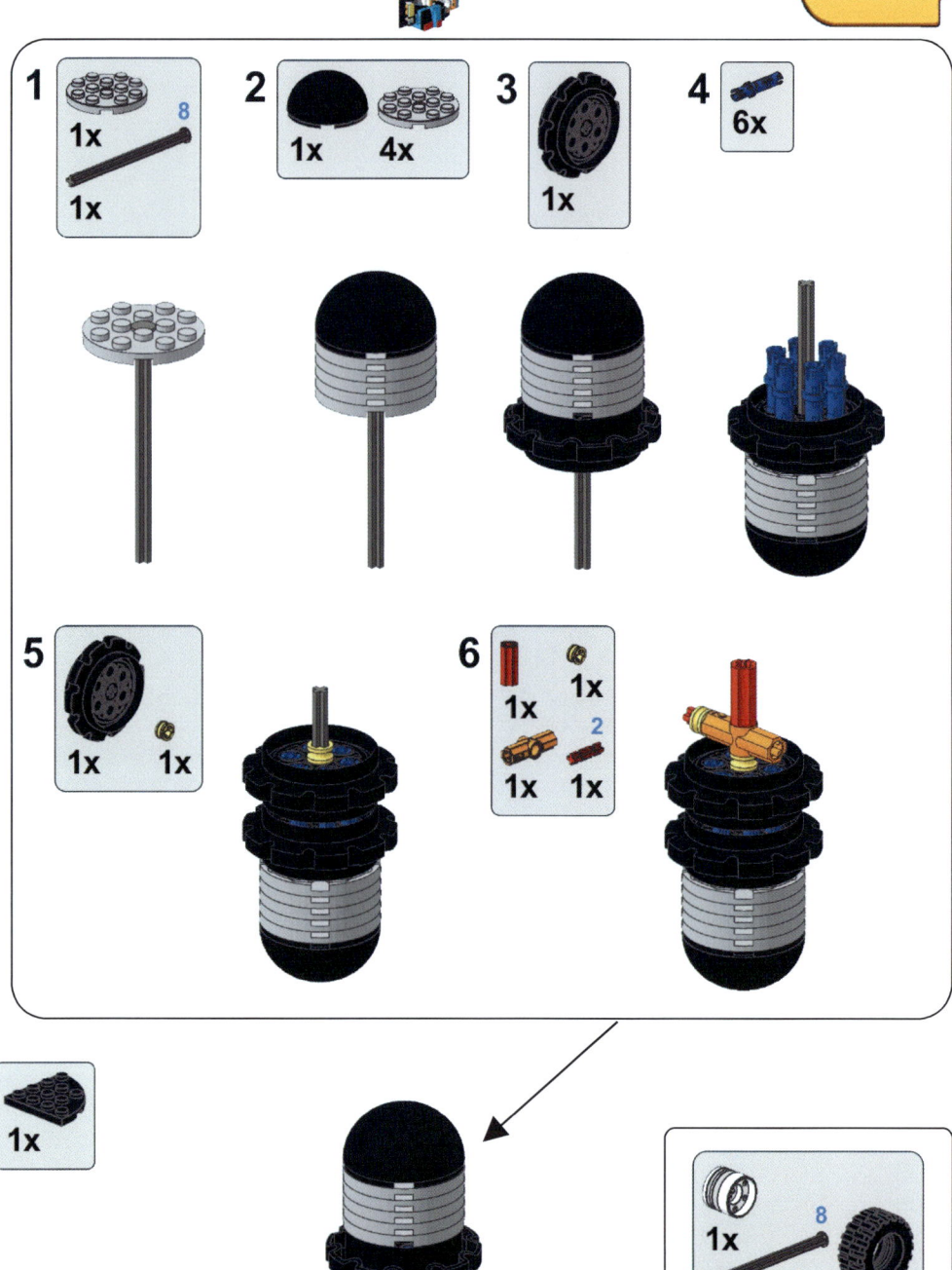

1 1x / 1x (8)
2 1x / 4x
3 1x
4 6x
5 1x / 1x
6 1x / 1x / 2 / 1x / 1x

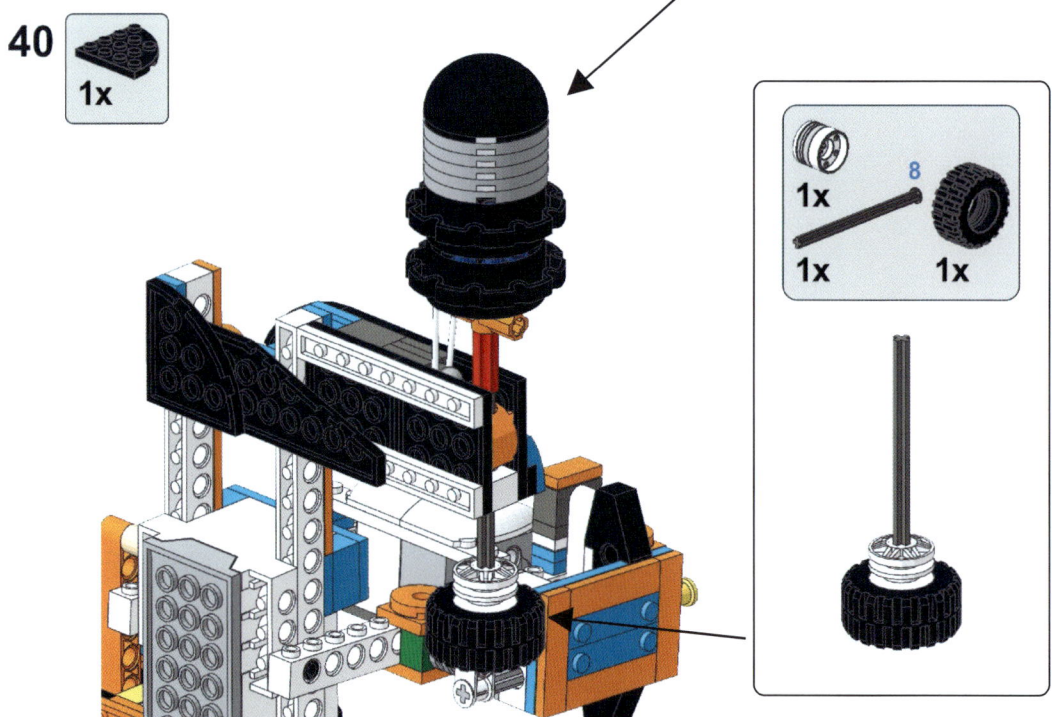

40 1x

1x / 1x (8) / 1x

Egg-Booster

BUILD

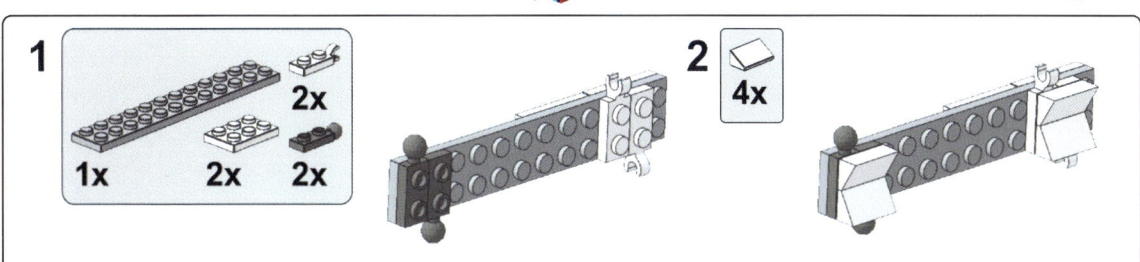

41

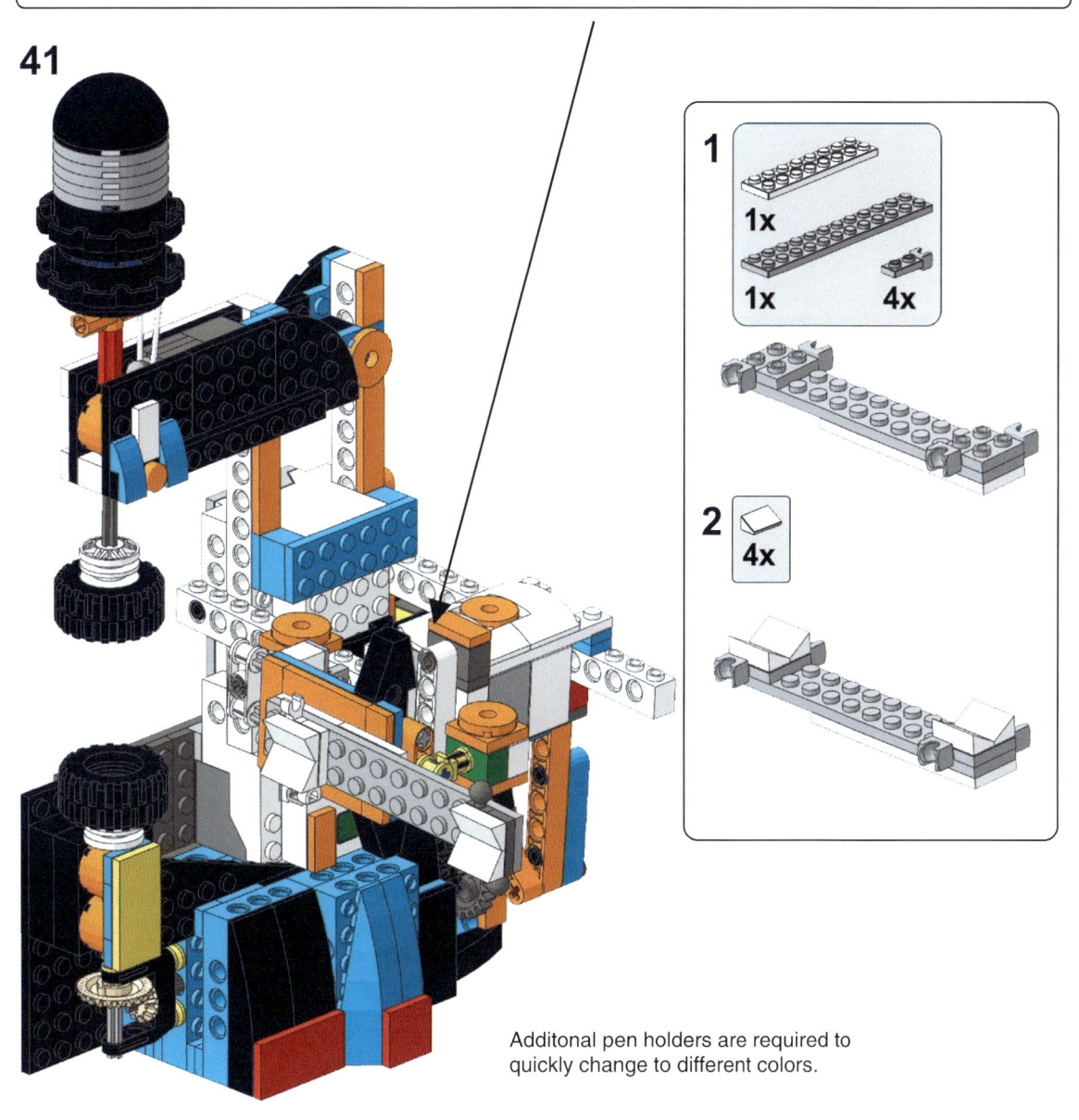

Additonal pen holders are required to quickly change to different colors.

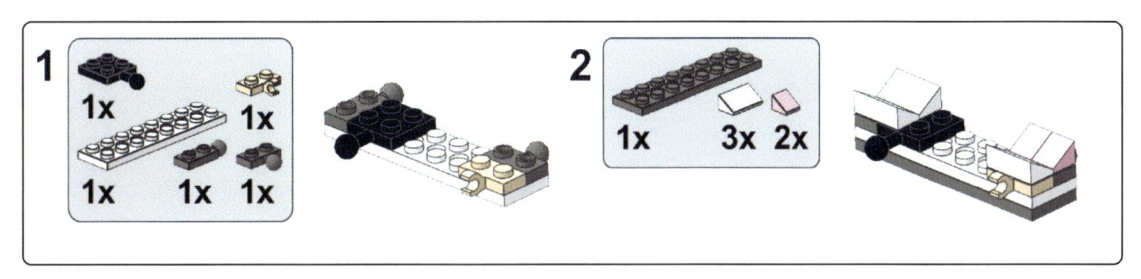

Egg-Booster

Code

For the egg-booster, there are two program types defined in this book:

    Egg-Paint - Pattern painting
    Egg-Print - Dot-Matrix printing

To initialize the Egg-Booster an initializing subroutine is to be created.

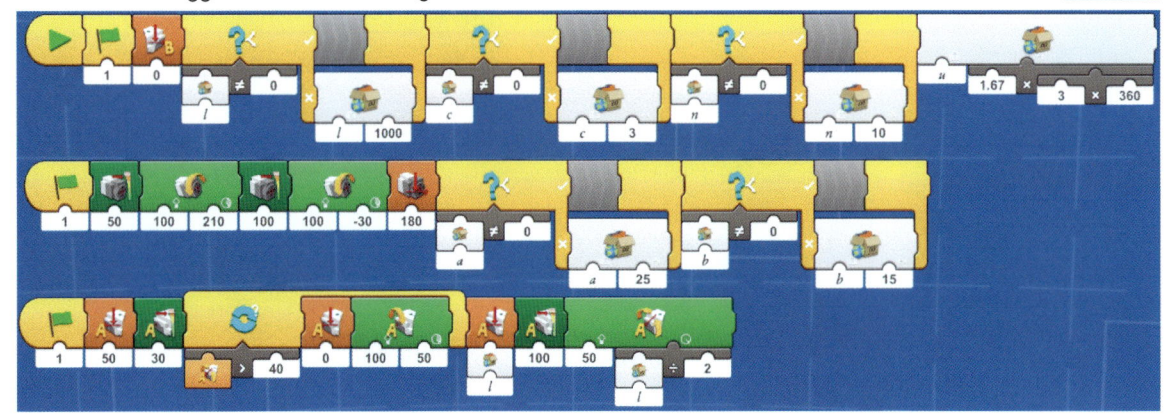

Before the start of the program you should equip all pen holders with differently colored pens. The tip of the pen is to be positioned with 3-5mm (approximately one stud) distance from the eggshell.

Egg-Booster

CODE

Egg-Paint – Pattern painting

Horizontal Circles

Vertical Lines

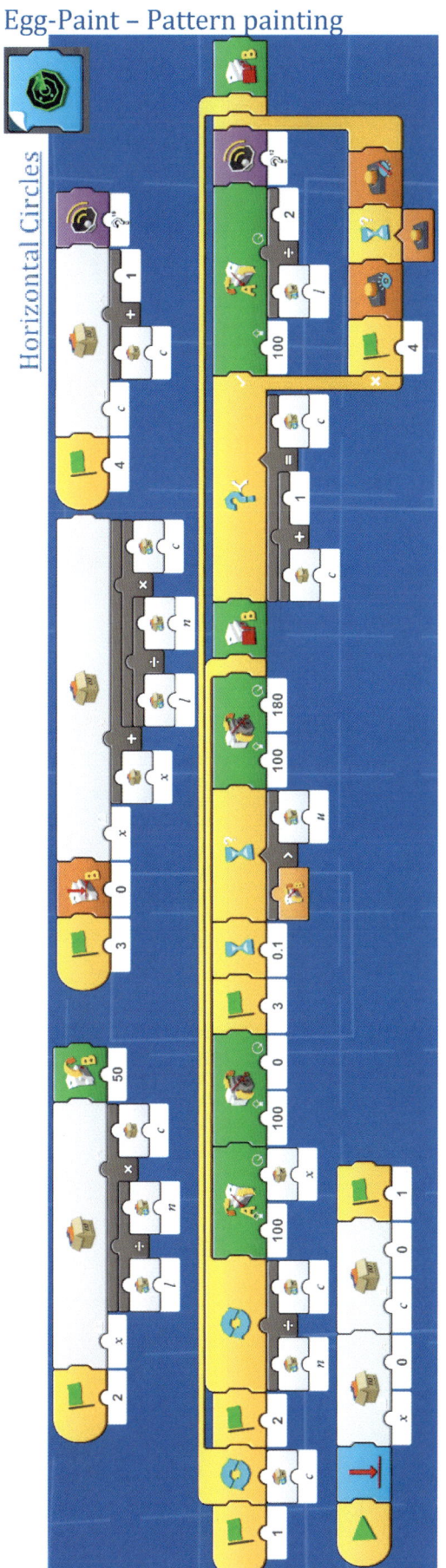

103

Egg-Booster

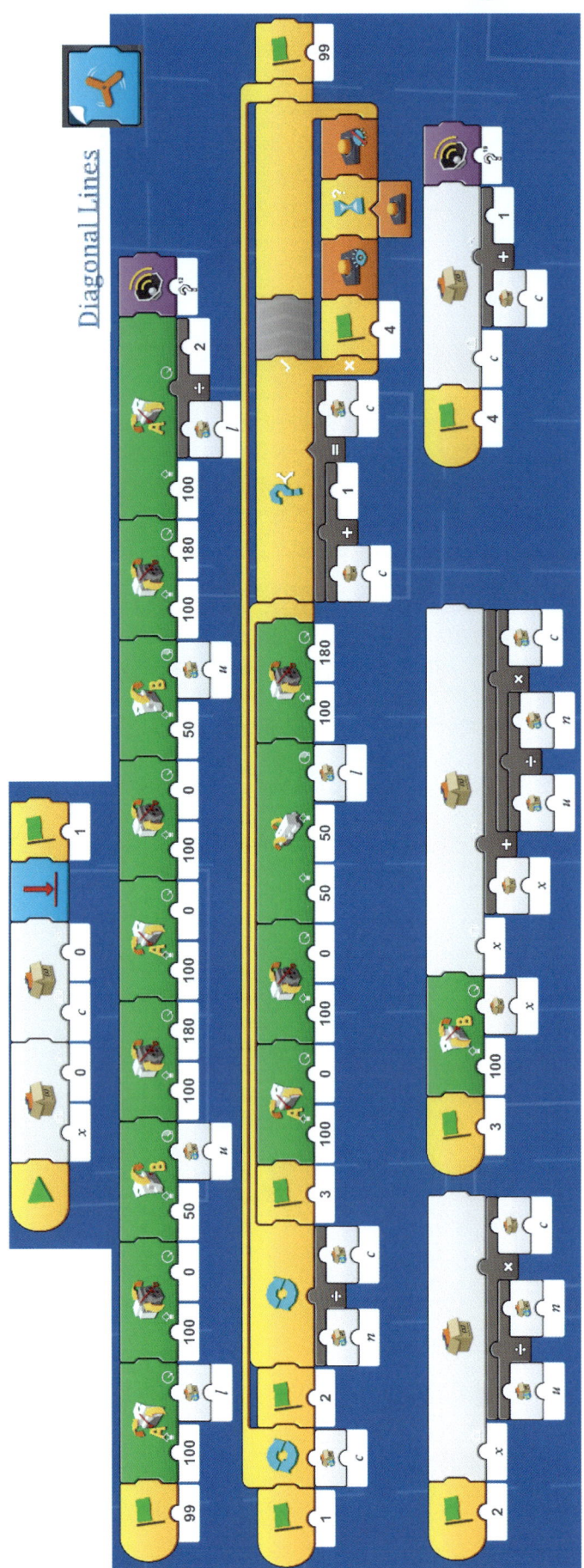

Diagonal Lines

The subroutines can be started without the need for any initializing subroutines.

Alternatively, the global variables can be defined to adjust the behavior of the program in terms of colors, number of lines and size of the egg.

104

Egg-Booster

Egg-Print - Dot-Matrix printer
Similar to the Dot-Matrix printing of the Boost-Writer, the Egg-Booster can print letters onto the eggshell. Each letter is to be defined in a seperate subroutine.

Egg-Booster

CODE

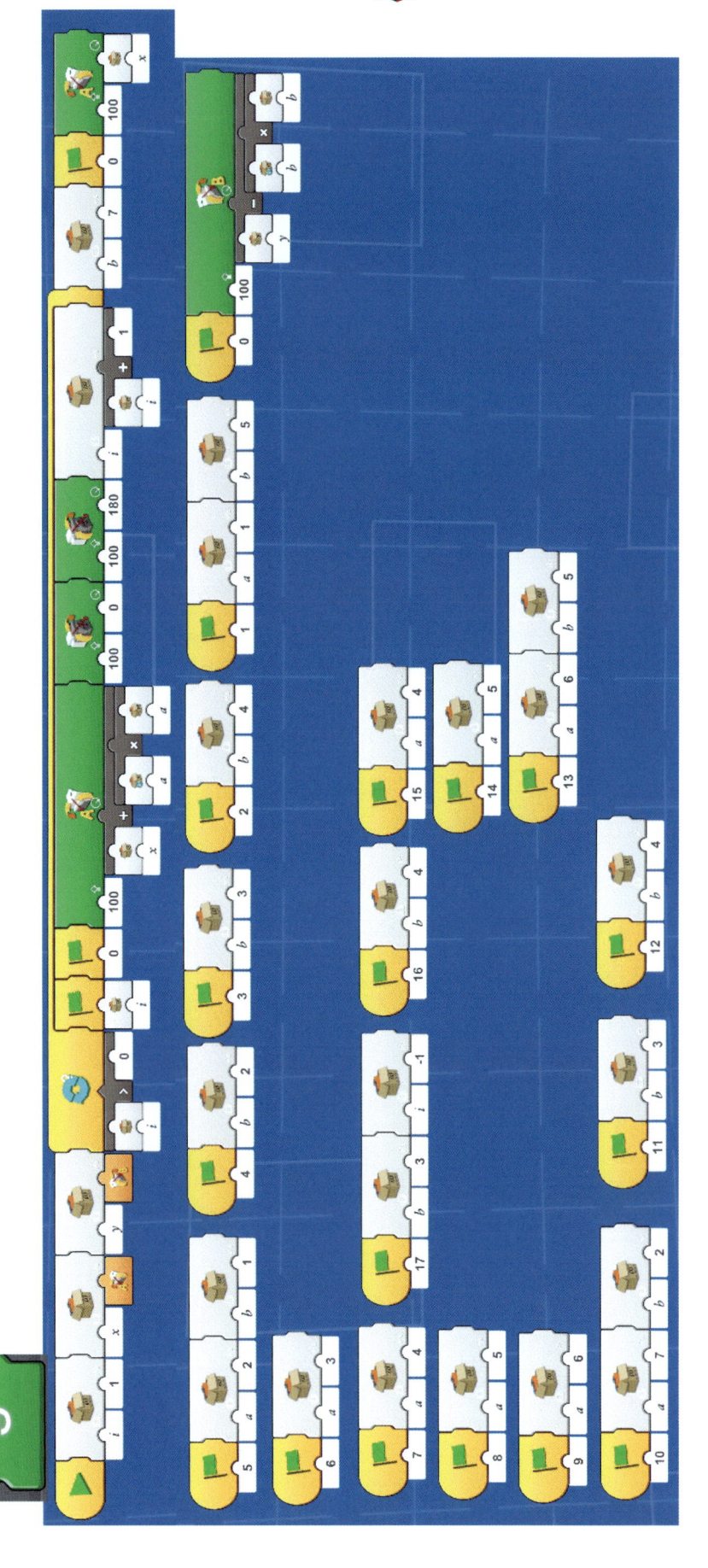

The main program can then look like this. The initializing subroutine is important to set all global variables and to move the pen in the correct position.

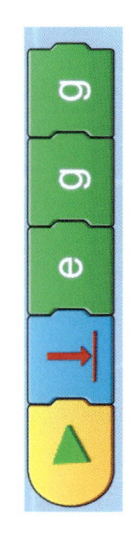

Egg-Booster

Play

The initializing subroutine moves the mechanical components to the starting position and stores a value in all global variables. Following table lists the purpose and recommended value for each global variable.

Variable	Recommended value	Purpose	Egg-Paint	Egg-Print
l	1000	Height of the egg. A medium egg is represented by 1000; a large egg is 1100-1200	✓	
c	3	Number of different colors in a pattern	✓	
n	15	Number of lines in a pattern	✓	
u	1800	Rotation angle of Motor B for a full 360° rotation of the egg	✓	
a	25	Vertical (A-Motor) distance of dots		✓
b	15	Horizontal (B-Motor) distance of dots		✓

Initializing

To start three parallel sequences, jump label 1 is used right at the start of the subroutine. Position of motor B is set to 0. The following three "if"-blocks check if the global variables l, c and n are already set to a value. If not, they are set to the recommended values. Finally, global variable u is set to the gear ratio for a full rotation of the egg (gear ration 1:1.67 for the bevel gears and 1:3 for the cylindrical gears.

In the sequence at jump label 1 the power of the external motor is set to 50%. The motor then turns 210° upwards till it hits the upper limit. After setting the motor power back to 100% the eccentric tappet is moved back 30° to bring it to its top dead center. The current motor position is set to 180°. The following "if"-blocks do check global variable a and b and set them to the recommended values if they do not contain any value, yet.

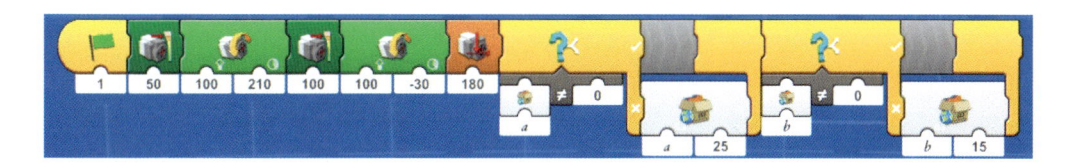

The second sequence which is also started via jump label 1 is initializing the vertical arm. The rotation angle of motor A is set to 50° and the motor power is reduced to 30%. The following loop is executed as long as the position of motor A is bigger than 40°. Within the loop, the current position of motor A is set back to 0 and the motor tries to rotate 50°. If the arm can freely move down, the motor A position will also be 50 at the end of the motion and the loop will be executed again. When the arm hits the lower limit, the position of motor A might be lower than 40 at the end of the loop and the loop is discontinued. This step-wise process is supposed to protect the model from excess stress or even breakage.

After the loop, when the arm is at its lowest position, the position of motor A is set to the value of the height of the egg and motor power is set back to 100%. The last block does not turn the motor by a certain angle but let the motor go to a certain position. Here it is half the height of the egg.

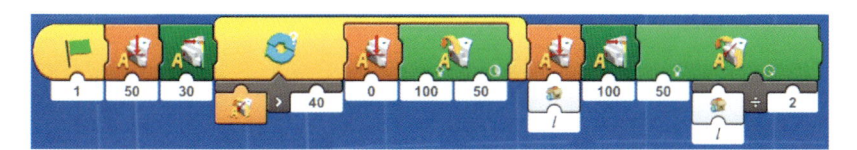

Egg-Booster

Egg-Paint – Pattern painting

The Egg-Paint programs all follow the same concept. We will look into the most interesting version for the diagonal line pattern.

First, the local variables x and c are set to 0 and the initializing subroutine is executed.

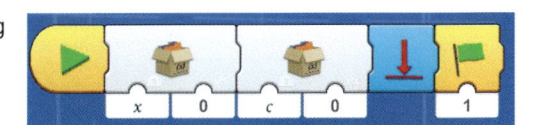

The loop at jump label 1 is executed for as many times as it is specified by the number of colors stored in global variable c. Within the loop, jump label 2 is used to store the starting angle of the first line in variable x. During the first execution, variable c is 0 and therefore also x will be 0. The pen will start at the current angle of the egg.
Number of lines (n) divided by colors (c) is the number of loop executions to draw lines in the current color. For uniform patterns, value n must be a multiple of c.

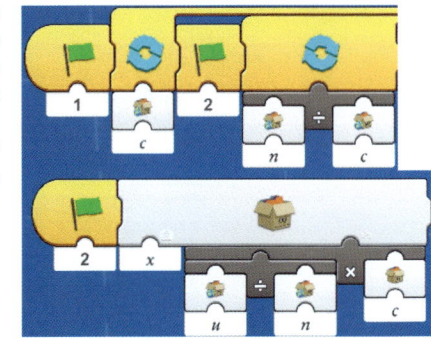

Within the inner loop jump label 3 turns the egg by motor B to the starting position (x) and writes the next starting position into variable x. At the same time, motor A moves the pen to the top position (0) of the egg. Then the pen is lowered to the eggshell by the external motor. The next programming block performs a synchronized motion of both motors A and B which results in uniform diagonal or curved lines which are not possible when both motors are addressed separately (as in the Boost-Writer). Changing the speed parameters in this block will result in a line of a different shape. After the line is produced, the external motor lifts the pen form the eggshell.

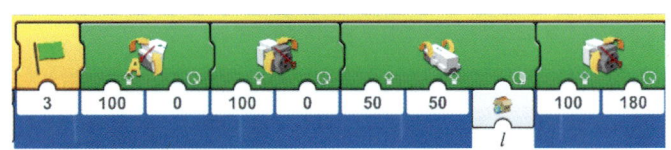

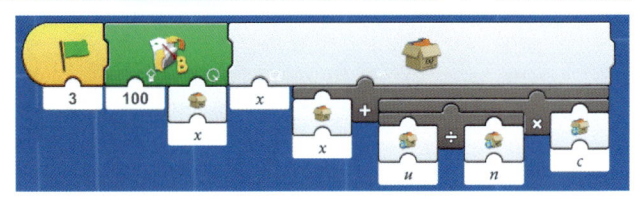

After all lines for one color have been applied, the inner loop is exited and an "if"-block checks if the current color was already the last color. If not, a button will be displayed on the screen and the program waits till the user has changed the pen and pushs the button. The button is removed from the screen and the program executes the outer loop again.

At jump label 4, which is executed parallel to the push button action, the current color c is increased by 1 and a sound (question mark 19) is played.

After all lines of all colors have been applied, the program ends the outer loop and continues at jump label 99.

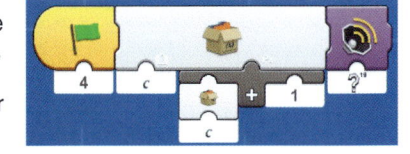

Jump label 99 moves the vertical arm (motor A) down to the lowest position (l). The pen is lowered to the eggshell (ext. motor to position 0) and the egg is turned by a full rotation (motor B turns for angle u). After lifting the pen from the egg, the vertical arm moves to the topmost position (motor A in position 0) and the pen draws another ring onto the eggshell. The last movement of motor A sets the vertical arm back to the middle position and a final sound (question mark 12) is played.

Egg-Booster

The Egg-Paint subroutines can be started without a preceding initializing subroutine or definition of variables. However, to define your own pattern, you can set the global variables for the number of colors (c), number of lines (n) and height of the egg (l) before the start of the actual egg-paint subroutine.

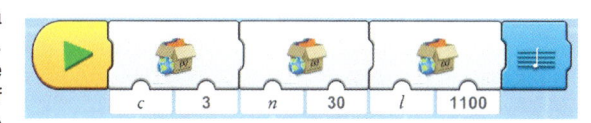

Egg-Print - Dot-Matrix printing

First the local variables are set. Variable i specifies the current number of the dot. Variables x and y store the starting position of motors A and B. The following loop is executed as long as variable i holds a positive number.

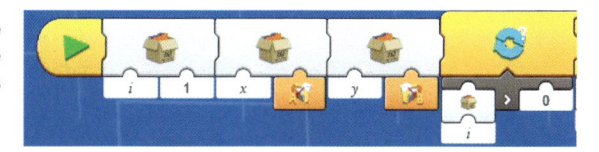

Within the loop, a jump to the label specified by variable i writes the coordinates of this dot into variables a and b. Then, motor A and B position the pen at these coordinates relative to the starting position (x and y) and with a dot spacing of global variables a and b. The pen is lowered (ext. motor at 0°) and immediately pulled back up to 180°.

As the last block of the loop, the dot number (i) is increased by 1. Within the definition of the last dot, variable i is set to a negative value and the loop will end. The following blocks move the pen to the starting position of the next letter. Letters have a spacing of 7 dots.

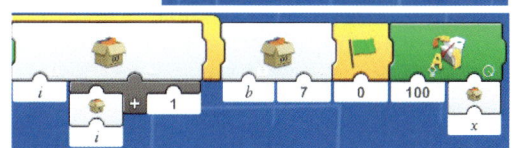

To define more letters, you can use the Dot-Matrix alphabet in the Boost-Writer chapter of this book.

To write text in multiple rows, the pen must be positioned accordingly before the subroutine of a letter is called. The following program writes „EGG" above „BOT". Using the global variables a and b for dot spacing this method will also work for different dot spacings.

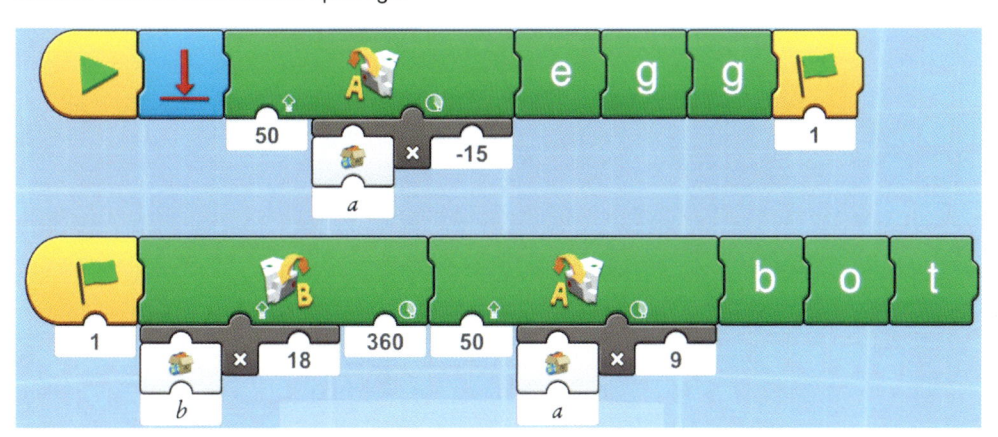

Cube-Booster

Cube Booster – The cube-solver

The cube booster can manipulate a cube with 3x3x3 segments. The cube is solved based on pre-defined movements. You must obtain the sequence of movements from one of the many cube-solving websites.

Build

To build the cube solver, you will need some additional Lego-Technic bricks. The list of these bricks is added at the end of the building instructions. These bricks are part of the Arctic Explorer Set (60194) which can be combined with the Boost set to another interesting model. Alternatively, you can use similar bricks from your Lego collection.

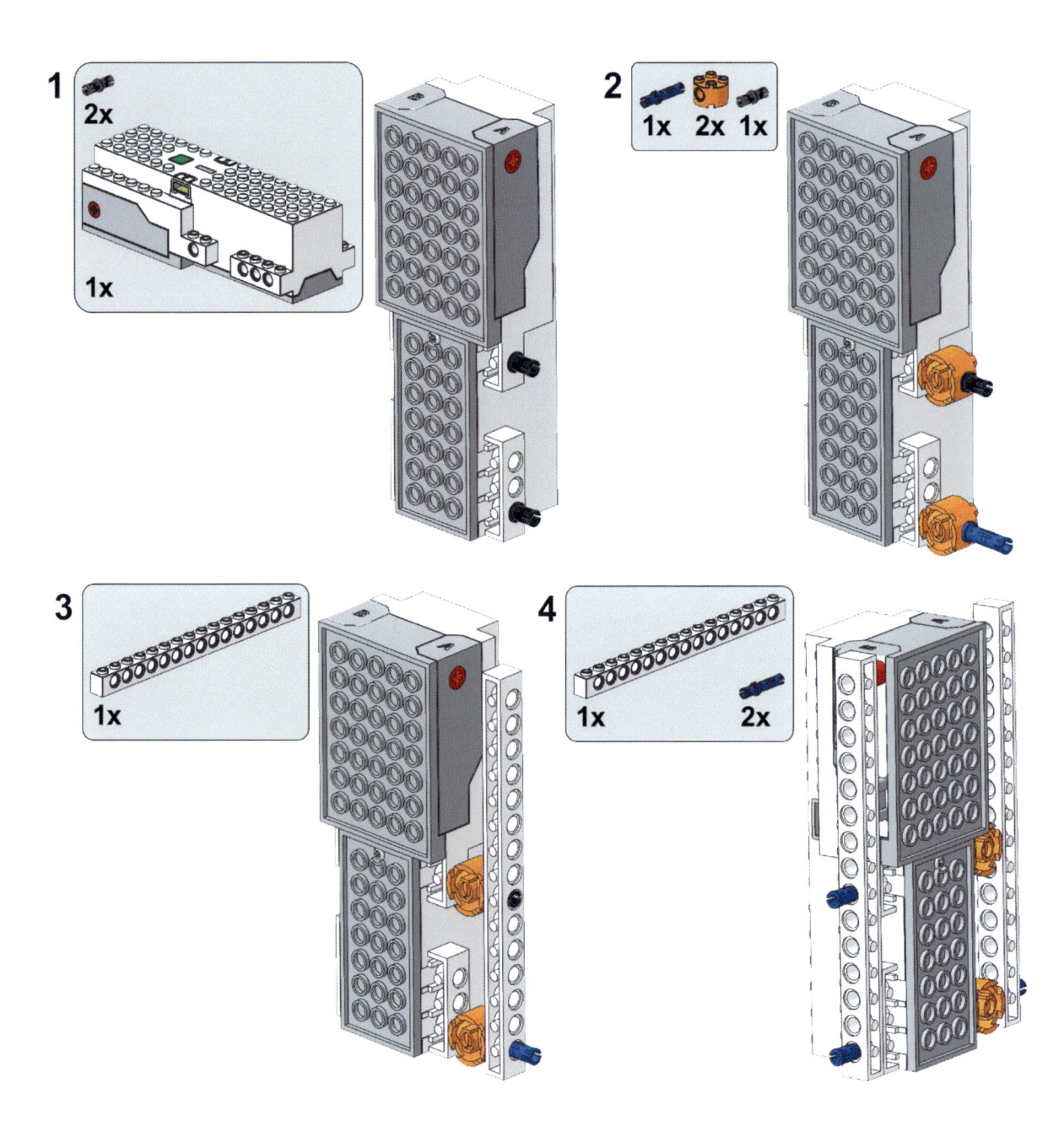

1
2x
1x

2
1x 2x 1x

3
1x

4
1x 2x

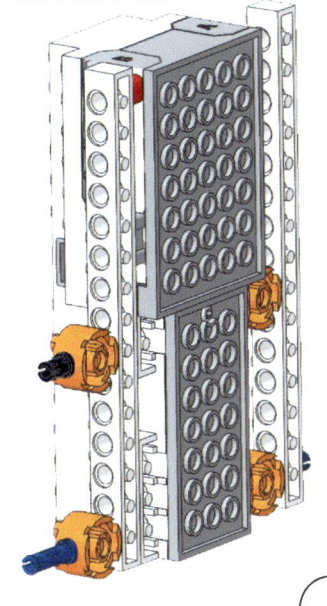

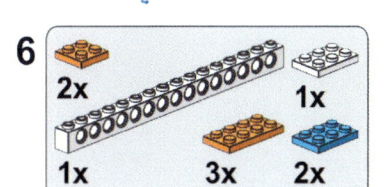

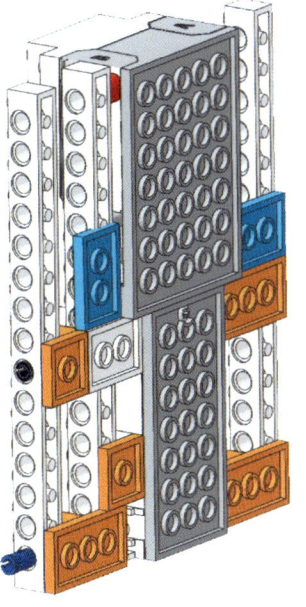

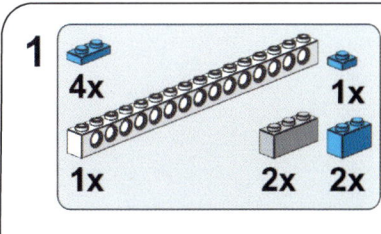

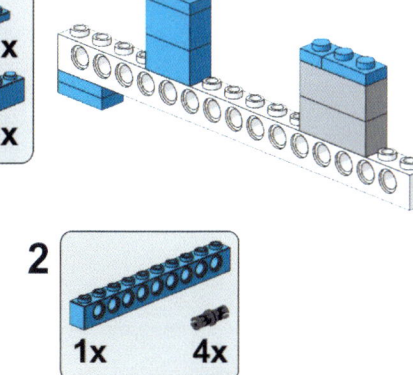

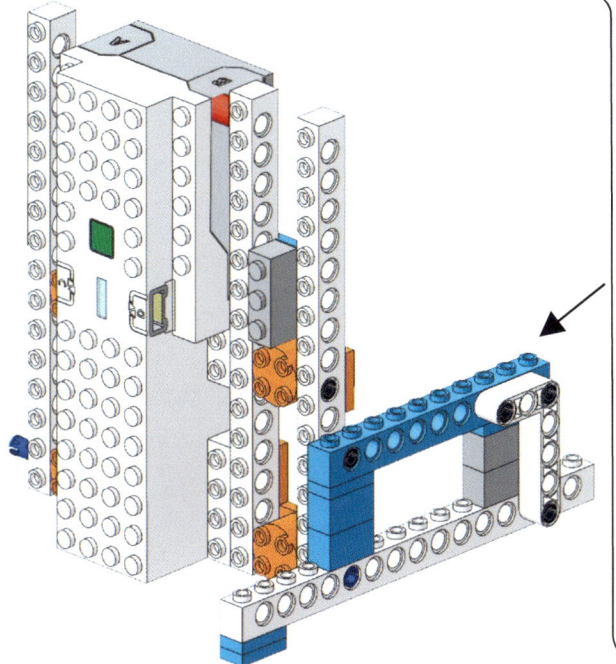

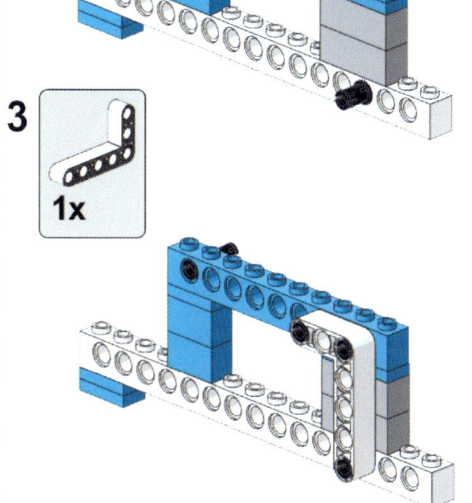

Cube-Booster

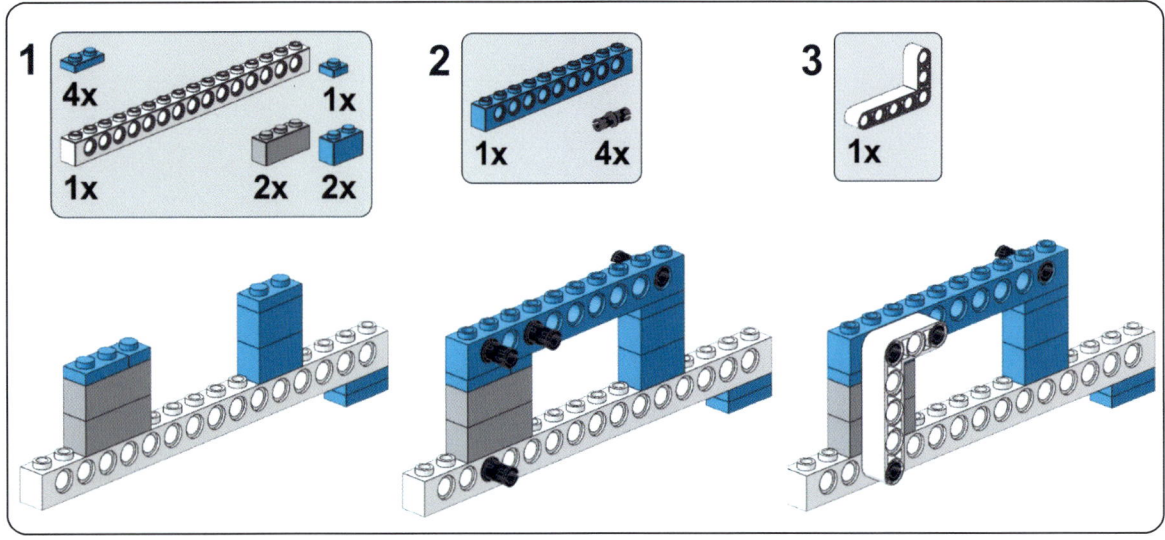

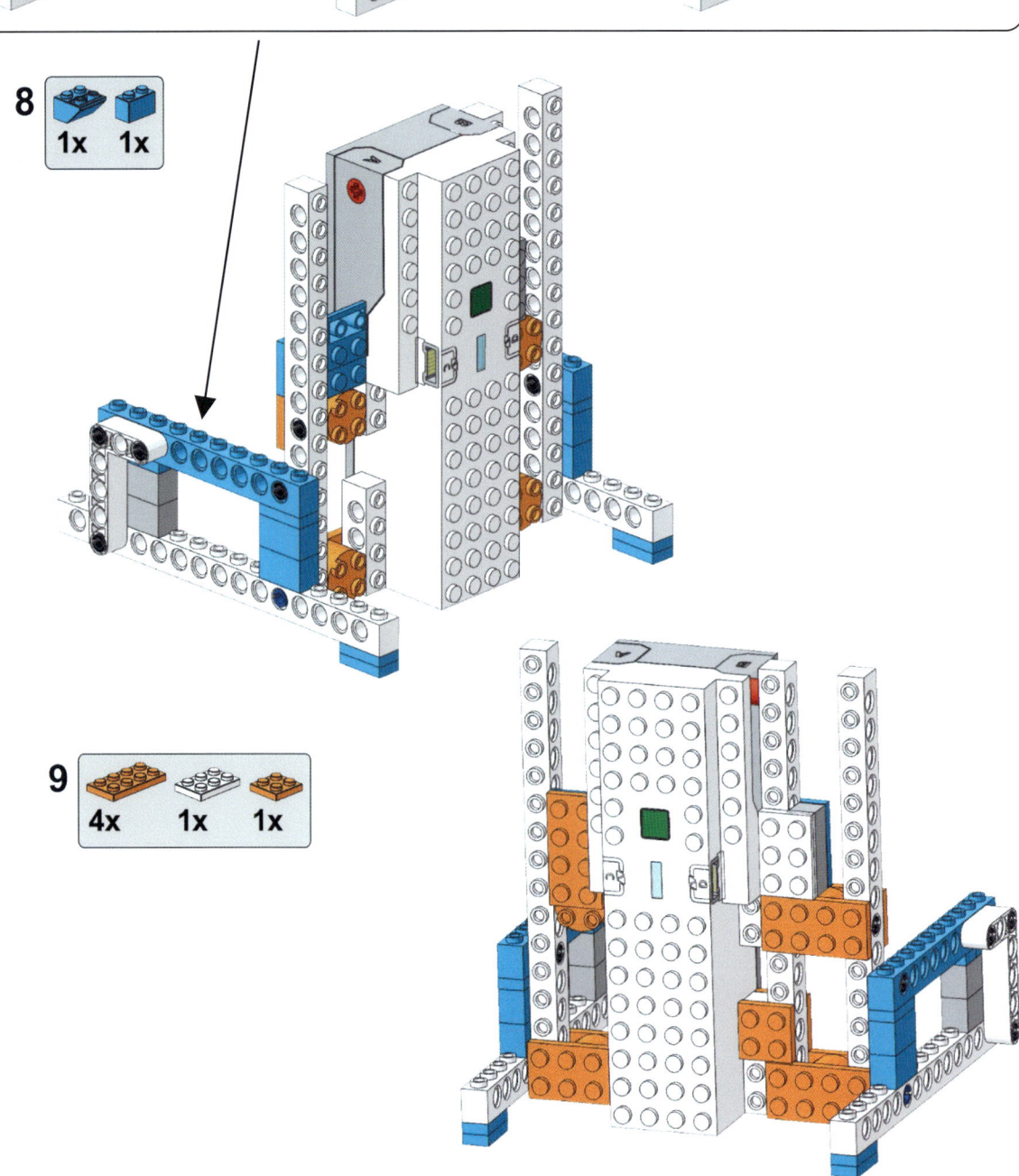

Cube-Booster

Cube-Booster

10
1x 2x 2x 2x 1x

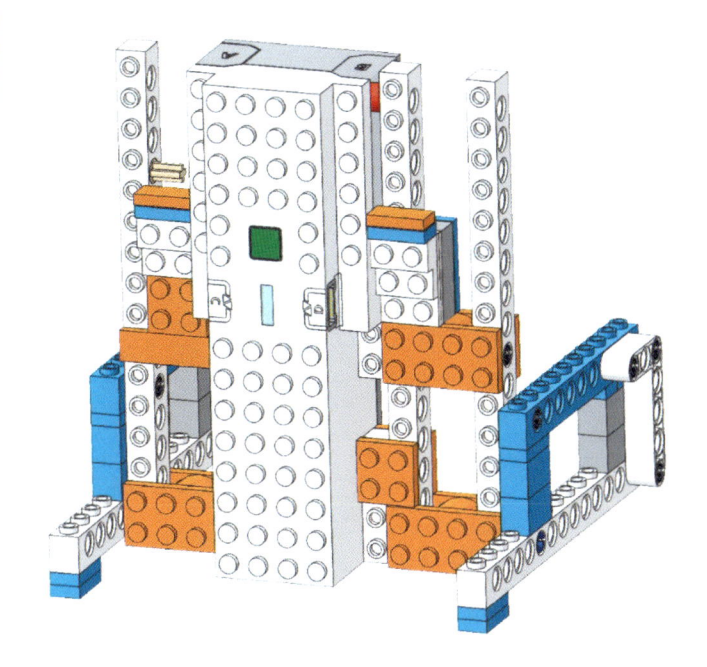

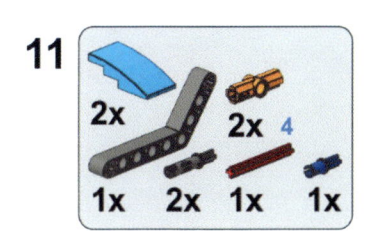

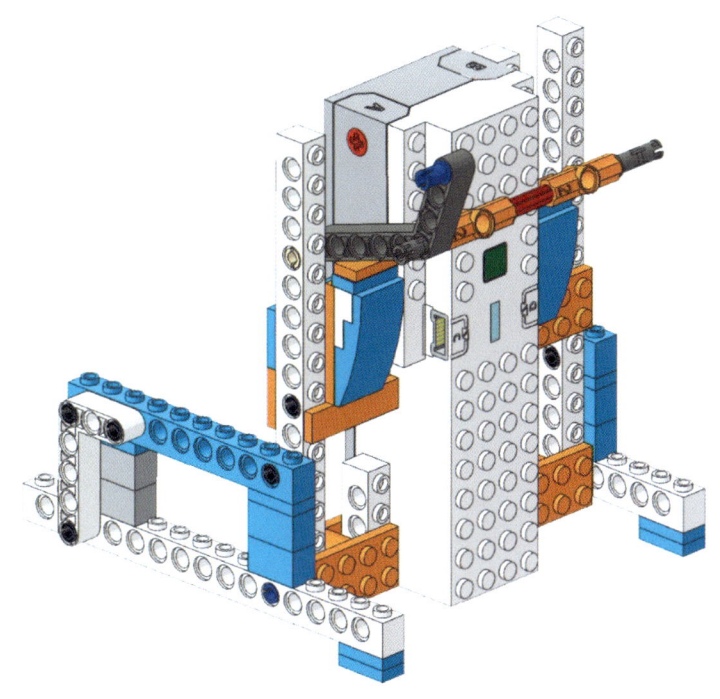

11
2x 2x 4
1x 2x 1x 1x

Cube-Booster

12 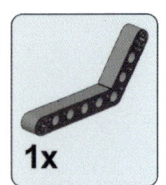 1x

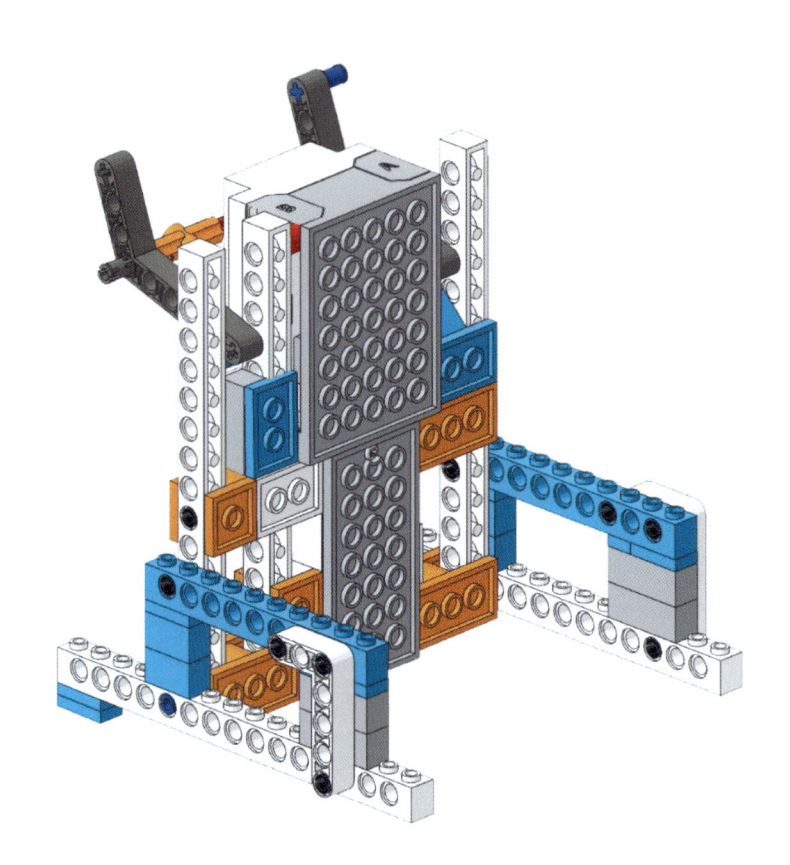

13 1x 1x 2x 2x 1x 4x 4

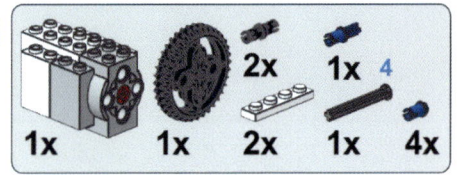

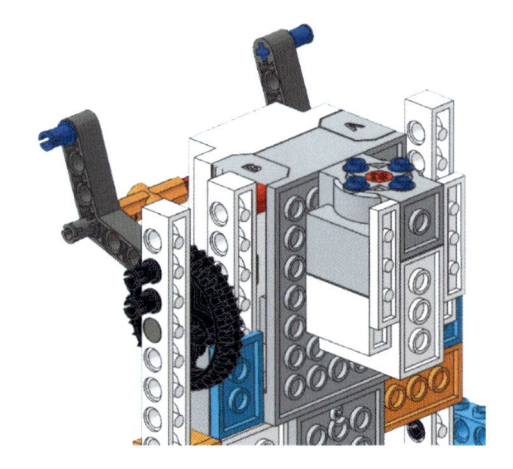

14 1x 1x 1x 2x

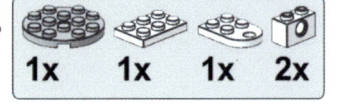

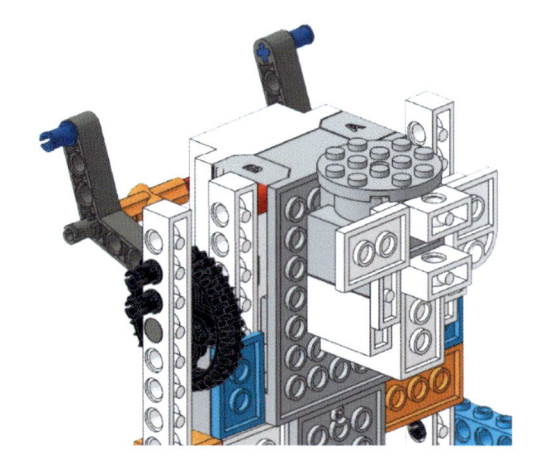

Cube-Booster

15
2x, 4x, 1x, 1x

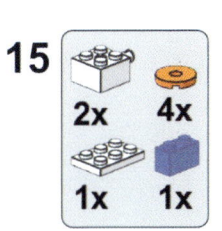

16
1x, 1x, 5
1x, 1x, 1x

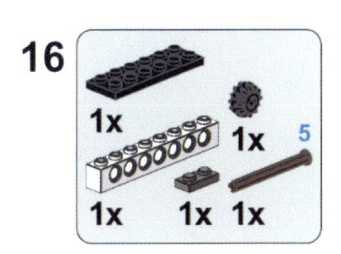

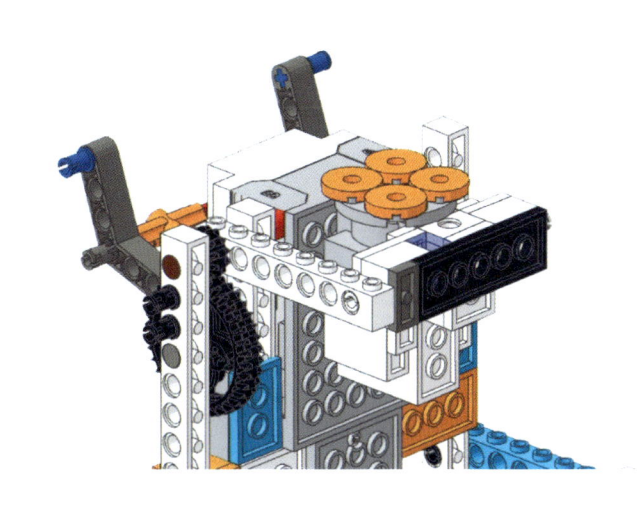

17
1x, 4
1x
1x
1x, 1x

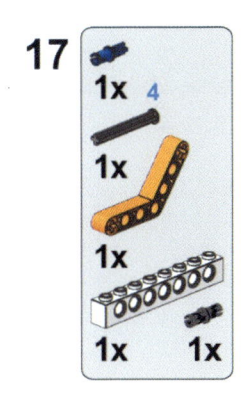

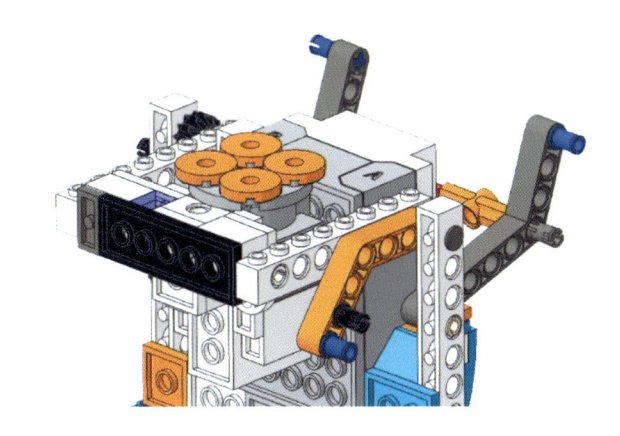

18
3
1x, 1x

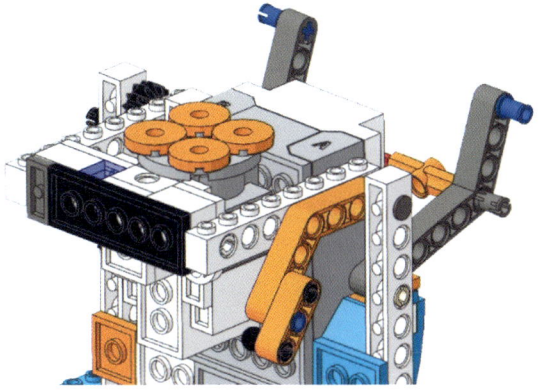

115

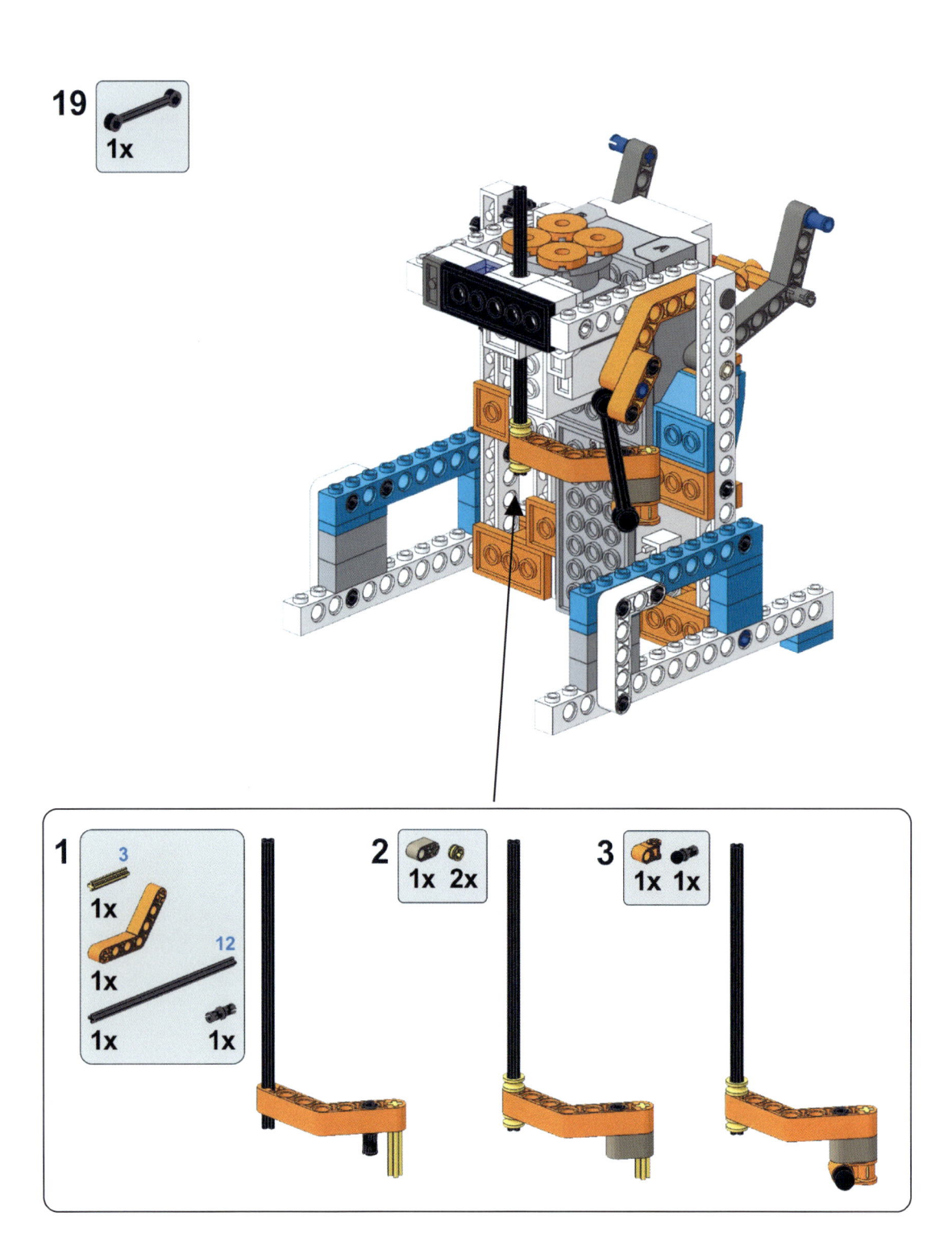

Cube-Booster

19 1x

Cube-Booster

BUILD

1. 1x, 1x, 1x, 1x, 2x, 3
2. 2x, 4x, 2x
3. 4x, 4x
4. 2x, 2x
5. 2x, 4x, 4x
6. 4x, 2x, 2x, 4x
7. 11x, 2x, 4x
8. 2x, 2x, 8x, 4x
9. 2x, 4x, 8x, 4x

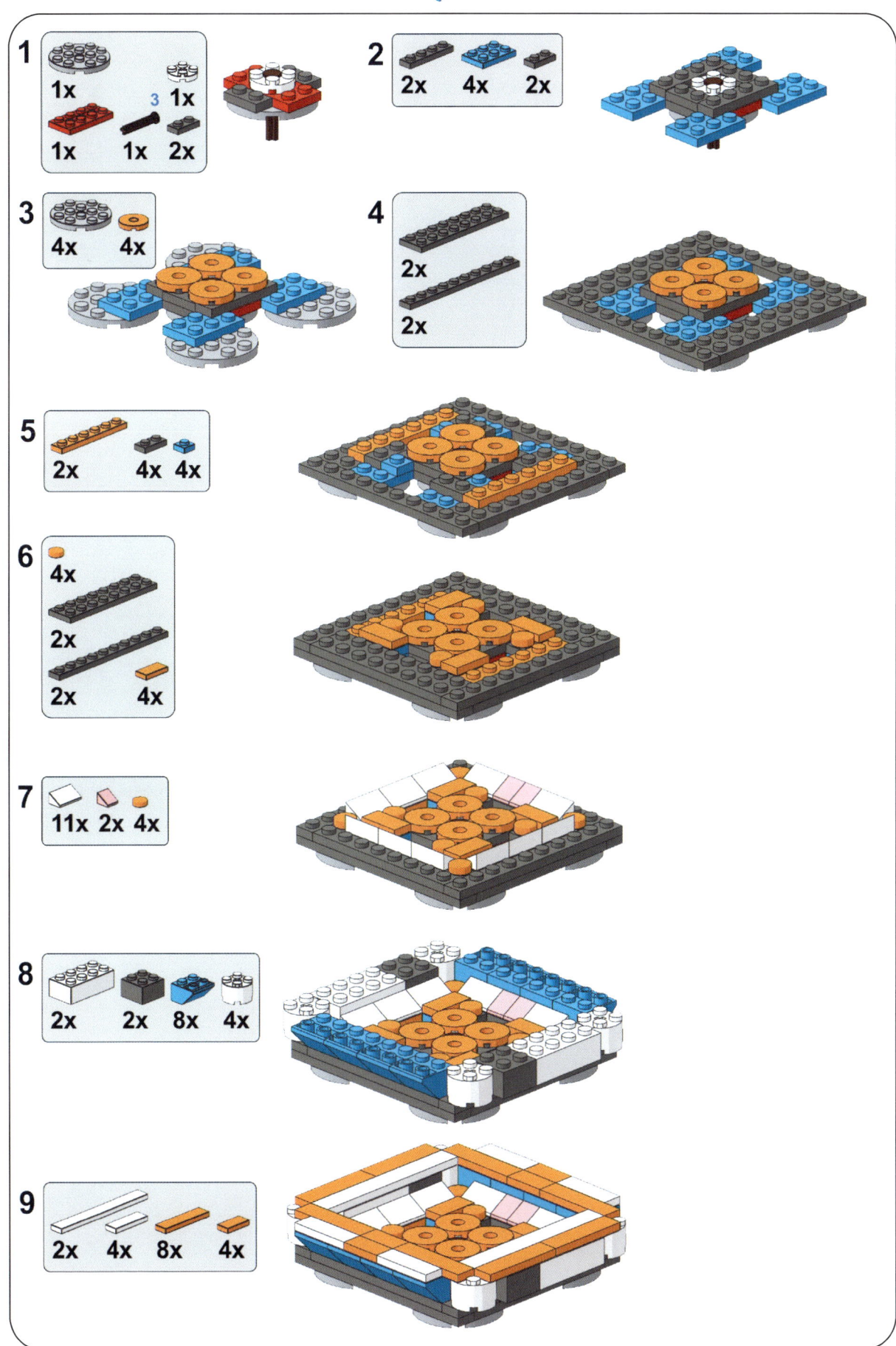

117

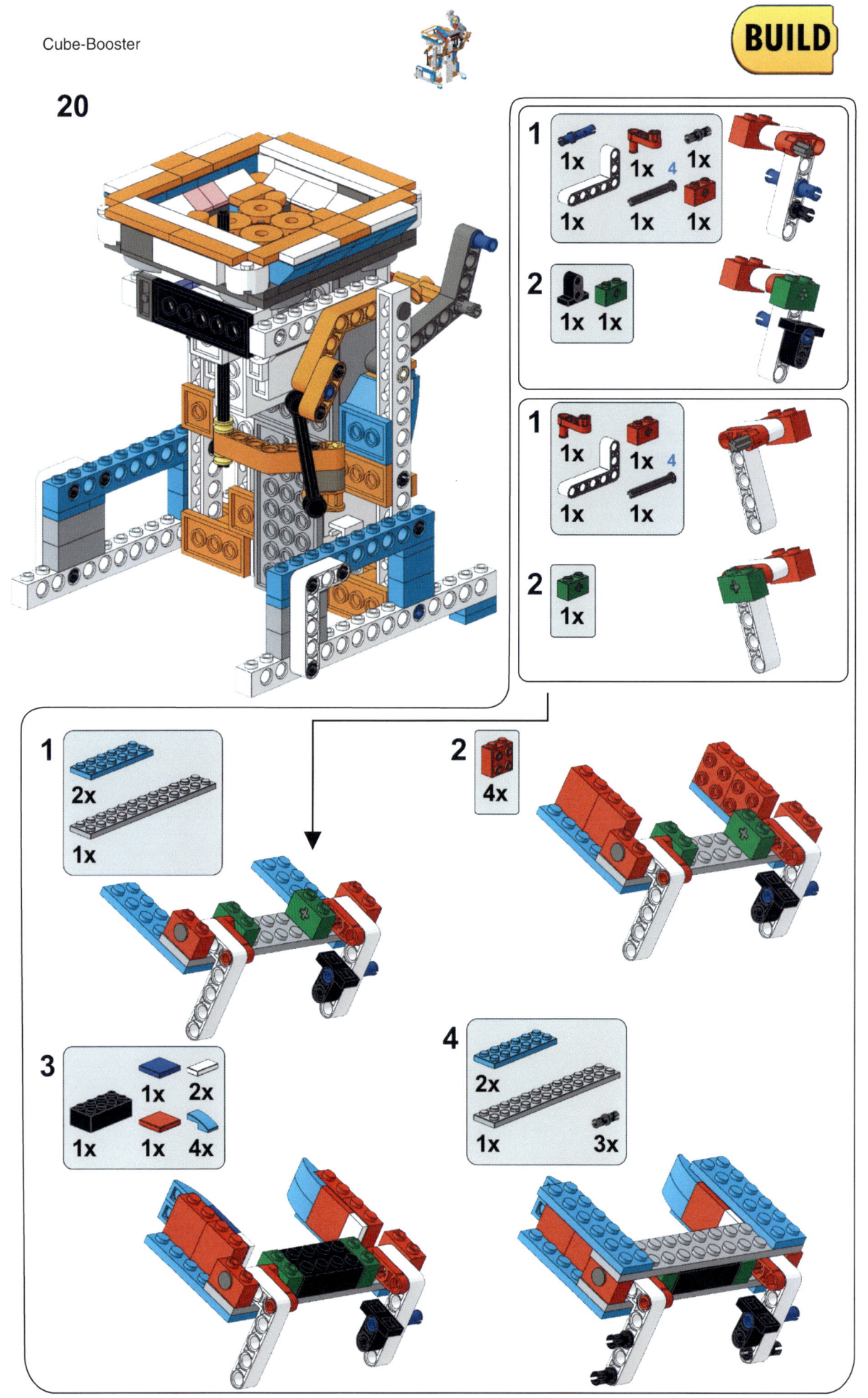

Cube-Booster

20

Cube-Booster

21

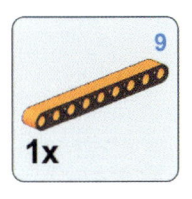

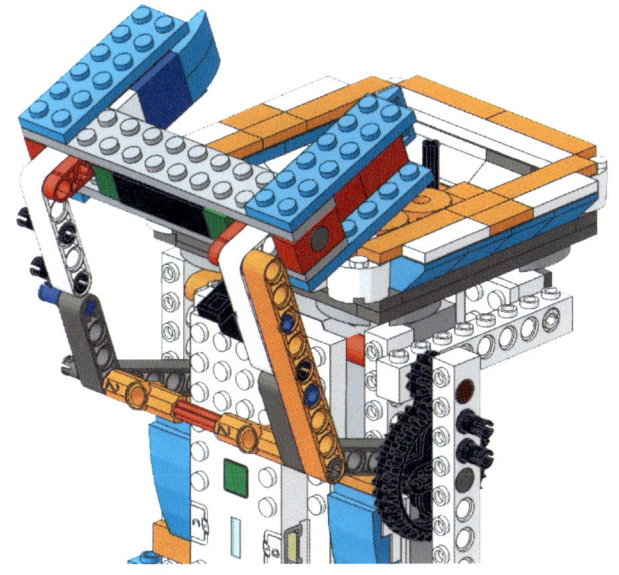

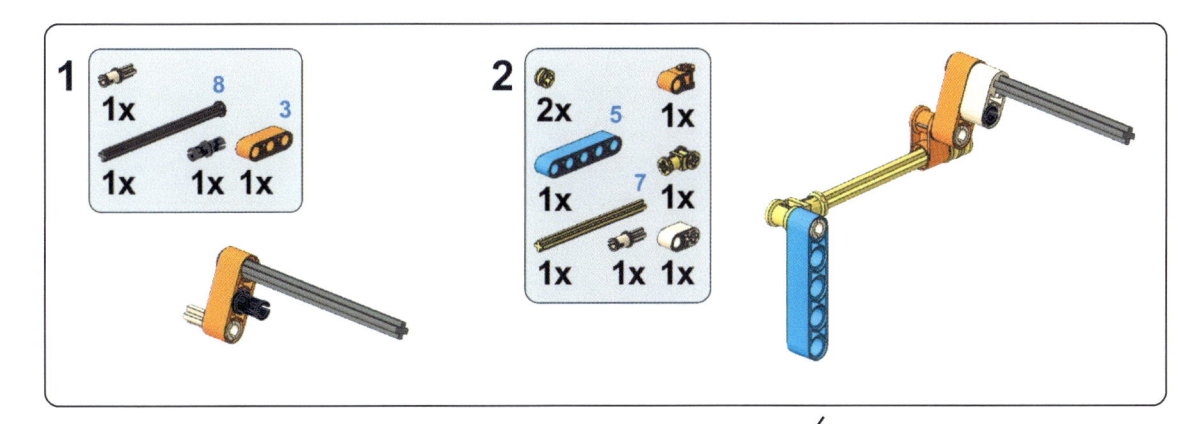

1x

22

1
1x
1x 1x 1x

2
2x 1x
1x 1x
1x 1x 1x

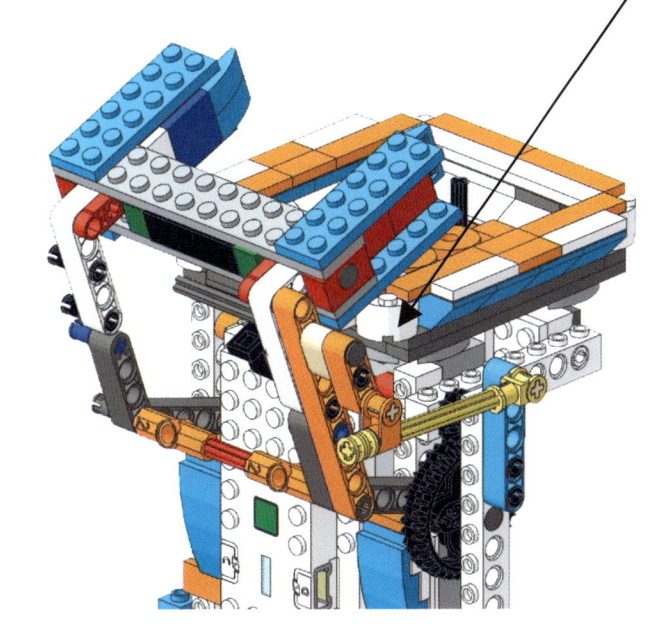

Cube-Booster

BUILD

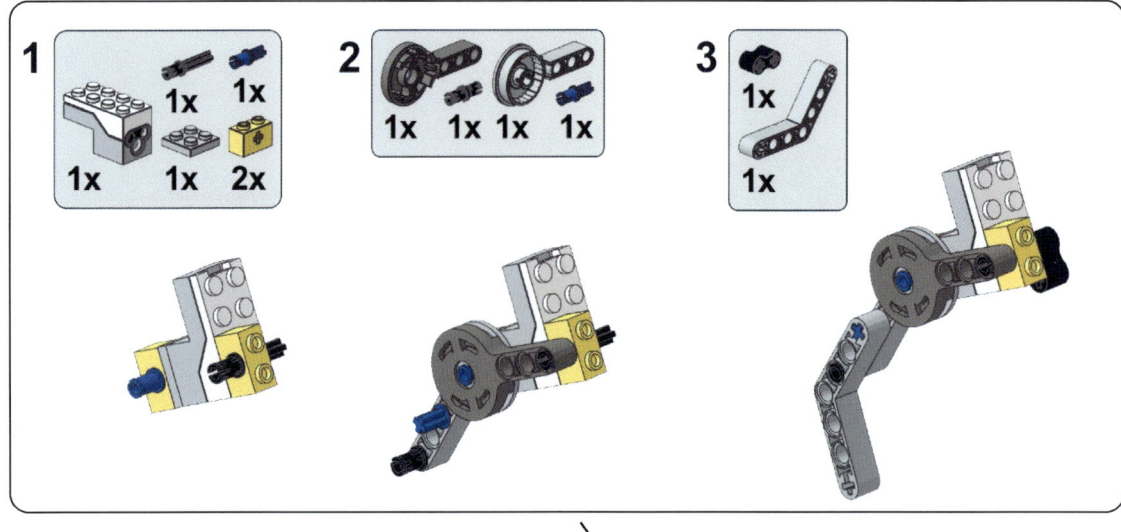

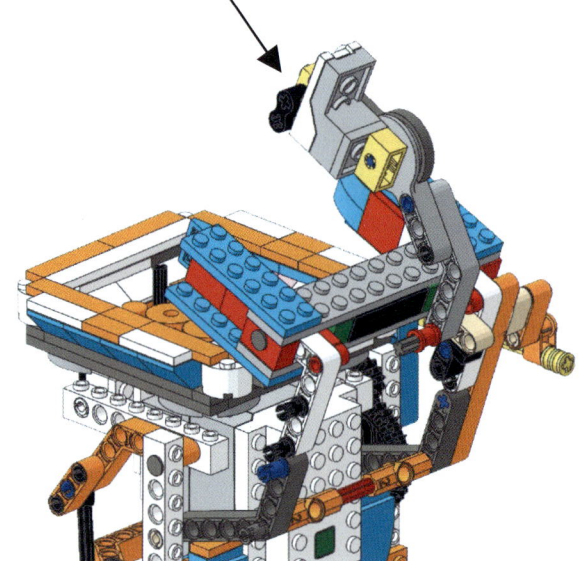

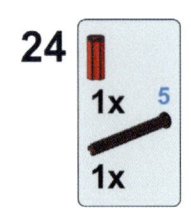

Cable run straight down outside the gripper arm

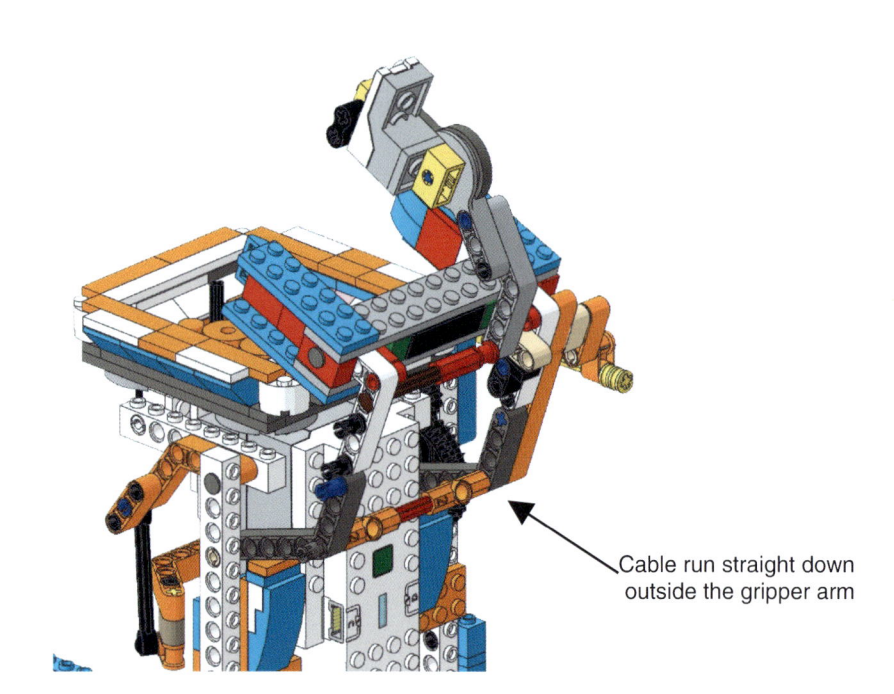

Cube-Booster

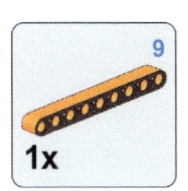

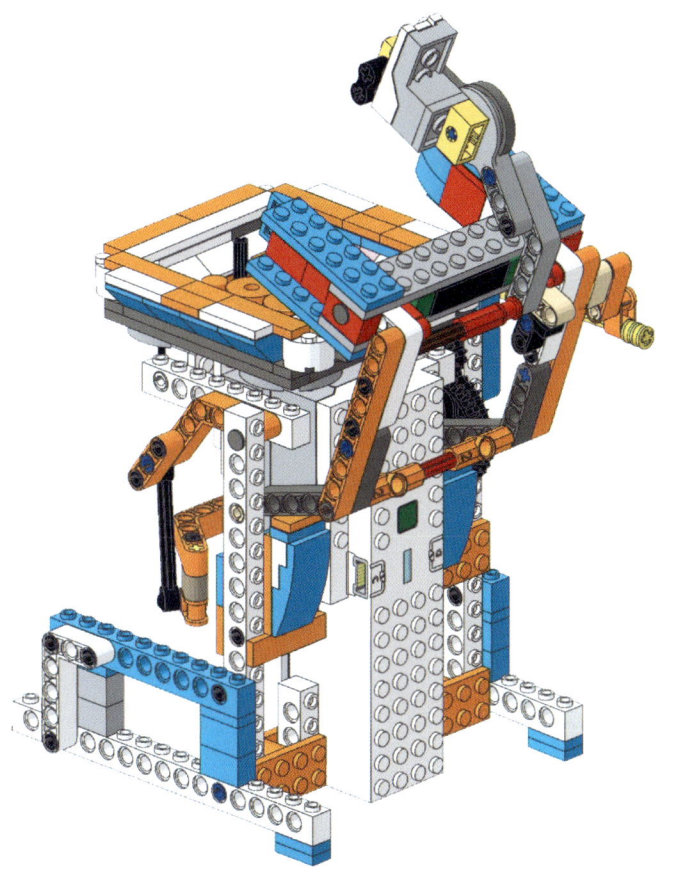

25 1x (9)

The following table shows the bricks you need in addition to the bricks of the Boost set (17101). These elements are part of the Arctic-Explorer-Set (60194). Alternatively, you can buy them for small money individually in numerous online shops. Colors do not play any role.

Amount	Part No.	Description	Picture
2	6629	Technic Beam 1 x 9 Bent	
1	32348	Technic Beam 1 x 7 Bent	

Cube-Booster

Code
To execute all movements for the solving of the cube you need to create several subroutines.

Initializing

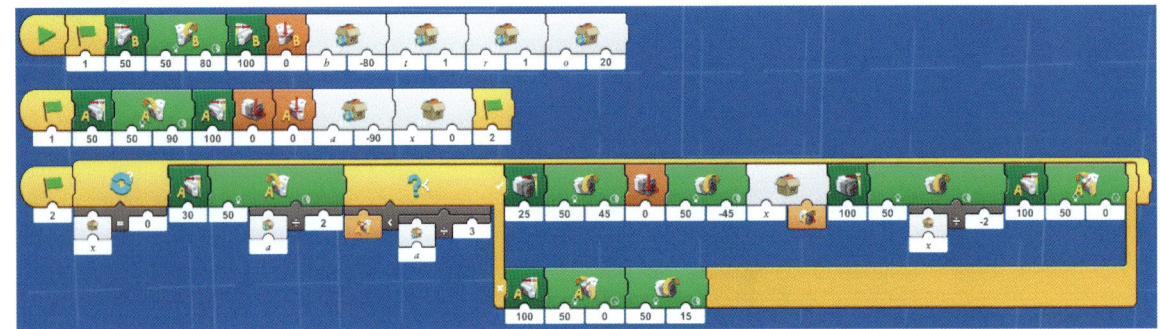

Generally, a cube can be solved with six basic movements. These movements are specified as a clockwise 90° rotation of one of the faces of the cube. A single letter specifies the face of the cube.

- D - Down - lower face
- U - Up - upper face
- R - Right - right face
- L - Left - left face
- F - Front - frontside
- B - Back - backside

A letter with an apostrophe specifies a counterclockwise rotation:
e.g. R' stands for a counterclockwise rotation of the right-hand side
A letter with a preceding „2" specifies a 180° rotation:
e.g. 2L stands for a 180° clockwise rotation of the left-hand side
In the following program, these prefixes are replaced by a value of 1, -1 or 2 to specify the rotation type.

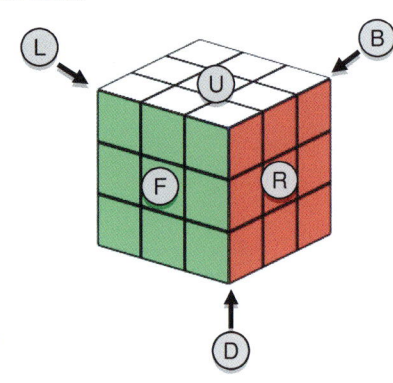

Subroutine for platform-rotation

Subroutine for cube tilting

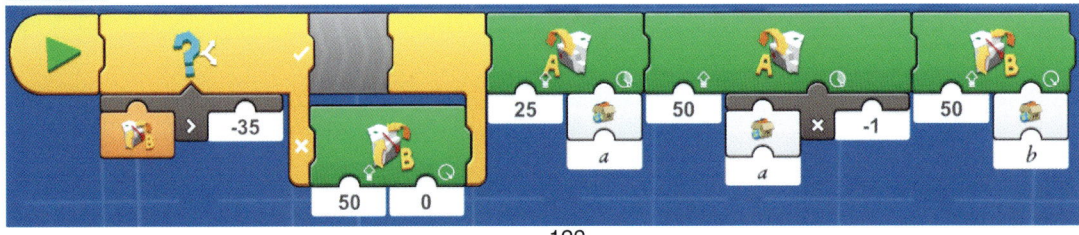

Cube-Booster

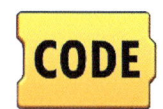

Subroutine for rotation down (D)

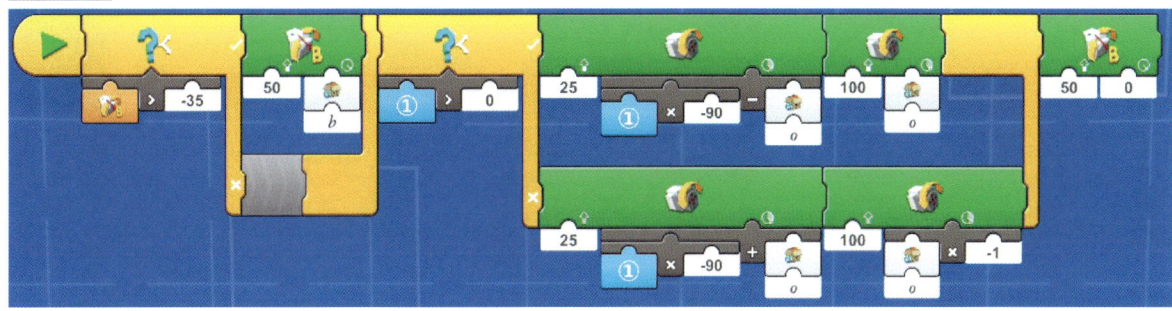

Subroutine for rotation up (U)

Subroutine for rotation right (R)

Subroutine for rotation left (L)

Subroutine for rotation frontside (F)

Subroutine for rotation backside (B)

Cube-Booster

Subroutine to check the correct solution
Although the mathematical functions of the App are not sufficient to create the solving algorithm, the following subroutine can be used to check the finished cube for correctness.

Cube-Booster

Main program
The algorithm for solving the cube must be provided to the program. You can obtain the algorithm for your cube from several websites. (e.g. rubiks-cube-solver.com, rubiks-cu.be or ruwix.com). First, you enter the current state of your cube on the website. The website will calculate the required movements and provide the algorithm in the form of a letter-based code. Based on these letters, you will have to put your main program together. The first block of each program must be the initializing subroutine.

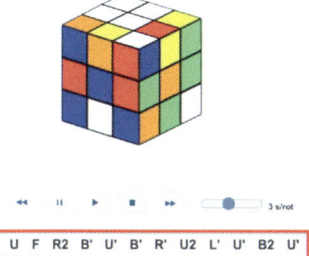

Attention: When entering the cube into the cube solver, you must make sure that the backside (B) of the cube points towards the gripper arm and the lower side (D) points downwards.

The cube booster works best with Speed-Cubes. Speed-Cubes offer a very smooth rotation with low friction and therefore need low power to turn their faces. The Cube-Booster will only be able to perform the rotations in the required way with a smoothly operating cube. Cubes which are not well manufactured or are hard to turn cannot be manipulated by the Cube-Booster. Even if you use a speed cube, you still must make sure that the batteries in the Move-Hub are in good condition. Otherwise the motors won't have enough power to manipulate the cube.

An example for a solving algorithm in the main program:

This is how the cube can be checked after solving:

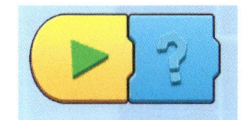

Advanced cube solving programs
Some advanced versions of the program are available on the websites of the author (see URLs on the first pages of this book). Scanning and solving the cube without the need to type the current state into a website is also possible using a PC and a Python program. You will need the right hardware (e.g. Low Energy Bluetooth dongle) and advanced programming skills to handle this type of program.

Cube-Booster

PLAY

Play

The subroutines use several variables. See the table below for their initial value and purpose.

Variable	Initial-Value	Purpose	Global	Local
a	90	Rotation angle for motor A to tilt the cube	✓	
b	80	Rotation angle for motor B to grip the cube.	✓	
o	20	Additional rotation angle beyond 90° to turn the cube.	✓	
x	0	Angle of rotation within the platform opening		✓
s	0	Face of the cube currently being checked		✓
f	0	Segment of the face currently being checked		✓
c	1,3	Multiple of variable b to detect center segment color		✓
k	0,72	Multiple of variable b to detect an edge segment color		✓
e	0,55	Multiple of variable b to detect a corner segment color		✓
m	-	Color of center segment		✓

Initializing

After jump label 1 is called, motor B power is reduced to 50%, motor B runs 80° against its lower limit and its power is raised back to 100%. This brings the gripper arm into the starting position. The position is stored as 0 for motor B. The standard values for global variables b and o are set. As these angles are used in several subroutines, the central setting of these variables makes it easier to experiment with other angle settings.

Jump label 1 sets power of motor A to 50%, turns motor A down by 90° against its lower limit and raises its power back to 100%. This brings the tilting rod to its starting position. The current position for motor A and the external motor is set to 0. The standard values for variables a and x are set and the program continues at jump label 2.

The program sequence at jump label 2 takes care of the platform positioning. A loop is repeated as long as variable x is still 0. Power of motor A is reduced to 30%. The tilting rod is moved up for half of its possible travel distance.

The following „if"-block checks if the rod is already below the opening of the platform and therefore was able to move up by more than 1/3 of its total travel. Is the rod hitting the platform and cannot freely move up, the program continues in the lower sequence of the "if"-block.

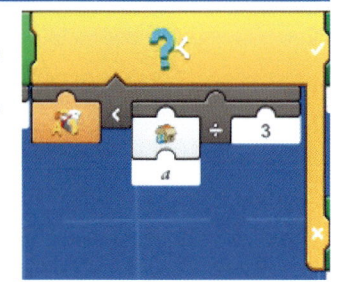

Cube-Booster

Was the rod not able to go through the opening, power of motor is set to 100% and motor A retracts the rod to its lowest position. The platform is turned by 15° for the next try.

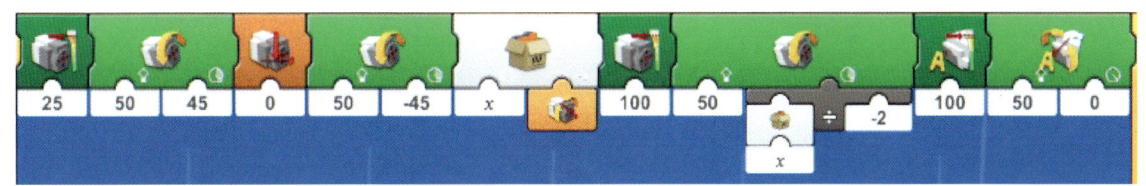

The upper sequence of the "if"-block is executed as soon as the rod was able to go through the opening. Power of the external motor is reduced to 25% and it tries to turn by 45° till the rod hits one side of the opening. The motor position is set to 0 and the motor tries to turn 45° in the other direction till the rod hits the other side of the opening. At this stop the current position of the external motor is stored in variable x. Motor power is set back to 100% and the motor turns by half of variable x to position the rod in the exact center of the opening. In this position, platform and cube are aligned with the gripper. The cube booster is ready to start manipulating the cube.

Subroutine for platform rotation

Before the actual rotation, the program checks if the gripper is in the lower position. If not, motor B turns the gripper to position 0 which is its starting position. The external motor then rotates the platform for a multiple of 90°. The multiplier is taken from the subroutine parameter 1. Each subroutine can have multiple parameters. In our case we only use one parameter in each subroutine, so we always use parameter number one.

Subroutine for cube tilting

Before tilting, the program also checks if the gripper is in its starting position and turns it down if necessary. To tilt the cube, motor A moves the rod quickly up and immediately back down. Then motor B moves the gripper to push the cube back onto the platform and complete the tilting. The gripper stays in the gripped position to prevent an unnecessary move in case the next move is a twist.

Cube-Booster

Subroutine for rotation down (D)

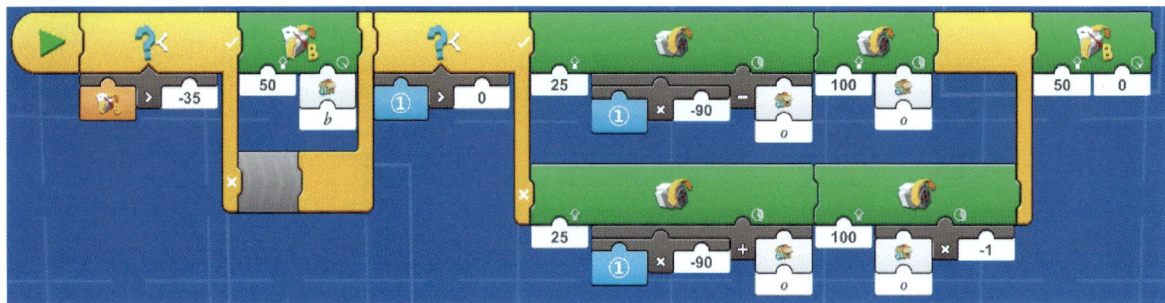

In this case, the gripper is moved if it is not already in the highest position defined by variable b. Is the subroutine parameter a positive number and a clockwise turn is required, the "if"-block executes the upper sequence. For negative parameters the lower sequence is executed. In both sequences, the external motor turns the platform by 90° plus the additional angle specified in variable o. This additional angle assures a full twist of the cube by considering the play in between platform and cube. To return the platform back to its correct position, the external motor turns back by the value in variable o. Finally, the gripper is moved back to its starting position.

Attention: If the twisting of the cube is not accurate enough you should first check the conditions of your batteries. The external motor might not develop enough power to twist the cube. Furthermore, the cube could have too much friction. Please always use a so-called Speed-Cube as mentioned above. If the twist is still not accurate enough, you can experiment with different values for variable o in the initializing subroutine.

Subroutines U, R, L, F, B

The other subroutines for cube rotations all work the same. First, the cube is tilted and rotated to have the face for the twist look downwards to the platform. Then the subroutine for rotation down (D) is executed and the cube is tilted and rotated back to its starting position.

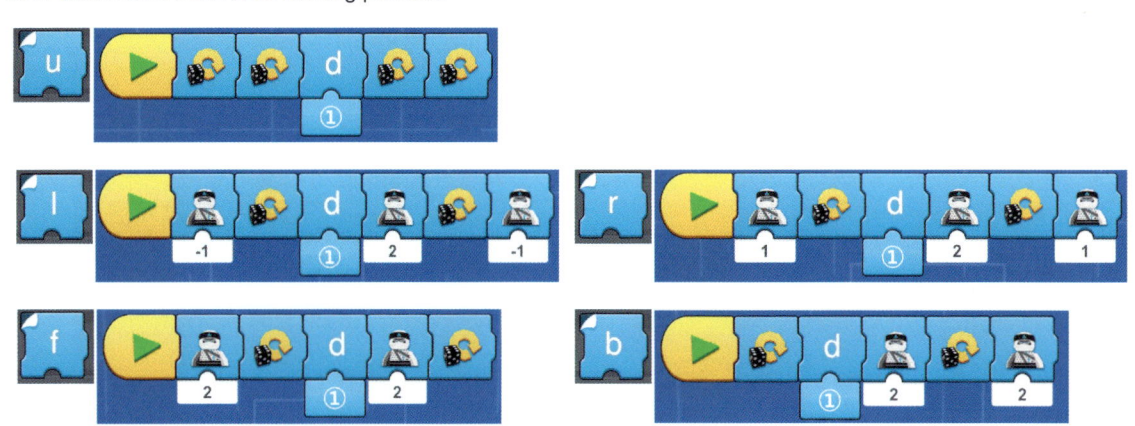

Above concept needs the cube back in its starting position before each move. This causes several additional moves which might be avoided if the cube-booster was able to remember the current position of the cube. Such a version of the program is available on the authors webpages (see URL on the first pages of the book).

Cube-Booster

Subroutine to check the correct solution
First, the initializing subroutine is executed and all required local variables are set.

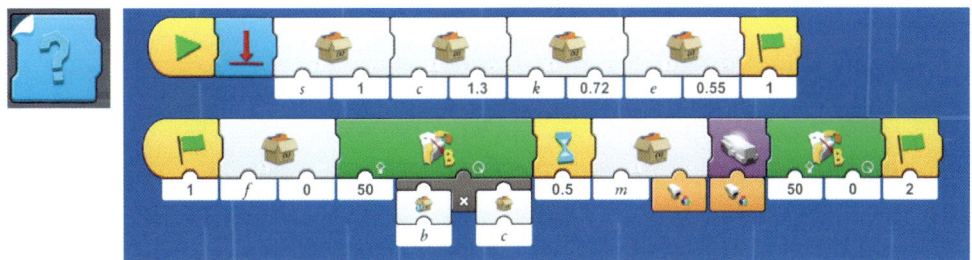

Jump label 1 sets local variable f to 0 which is the number of the center segment of the cube.
The sensor is moved over the center segment. After a short waiting time to assure that the sensor is not shaking anymore, the sensor reading is stored in variable m and the color is displayed by the Move-Hub LED. Motor B turns the senor back and the program continues at jump label 2.

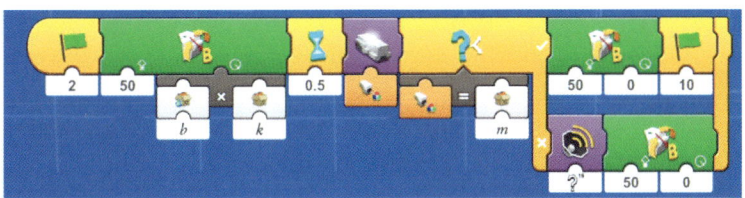

Jump label 2 checks the edge color against the center color stored in variable m. If the check is successful, the program continues at jump label 10. If not, a sound is played (question mark 19) and the program ends.

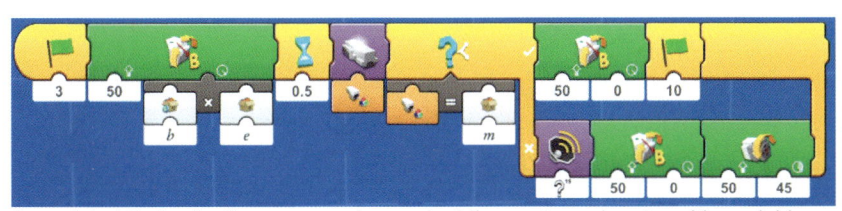

Jump label 3 checks the corner color against the center color stored in variable m. If the check is successful, the program continues at jump label 10. If not, a sound is played (question mark 19), the platform is turned by 45° and the program ends.

Cube-Booster

PLAY

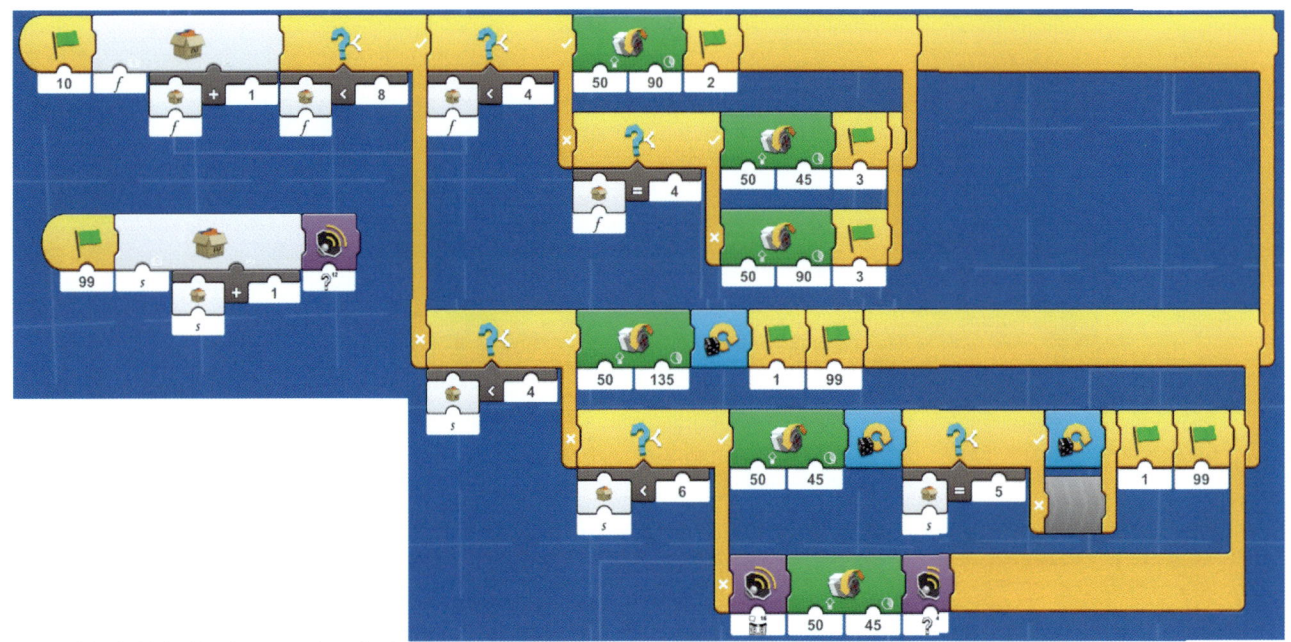

Jump label 10 holds the complete logic to move the sensor around the cube. At each call of the jump label, the number of the current segment (variable f) is increased by 1. Is the current segment still among the first four segments, the platform is turned by 90° between each check at jump label 2. When segment 4 is reached the platform is turned by 45° and jump label 3 checks the first corner. For the next 3 segments, the platform is turned by 90° and jump label 3 checks the remaining three corners. The illustration on the right (one face of the cube) shows the sequence of the segment checks.

8	3	7
4	0	2
5	1	6

As soon as variable f increased to 8, all segments have been checked and the cube must be tilted. For the first four faces of the cube the cube is turned by 135° to its starting position and tilted to the next face. For faces 5 and 6, the cube is tilted over other edges. After each change of face, jump label 99 increases variable s by 1 and plays a sound (Question mark 12) to celebrate the successful check of the face.
Are all faces of the cube successfully checked, the platform is turned by 45° to the starting position and two sounds (Vernie 16 and Question mark 4)

Attention: For a complete check you need to put fresh batteries into the Move-Hub. This is required to make sure, the sensor can be accurately positioned above the different color segments. Furthermore, the sensor is quite sensitive for the ambient lighting. If you experience problems with positioning despite good batteries, you can adapt the variables c, k and e to change the sensor positions for center, edges and corners.

Controlling the Move-Hub by PC and Python

To realize truly complex projects and realize code with additional connectivity options, it is possible to use a PC to directly access the BLE interface of the Move-Hub. You will need some special hardware to connect to the Move-Hub as the BLE interface does not work well with some BLE devices. A Raspberry Pi 3 Model B+ is well suited for the job.

You can access some program examples on the authors webpages. The webpages also offer an installation and setup guide for the Raspberry Pi and the connection to the Move-Hub.

Acknowledgements

This book is dedicated to my family and to my Kids. They are sharing their enthusiasm for Lego with me and let me play and experiment with it for several hundred hours to make the development of this book possible. I also want to thank my parents for providing my brother and me with lots of Lego in the 70s and 80s. As teenagers, they convinced us to keep our Lego for our own kids. Together with my wife I spend some amusing hours in our basement to re-assemble the old Lego sets and their building instructions. Our kids (and myself) still enjoy these old sets and I hope that my readers will also enjoy this book and the models. I am looking forward to your feedback.

About the author

Björn Bundschuh, born in Germany 1974, holds a degree in mechanical engineering and spent most of his professional career in mechanical design, automation and project management. Raised with Lego, he was interested in Lego Technic from the start but did not own a Lego Technic set before it was brought to him for his 40th birthday by his brother. Especially the Boost-Set revitalized his love for building with Lego. Today, his Lego creations are discussed on several internet platforms.

Printed in Poland
by Amazon Fulfillment
Poland Sp. z o.o., Wrocław